Today's American

Today's American

HOW FREE?

Edited by
ARCH PUDDINGTON,
THOMAS O. MELIA,
AND JASON KELLY

FREEDOM HOUSE
New York • Washington, D.C.

ROWMAN & LITTLEFIELD PUBLISHERS, INC.
Lanham • Boulder • New York • Toronto • Plymouth, UK

ROWMAN & LITTLEFIELD PUBLISHERS, INC.

Published in the United States of America
by Rowman & Littlefield Publishers, Inc.
A wholly owned subsidary of The Rowman & Littlefield Publishing Group, Inc.
4501 Forbes Boulevard, Suite 200, Lanham, Maryland 20706
www.rowmanlittlefield.com

Estover Road
Plymouth PL6 7PY
United Kingdom

British Library Cataloguing in Publication Information Available

Library of Congress Cataloging-in-Publication Data:

Today's American : how free? / edited by Arch Puddington, Thomas O. Melia, and Jason
Kelly.
    p. cm.
Includes bibliographical references.
ISBN-13: 978-0-7425-6290-5 (cloth : alk. paper)
ISBN-10: 0-7425-6290-5 (cloth : alk. paper)
1. Civil rights—United States. 2. Discrimination—Law and legislation—United States.
I. Puddington, Arch. II. Melia, Thomas O. III. Kelly, Jason.
    KF4749.T63 2008
    342.7308'5—dc22   2007051924

Printed in the United States of America

♾™ The paper used in this publication meets the minimum requirements of American
National Standard for Information Sciences—Permanence of Paper for Printed Library
Materials, ANSI/NISO Z39.48-1992.

Table of Contents

Table of Contents, *continued*

Acknowledgments

The publication of *Today's American: How Free?* would not have been possible without the support of the Freedom House Board of Trustees and staff. Two members of the board—Peter Ackerman, chairman, and Stuart Eizenstat, vice chairman of the executive committee—provided critical moral and intellectual support to the editors. The report benefited immensely from their enthusiasm, insight, and sound judgment.

Jennifer Windsor, Freedom House executive director, played an indispensable role at every stage of the project. A number of current and former Freedom House staff members were helpful in providing advice on particular issues. They include Daniel Calingaert, Robert Herman, Niaz Kasravi, Mariam Memarsadeghi, Damian Murphy, and Christopher Walker.

Elizabeth Floyd and Thomas Webb kept the research and editorial process moving along efficiently. Extensive research, editorial, proofreading, and administrative assistance was provided by Jessica Beess und Chrostin, David Emery, Shaina Greiff, Kathryn Hannah, Astrid Larson, Amanda Lorman, Katrina Neubauer, Rebecca Vo, and Thomas Webb. Anne Green, of Greenways Graphic Design, was responsible for the design and layout of the book. Tyler Roylance and Rachel Wildavsky were responsible for editing the manuscript, and Holly Zimmerman served as proofreader.

Introduction

By Peter Ackerman, Stuart Eizenstat, and Mark Palmer

Freedom House was established in 1941 by a distinguished group of Americans who were committed to the defense of freedom, then under grave assault by fascism in Europe and the Far East. The Freedom House Board of Trustees saw and continues to see world freedom as indivisible, understanding that to preserve freedom at home, Americans must be willing to protect and advance it in other societies.

The reverse is also true. Freedom House has always believed that American democracy must be robust and secure if the United States is to sustain its position as the most significant supporter of freedom around the world.

Freedom House does not view freedom as an abstraction, but rather as a tangible, meaningful set of rights to which every human being is entitled, no matter the country or circumstances of his or her birth. By its very nature, freedom is never fully attained in any country. It must constantly be defended and refined.

Evaluating the extent to which human rights are protected is essential to freedom's progress. That is why we have published *Freedom in the World*, our flagship survey of political rights and civil liberties in every country in the world, for the past three decades. These and other assessments serve as a platform for spurring constructive and vigorous dialogue within societies as to how they can advance further toward freedom.

One of America's greatest strengths is its willingness to turn the spotlight on its own practices and critically evaluate its democratic institutions. At Freedom House, we think that now is an ideal time for reflection about the health of American democracy.

The upcoming U.S. elections offer a unique opportunity to debate the state of the union and especially the freedoms enjoyed by its citizens. But this debate cannot be advanced only through partisan politics. The excessive polarization in American politics today too often caricatures the serious problems that we confront as a nation and underestimates what we are capable of as a society.

In the hope of prompting a broader discussion about the state of freedom in America, Freedom House is publishing *Today's American: How Free?* The study evaluates the current on-the-ground condition of democratic institutions in the United States, describes their historical context, and, where relevant, gauges American performance in comparison with other developed democracies. The title comes from a 1986 book published by Freedom House, which consisted of essays written by eminent intellectuals about various challenges to American democracy.

Though consistent in spirit with that earlier work, the present version differs in that it subjects the basic institutions of American democracy to a comprehensive assessment. *Today's American: How Free?* is organized into 10 chapters, each of which addresses a discrete institution or topic: the political process, political corruption, the effect of counterterrorism policies on civil liberties, freedom of expression and the press, race relations, the status of immigrants, criminal justice and property rights, equality of opportunity, freedom of religion, and academic freedom.

Many of the issues in the report are also evaluated in *Freedom in the World*, which assesses the strength or weakness of the core characteristics of freedom in every country, including in the United States. But the narratives in an annual global survey are naturally too brief to provide the sort of fulsome examination that we feel would be useful in catalyzing a richer dialogue. Therefore Freedom House has produced its first book-length study assessing the state of freedom in a single country.

The methodology used in this report is similar to those of other Freedom House publications. Freedom House analysts prepared initial drafts of the chapters, which were then reviewed by the distinguished scholars and experts noted in the Acknowledgements.

The Freedom House Board of Trustees has approved the methodology and approach undertaken in this study. Many members of the board provided extensive input and made important contributions that have greatly enhanced the quality of the report.

The diversity of views represented on the Freedom House board—one of the great strengths of the organization—helped to stimulate vigorous discussion and debate on various issues in this report. While the board as a whole has approved the overall findings of the study, individual trustees may not agree with each and every statement or conclusion. The final editorial judgments, as with all Freedom House publications, were made by the Freedom House editorial staff.

It is our hope that *Today's American: How Free?* will spark renewed and informed dialogue about the state of freedom in America, and how it can be further enhanced. We also urge other societies to undertake their own self-evaluations. Freedom House would be happy to facilitate the process, and to provide needed support and assistance.

Peter Ackerman is chairman of the Freedom House Board of Trustees; Stuart Eizenstat and Mark Palmer are vice chairmen.

Today's American: How Free?

By Arch Puddington and Thomas O. Melia

How free is today's American? The state of freedom within the United States has been a matter of considerable contention, especially in the years since September 11, 2001. Some elements of President George W. Bush's counterterrorism effort—such as the monitoring of domestic telecommunications and the detention and interrogation of suspected terrorists—have drawn criticism from the public as well as multiple and ongoing challenges in the courts and by Congress. These concerns, coupled with other, long-standing critiques of the American system, have led some to ask whether Americans are facing an erosion of the rights and freedoms that are central to our national identity.

In the following pages, Freedom House presents its views on the state of freedom in the United States. In addition to addressing the effects of recent counterterrorism programs on civil liberties, it examines crucial topics including religious freedom, immigration, race relations, academic freedom, equality of opportunity, criminal justice, property rights, corruption, the political process, and freedom of expression and the press.

Having undertaken this examination over many months, Freedom House concludes that today's American is quite free. The United States in 2008 remains a society in which political rights and civil liberties are widely though not universally respected. Challenges to those freedoms by government officials or other actors encounter vigorous and often successful resistance from civil society and the press, the political opposition, and a judiciary that is mindful of its role as a restraint on executive and legislative excess. Indeed, the dynamic, self-correcting nature of American democracy—the resilience of its core institutions and habits even in a time of military conflict—is the most significant finding of *Today's American: How Free?*

The study draws three broad conclusions that go to the heart of both the strengths of the American system and the challenges confronting it.

The United States has been relatively successful in managing the inevitable tensions of a society characterized by substantial racial, ethnic, and religious diversity. Unlike the European democracies, for instance, America has been a destination for immigrants throughout its history. Indeed, it has been defined by its continually changing demography. The country's ability to receive and integrate tens of millions of non-Europeans in recent decades is an impressive testament to the flexibility, fairness, and pragmatism of the American system. One might consider the United States to be the world's first truly globalized nation, given the origins of its people and its increasing economic and communications integration with their many homelands.

Nevertheless, America's comparative success in creating a multiracial and, in a sense, multinational society should not obscure the very real problems associated with such diversity. Racial minorities and immigrants are central to practically every issue that confronts the country today, including the difficult relationship between African Americans and the criminal justice system, the debate over the role of Muslims in American society, and the recurring controversy over illegal immigrants. Racial and religious differences give rise to demagogues on all sides. Angry arguments about "controlling our borders" and affirmative action are vivid reminders that pluralism makes hard demands on the institutions of free societies. The tensions and debates over the status of minorities and immigrants will remain with the United States long after the current contention over issues like the PATRIOT Act has been put to rest.

The restrictions on freedom posed by counterterrorism measures are worrying. This study expresses grave concern about attempts to extend executive authority without the usual congressional and judicial review, extraordinary renditions, mistreatment of those in U.S. custody, and warrantless wiretaps in contravention of the requirements of U.S. law.

However, the controversy surrounding the Bush administration's counterterrorism policies must be assessed at least in part within the context of the strains on civil liberties in previous times of war. To be sure, the United States should be judged by the standards of the 21st century, and not by those of yesteryear. It is important and heartening to note the extent to which the response of civil liberties advocates has been both crisp and ultimately persuasive with judges, including those presiding in military courts. But it is also worthwhile to acknowledge the great distance our society has traveled in the evolution of its democracy. In 1798, newspaper editors were jailed under the Sedition Act; during the Civil War, habeas corpus privileges were suspended; during World War I, women peaceably picketing at the White House for suffrage were imprisoned for "disrupting the war effort"; during World War II, censorship was imposed and Japanese Americans were placed in internment camps; and in the Vietnam War era, the FBI and CIA investigated thousands of Americans whose patriotism was questioned because of their antiwar opinions. Today, none of these practices would be tolerated, or even seriously considered.

The excesses of these earlier periods of conflict were each addressed and resolved by the normal workings of the American system, though often after some delay. Regarding today's civil liberties controversies, a process of rethinking and adjustment is already under way as this work goes to print. The executive branch is being challenged by the courts and by Congress, and

Congress is being challenged by the voters. Further corrections can be expected in the coming months and years. This is the larger, more important reality that gives Freedom House confidence in the democratic future of the United States. The American democracy responds to transgressions and is constantly reinvigorated.

A free press and an independent judiciary continue to be linchpins of the American system and are essential to preserving freedom in our society. The judiciary's role in repeatedly defending individual rights can be seen throughout this study. The rights of religious and racial minorities, the free speech protections for students and academics, the due process rights of American citizens (and others) detained as enemy combatants, the ability of accused criminals to mount an effective defense, the rights of women to secure equal access to economic opportunity—these are but a few examples of the many aspects of democratic fairness that are regularly addressed by the courts. The judiciary's function as guardian of minority rights is visible now in the national discussion about the rights of gay men and lesbians to marry, adopt, and inherit. The role of the press as a vital bulwark of freedom appears throughout this study in much the same way, and with respect to many of the same issues. The strength and independence of these two institutions has long been crucial to the protection of American freedoms, and is no less so in the current period of conflict and uncertainty.

Assessment Of Major Findings——The study highlights a number of enduring and systemic challenges to American democracy and the condition of individual freedom in the United States:

Racial Inequality

The United States has made important progress in race relations since the civil rights revolution. The fact that two African Americans, Colin Powell and Condoleezza Rice, have served as secretary of state in the administration of a Republican president, and that, as this study goes to press, Senator Barack Obama is a serious contender for the presidency, reflects the sweeping changes that have taken place over the past half century. Black Americans today are more prosperous and more visible at the upper echelons of society—in business, the professions, and politics—than at any time in our history. That Hispanics and Asian Americans have also served in important cabinet positions and at the heights of the corporate world, the armed forces, journalism, and academia is further evidence of the acceptance of racial and ethnic diversity as a fact of American life.

The justified celebration of pluralism, however, can obscure the substantial and enduring gap between whites and blacks in the United States. Racial inequality is a reality across a broad set of institutions, but is most notable in three areas: living standards, education, and criminal justice. African Americans are more likely than whites to be born out of wedlock, drop out of high school, fail to obtain a college degree, and be unemployed, and are much more likely to have spent time in prison or jail. On average they earn less than whites, and are less likely to work in high-paying professions. To be sure, most indicators are changing for the better. But for the sizeable segment of blacks who are living in poverty or in near poverty, the prospects remain bleak. This is especially the case for young black men in inner-city neighborhoods. There is in fact an emerging gender divide among young blacks, with women much more likely than men to graduate from high school and enter college.

Hispanics, the other of America's two largest minority groups, share with blacks a number of socioeconomic problems, including high rates of incarceration, substantial levels of poverty, and worryingly low rates of high school graduation. Since many are relatively recent immigrants, Hispanics are in certain respects following a pattern established by previous waves of immigrants from Southern and Eastern Europe, especially given the large portion of unskilled workers among Hispanic newcomers. But in an era in which education represents the most significant vehicle for joining the economic mainstream, the lag in Hispanic school achievement is a cause for concern.

Clearly the legacy of America's sordid history of slavery and segregation is an important factor in the problems that blacks confront today. The degree to which outright racial bias continues to be responsible for inequality is less obvious. The United States has done a lot over the past 40 years to expunge racism from its public institutions, economic life, and popular culture. In addition to the basic set of antidiscrimination laws, the country has mandated affirmative action in hiring and promotion policies, rewritten employment criteria (and exams for public-sector jobs) to eliminate potential cultural bias, adopted policies to ensure that minority political influence is not diluted by election laws or redistricting plans, and established a broad array of projects to encourage young blacks to enroll in higher education. The Justice Department continues to investigate and prosecute crimes committed against blacks and activists during the civil rights era, and various states have established the equivalents of truth commissions or otherwise acted to acknowledge historical wrongs, bringing a measure of belated justice for past crimes against African American citizens.

These measures have changed America in fundamental ways. But they have not contributed significantly to an improvement in the state of the inner-city poor. Increasingly, policymakers and African American community leaders have identified education as the key to future movement toward equality. Some within the black community have also pointed to aspects of black youth culture as an obstacle to achievement, especially for boys. Moreover, two of the most cherished goals of the movement for racial equality, residential integration and school desegregation, remain stubbornly out of reach. While some of the other pressing problems identified in this study—deficiencies in the electoral process and the civil liberties excesses of America's counterterrorism policies, to take two important examples—can clearly be addressed by policymakers, the solutions to America's racial divide are more elusive and appear at this juncture to be less obviously dependent on government action than was the case in the past.

Counterterrorism and Civil Liberties

There are many reasons to be critical of the Bush administration's counterterrorism policies, and these issues are addressed in some detail in the chapter on civil liberties. The central question of this assessment, however, is the state of Americans' individual freedom and the degree to which that freedom has been undermined or threatened by government actions. Generally speaking, the controversies over counterterrorism policies can be traced to the Bush administration's assertion of a degree of executive authority that is extraordinary even in wartime. A number of specific policy debates arose belatedly due to the administration's efforts to circumvent the normal checks and balances provided by Congress and the judiciary. We want to note the damage that some of the policies could cause if permitted to stand, but we do not want to exaggerate the extent to which they have actually affected Americans' civil liberties in the past few years.

The war on terrorism has resulted in significantly fewer violations of individual freedom than previous conflicts. In particular, American officials and the mainstream media have gone to great lengths to avoid demonization of Arab Americans and Muslims, in stark contrast to the treatment of German Americans during World War I and the placement of Japanese Americans in internment camps just over two decades later. During World War II, political leaders and the press routinely smeared the Japanese and Japanese Americans with crude, blatantly racist remarks. In the current situation, those few prominent Americans (including politicians, media commentators, and civic leaders) who have impugned the patriotism of Muslims and Arabs in America have themselves often been sharply rebuked by high officials from both parties and other leaders.

Similarly, there have been no efforts to curb political dissent in ways comparable to what transpired during both world wars and the Vietnam War. A series of huge antiwar rallies have been held since the invasion of Iraq, with no significant obstruction by federal or state authorities.

It remains to be seen whether evolving approaches to protecting national security will in the end prove equal to the task of countering the new and more lethal form of terrorism, and whether the existing body of international and domestic law takes the terrorism challenge sufficiently into account. Nonetheless, this study concludes that the international reputation of the United States, and thus its ability to pursue the "Freedom Agenda" that President Bush has so eloquently articulated in his foreign policy, has suffered a significant setback due to policies attributed to the war on terrorism. Of particular concern for this examination of the state of freedom in the United States are those policies that have led to the mistreatment of foreigners in American custody—including extraordinary rendition of suspects to countries with unsavory reputations regarding due process and torture, the acknowledged American use of interrogation techniques that are widely viewed as torture, and the long-term lack of legal status for those detained at Guantanamo—along with the growing use of warrantless wiretapping and computerized "data mining" on American citizens.

The direct impact of the USA PATRIOT Act and other counterterrorism measures on the civil liberties of American citizens overall is uncertain, although the electronic surveillance actions could involve millions of Americans. In addition, new revelations regularly point to overreach in antiterrorism cases by law enforcement agencies. While there is as yet little evidence to suggest that counterterrorism programs have severely impinged on the rights of substantial numbers of Americans, the potential for more widespread violations must be taken seriously. The judiciary (including military courts) has struck down some aspects of counterterrorism policy, and the prospects are good for further action by the courts and Congress to curtail or terminate initiatives that pose threats to individual rights.

Criminal Justice

The findings on the functioning of the criminal justice system are perhaps the most disquieting in this study. This is especially the case because, in so many other areas, the United States stands as a model rule-of-law society. Analysts consistently point to strong evidence of unequal treatment of blacks and Hispanics compared with whites, prison overcrowding and mistreatment of prisoners, and excessively long sentences, especially for non-violent drug offenders.

The increase in incarceration rates is jarring. In 1980, the rate of incarceration overall in America was 1.39 per thousand residents; by 2006, that figure had risen to 7.5. Also disturbing is the fact that a black man today has a one in three chance of being behind bars at some point during his lifetime. (If he has not completed high school, he has a 60 percent chance of going to prison.) In contrast, a white man has only a 1 in 17 chance of going to prison.

Those who defend recent American policies note that stricter enforcement and sentencing practices coincided with a major reduction in crime over the past quarter century. This is an important point. Public fears that crime is out of control have contributed to a lack of faith in democracy in a number of countries around the globe. While the effects of crime had not reached that level in America, the law-and-order issue was certainly a factor in political life, and violent crime was clearly contributing to the decline of major American cities and the impoverishment of minority neighborhoods. High rates of violent crime, and the sense that the country's political leadership was unable to offer effective remedies, enhanced cynicism toward the political process among many Americans.

Yet while one would expect some degree of correlation between crime rates and the rate of incarceration, in recent years the prison population has continued to expand despite the preceding drop in crime. Moreover, new policing initiatives have relied heavily on methods that some deem discriminatory toward blacks and Hispanics, such as stop-and-frisks and saturation-level police presence in certain neighborhoods.

Looking more broadly at the criminal justice system in America, important concerns have also been raised about prosecutorial tactics in cases of white-collar crime. Some have questioned whether the criminalization of certain business practices is appropriate, and whether due process is observed in the seizure of assets during the investigation and prosecution of alleged crimes. The zealous pursuit of particular white-collar cases has even drawn accusations of political motivation.

Political Process

The American political system is, in many critical aspects, either a work in progress or in need of serious repair. Some points of concern date back several decades (low voter turnout) and some date to the adoption of the Constitution (the Electoral College). Other issues, such as the effects of our decentralized system on the fairness of voting procedures, have come to the forefront more recently, as systemic barriers to participation and inequities within and across states have become better appreciated. The pervasive role of money in politics pits libertarian defenders of donors' First Amendment freedoms against those seeking to regulate campaign finance. The desire to regulate is in part a response to the apparently corrupting influence of candidates' perpetual search for campaign funds. It is also rooted in the notion that all Americans should have equal access to their government officials, regardless of personal wealth. Libertarians argue that such restrictions limit the choices available to voters, and that the only regulation needed is full disclosure of all contributions, allowing voters to decide whether a candidate may be unduly obligated to a particular donor or group of donors.

No American would say that the United States is a perfect democracy, or even that it administers elections as well it should. Indeed, controversies arising from electoral practices that could be corrected have in recent years dismayed America's admirers, and brought glee to its critics.

Notwithstanding the flaws discussed in the chapter on this topic, the American political system essentially works, in that new actors constantly enter the arena while incumbents and party majorities are ousted at each election; public opinion matters, and those citizens who choose to mobilize can affect outcomes very directly. The midterm elections of 2006 demonstrated anew that—despite concerns about the impact of gerrymandering, the presumed fund-raising advantages of incumbency, and efforts at vote suppression in key areas—the American people retain the power to change their leaders democratically.

Immigration

After the September 11, 2001, terrorist attacks, some feared that the United States would experience a new wave of anti-immigrant nativism that would threaten the country's tradition as a home for immigrants from around the world. There is ample precedent in American history to justify such fears. The anti-German sentiment associated with World War I and the political radicalism that followed the conflict played important roles in triggering three decades of highly restrictive immigration policy. Similarly, as noted above, World War II led to an upsurge in anti-Japanese feeling and the internment of more than 120,000 Japanese and Japanese Americans.

Furthermore, worries about the loyalty of immigrants from Muslim countries in the post-9/11 period dovetailed with a growing unease about the porousness of America's border with Mexico. Fears of terrorist infiltration combined with concern over the economic and social impact of millions of undocumented workers from Mexico and other Latin American countries elevated immigration to the top of the political agenda while this study was being prepared.

The tone and content of the debate is at times disturbing, especially the depiction of undocumented workers as lawbreaking economic burdens to American society. Some public officials have even advocated the deportation of the estimated 12 million illegal immigrants currently in the country. If this were seriously attempted, it would entail massive human injustice and violations of civil liberties. Still, unlike past periods of intense debate over immigration, the current controversy has not triggered widespread nativism or racism (although there have been localized incidents). And while failure to gain control over America's borders could obviously weaken public support for continuing substantial legal immigration, it is noteworthy that the main thrust of the restrictionist argument has been directed at illegal aliens and not at the basic U.S. policy of welcoming robust, legal inflows in a nondiscriminatory manner. The leading proposals for coping with existing undocumented immigrants have focused on ways to guide them toward legal status and citizenship. The events of 9/11 have reinforced the conviction that a principal objective of immigration policy should be the assimilation of new residents into the social and economic mainstream. Thus there has been a renewed emphasis on all immigrants learning the English language, moving toward citizenship, and integrating into the American workplace.

The treatment of immigrant Muslims and Arabs has been a concern in the post-9/11 period. In the months following the attacks, hate crimes against Muslims, which had been at a relatively low level, increased substantially. In a blatant violation of civil rights, the federal government rounded up and imprisoned some 1,200 Muslim men. Those detained were, with few exceptions, never charged with a crime and were often deprived of access to legal counsel. Many had overstayed their visas and were eventually sent back to their countries of origin. Other Muslims who were in the United States legally as immigrants or students were subjected to heightened scrutiny, and occasionally investigation, by the federal government.

While many Muslims complained that they were victims of unwarranted suspicion and or outright discrimination, the overall impact on their status in the United States was limited. Almost immediately after the attacks, the leaders of Muslim and Arab American organizations were consulted by senior federal officials and were often asked to appear at forums sponsored by Republicans and Democrats, public policy organizations, and interfaith groups. Within two years, the number of hate crimes against Muslims declined significantly. A survey published by the Pew Research Center in May 2007 found that the vast majority of Muslims in America are "pretty happy" or "very happy." The findings suggested widespread contentment with their economic status and indicated considerable intermingling with other groups. As Muslim and Arab immigrants continue to seek admission to the United States, established residents from both groups have increased their participation in the American political process since 9/11. Significantly, the Pew study found important differences between Muslim immigrants, who seemed to feel that they had in important ways attained the American dream, and U.S.-born Muslims, who were far less satisfied with their situation. This latter group primarily consists of African Americans, and their views thus reinforce this study's conclusion that reducing the black-white divide remains America's most formidable long-term challenge.

Equality of Opportunity Amid Economic Globalization

Among major liberal democracies, no country has been more aggressive in embracing the global economy than the United States. America's policies have had tangible benefits: the country is well positioned for global economic competition, has enjoyed several decades of low inflation, and has maintained a rate of unemployment that is low by the standards of the developed free-market world.

Most jobs in America are created by private businesses, large and small. The legal and cultural climate in the United States—which permits an individual to develop an idea and seize an economic opportunity by launching a new business, often aided by infusions of capital from risk-taking investors—is unparalleled in the world today, and is the foundation upon which American prosperity is built.

America's economic course, however, has also had its negative side. Most notable is the widening gap between those in the minority with the skills and training to take advantage of the new economic environment, and the rest of society. While rising inequality was initially put forward as a concern by liberals, conservatives too have recently begun to comment on the phenomenon. Even former Federal Reserve chairman Alan Greenspan has recently said that the growing differentials in income and wealth constitute potential threats to the future of capitalism.

In the United States, organized labor has traditionally worked to defend the rights of workers and soften capitalism's sharp edges. The steep decline in union membership over the past few decades is therefore unsettling. In 2006, only 12 percent of American workers were represented by unions, a remarkably low figure for a developed industrial democracy. An even more telling statistic is the unionization figure for the private sector: 7.4 percent (36.2 percent of public employees are unionized).

Unions in practically every liberal democracy have suffered losses in recent decades, due to the evolution of their economies away from industrial production and toward the provision of services. Yet in most of these countries, unions continue to represent a quarter or more of the private workforce and play a vital role, in partnership with management and government, in ensuring that the benefits of a productive economy are widely shared. In Canada, for instance, workers in the private sector are four times more likely to be unionized than their U.S. counterparts. The decline of unions is not in itself evidence that the rights of employees are being trampled or that workers are unhappy in their jobs. If workers choose to reject unions, that is their right in a democratic society. In the United States, however, the playing field has tilted against organized labor over the past three decades. Management resistance to unionization has increased, and both federal policies and the decisions of the National Labor Relations Board have narrowed the ability of unions to secure bargaining rights for workers.

Antidiscrimination Laws

Since the adoption of the 1964 Civil Rights Act, the United States has established an elaborate framework of laws and policies that are designed to prevent discrimination against women and racial and ethnic minorities. These laws have played an important role in transforming the status of groups that had previously played subordinate roles in the nation's economic life and had often been excluded from institutions of higher education.

Women in particular have gained from policies meant to accelerate their participation in the economy. While they are still grossly underrepresented in the halls of Congress, executive mansions, and corporate boardrooms across the country, women today are more likely than men to attend college, and their presence in medicine, law, and other professions has increased exponentially over the past several decades. We are confident that this will continue, as glass ceilings are broken by the pressures of meritocracy, targeted legal action, and the continuing evolution of cultural sensibilities on the part of men and women alike.

America's antidiscrimination legislation also applies to certain immigrant groups, and has thus had an impact on Hispanics and, to a lesser extent, Asians. Affirmative action plans for university admissions have generally lumped Hispanics with African Americans as beneficiaries of preferential treatment. The inclusion of Hispanics in such plans has generated controversy above and beyond the basic divisions over giving preference based on group identity. Some question whether Hispanics and other immigrant groups should be included in programs originally designed to compensate for the historical injustices endured by black Americans during and after slavery.

While 19 states, the District of Columbia, and numerous municipalities have enacted laws barring discrimination based on sexual orientation, federal law in this area offers nothing comparable to the antidiscrimination legislation covering race, religion, ethnicity, sex, age, disability, and pregnancy. As this report was finalized in November 2007, the U.S. House of Representatives passed, 235 to 184, the Employment Nondiscrimination Act. If cleared by the Senate and signed into law, it would grant broad protections against discrimination in the workplace for gay men, lesbians, and bisexuals. Opinion surveys show that a plurality of Americans oppose discrimination against homosexuals, but a majority still reject same-sex marriage, a matter with which state legislatures and the courts continue to grapple.

Religious Freedom After 9/11

The American tradition of tolerance and protection for religious minorities has held firm despite a measure of popular resentment aimed at Muslims in the wake of the 2001 terrorist attacks. Muslims, like Catholics, Jews, and adherents of other faiths and denominations, are free to practice their religion in what remains a predominantly Protestant country. While new policies established under the PATRIOT Act allow federal authorities to monitor religious institutions, there have been few complaints that the state is interfering with the normal routines of churches, synagogues, and mosques. Indeed, the religious life of today's American is robust, with one of the highest rates of regular attendance at religious services in the developed world. Aside from the unhappiness in the Sikh community in the summer of 2007, when airport security-screening procedures were extended to head coverings including the turbans worn by Sikh men, the United States has largely avoided major controversies of the sort that have erupted in some European countries over the wearing of headscarves, veils, or other items that have a religious significance. Likewise, the American tradition of church-state separation has been maintained, despite some efforts to weaken it.

Press Freedom

The American media face a number of problems, some of which emerged after 9/11, but they remain free to collect and report news and information. The press long ago established itself as an indispensable guarantor of the broader array of democratic freedoms in the United States. While some have complained that the mainstream media were insufficiently skeptical of the government's case for the invasion of Iraq, the press has been notably independent and vigorous in its overall reporting on controversial aspects of the war on terrorism. Major newspapers and television networks have devoted extensive coverage to the administration's surveillance program, the detention of terrorism suspects in foreign jails, the prison camp at Guantanamo, and the Abu Ghraib scandal. There was some debate over the practice of reporters being embedded with American military units during the initial phases of the Iraq war, but even then the press was subject to very little censorship. In the years since the invasion, American media have provided fulsome coverage of the escalating civil strife and the succession of American setbacks in the country. Separately, the press has closely followed a series of domestic scandals involving corporate leaders, elected officials, and lobbyists.

Freedom of information has been threatened in recent years by the Bush administration's pronounced tendency toward enhanced secrecy. The manifestations of this shift have included limited press access to administration officials and a major increase in the volume of documents that have been classified and thus made unavailable to the public. Indeed, according to press reports, a program to reclassify previously declassified documents was launched at the behest of Vice President Dick Cheney. Meanwhile, there have been a number of cases in which the press has published information that had been classified for national security reasons, and journalists have faced an increase in demands by prosecutors and judges to reveal the identity of confidential sources and turn over investigative notes. Although a direct confrontation between the government and the press has been avoided during the post-9/11 period, the issue of the media's right to publish classified material may yet require the attention of policymakers and the courts.

An accelerated decline in the economic conditions of the newspaper industry and the continued consolidation of major media outlets have raised concerns about media diversity. Critics have also highlighted the power of certain media, such as talk radio and political blogs, to polarize public opinion on various matters. These problems, however, are perhaps more than offset by the exponential growth in information options driven by cable and satellite services; the internet, including opinion and commentary venues like blogs; and better access to the remaining variety of U.S. and foreign newspapers, magazines, and wire services.

Conclusion

While this study examines the deficiencies in American democracy today, our conclusions about the overall state of freedom are optimistic. More than six years after 9/11, the American people are blessed with a society dedicated to the protection of liberty and committed to the institutions of democratic politics and the rule of law.

This publication is not meant to be prescriptive. We have not included a list of proposals and policies to deal with the weaknesses that are identified. Some problems, in fact, appear to lie beyond the scope of traditional government action. Thus while we have cited racial inequality as perhaps the most important problem facing American democracy, we do not see a direct and obvious link between the poverty that continues to afflict African Americans disproportionately and any particular legislative remedy.

However, other problems highlighted in this study could certainly be ameliorated, if not entirely resolved, through a change in administration policies or in the law. The courts have issued decisions to deal with certain excesses of counterterrorism policy, but more can and should be done by Congress. Likewise, state legislatures can and should enact measures to develop a more equitable and humane criminal justice system.

Finally, as the world's leading democracy, the United States has a special obligation to ensure that its own electoral and political processes adhere to the highest standards of fairness, inclusion, and transparency. The aftermath of the 2000 presidential election brought national and international attention to a number of problems with the conduct of elections, campaign funding, and the selection of nominees that had been festering for years. While Congress has addressed a few of these deficiencies, more aggressive action is called for if the American method of choosing political leaders is to match our nation's democratic ideals.

Today's American lives in freedom. The self-correcting democratic system will continue to protect that freedom so long as its institutions remain robust and Americans remain willing to scrutinize and improve their own conditions and practices. It is our hope that this report helps to catalyze that process.

The Civil Liberties Implications
of Counterterrorism Policies

In the history of the United States, the American commitment to civil liberties has frequently been put to the test. The Alien and Sedition Acts of the late eighteenth century, the suspension of habeas corpus during the Civil War, the persecution of war critics during World War I and the Red Scare that followed it, the internment of Japanese Americans during World War II, the McCarthyite phenomenon during the early cold war, and the government's campaign of surveillance targeting opponents of the Vietnam War—all were driven by a perceived need to protect the United States against foreign adversaries or internal subversion. The darker chapters of American history, especially those involving crackdowns against immigrants and political dissent, have almost always occurred during times of war or the threat of war.

It is within the context of a history in which the rights of the individual have been placed in jeopardy mainly during wartime that we must assess American counterterrorism policies in the wake of the September 11, 2001, attacks on the United States.

This chapter deals with those aspects of President George W. Bush's counterterrorism agenda that have drawn criticism from civil libertarians and others in the United States and abroad, including the USA PATRIOT Act, warrantless domestic surveillance, extraordinary renditions, harsh detention and interrogation policies, the opening of a special detention facility at Guantanamo Bay, and efforts to curtail judicial review of such matters. The report details the arguments advanced against these policies as well as those articulated by the Bush administration and its supporters. But this is not a simple "on the one hand, on the other hand" assessment. The chapter shows that a number of the actions taken by the administration in its war on terrorism present genuine threats to the individual rights of American citizens and of foreign citizens caught up in the counterterrorism net.

At the same time, it is important to point out that the setbacks to individual rights during the war on terrorism pose less severe threats to American liberty than those that arose during the major conflicts of the past. The United States has not declared a wholesale suspension of habeas corpus rights, outlawed political dissent, placed tens of thousands of non-white residents in domestic detention centers, ordered security services to conduct campaigns of surveillance against war critics, or blacklisted entertainers and academics who differed with the policies of the federal government. Nor has the government taken sweeping action against the press, despite article after article that revealed sensitive information about counterterrorism initiatives.

In an evaluation of the administration's policies, there is also the question of whether the laws and techniques developed to cope with traditional military conflicts and espionage tactics are suited to a conflict involving inchoate, global terrorist networks that disregard the traditional rules of warfare and are committed to inflicting massive casualties on the civilian population of the United States and other countries. Civil libertarians and others have argued strongly that the laws and policies devised to deal with traditional warfare are sufficient to cope with the threat of terrorism. They may be right. But at this point the United States and other democratic societies are still grappling with this extremely important issue.

Finally, as this chapter points out, the countervailing forces of American democracy have tempered a number of the administration's more ambitious initiatives and will no doubt have an important impact on the shape of America's counterterrorism regime in the future. The courts, Congress, and the press have all played an important role in forcing changes in the administration's approach; their role will, if anything, become more significant as counterterrorism policies are further refined and moderated.

The USA PATRIOT Act

The Uniting and Strengthening America by Providing Appropriate Tools Required to Intercept and Obstruct Terrorism Act (known as the USA PATRIOT Act, or simply the PATRIOT Act) was signed into law by President Bush on October 26, 2001. It was sought by the administration and passed by Congress in response to 9/11, and was intended to expand the authority of law enforcement officials and intelligence agents to combat terrorism in the United States and abroad. The PATRIOT Act amended many existing U.S. statutes, including immigration laws, banking laws, anti–money laundering laws, and the 1978 Foreign Intelligence Surveillance Act (FISA). Although the law enjoyed widespread approval in Congress when it was passed, and despite its renewal in March 2006 by a vote of 280 to 138 in the House, many of its provisions are still highly controversial and have been challenged in court.

This controversy is particularly important because the use of the PATRIOT Act both leads and perpetuates a long-term broadening of governmental powers. Many of the most hotly disputed provisions are modeled on preexisting antiracketeering statutes. These statutes had strengthened the penalties for certain offenses committed by members of criminal organizations, and lowered the government's burden of proof in criminal investigations and trials.[1] Although they are controversial even as applied to their original target, organized crime, antiracketeering laws are now being used to prosecute other crimes as well. In a similar way, many of the antiterrorism tools provided in the PATRIOT Act are now being used to pursue those suspected of other crimes, particularly drug crimes.

The PATRIOT Act is divided into 10 titles. Title I establishes a federal fund for counterterrorism efforts and authorizes the president to seize funds belonging to any "foreign person, foreign organization, or foreign country" which he finds has participated in a terrorist attack against the United States. This provision is modeled on criminal asset forfeiture laws, which allow the government to seize the assets of accused criminals without due process.

Title II amends FISA to allow greater surveillance of suspected terrorists and spies, both foreign and domestic. The provisions of Title II are among the most contentious parts of the act. Detractors argue that the increased surveillance they permit impinges on individual rights without meaningfully increasing protection from terrorism.

Under the U.S. Constitution's Fourth Amendment and Title III of the Omnibus Crime Control and Safe Streets Act of 1968, government searches in criminal investigations cannot be undertaken without warrants specifying the place to be examined and the reasons for the action. FISA allows the government to conduct warrantless searches if a federal judge finds probable cause that the target is conducting espionage for a foreign power. However, according to Title II of the PATRIOT Act, if the government merely certifies to a judge that a search is related to terrorism, the judge has no authority to reject the search application. In July 2002, the Justice Department said of this provision, "Such an order could conceivably be served on a public library, bookstore, or newspaper."[2] The University of Illinois reported that in the months following 9/11, 10.7 percent of all libraries received requests for reports about patrons' reading materials. Because the recipients are gagged under the law, such requests may be significantly underreported.[3]

Title II specifically authorizes the government to use "trap and trace" devices and pen registers—which provide information about telecommunications sent and received from a given source—against any non–U.S. citizen in the United States or against any person suspected of involvement with international terrorism or clandestine intelligence activities. Title II also authorizes "roving surveillance," permitting the government to intercept communications without specifying the facility or location. Instead, the government may avail itself of all the information, facilities, or technical assistance necessary to monitor a given target while protecting the secrecy of its investigation. Critics have noted that under the PATRIOT Act, authorities need not identify the target to obtain a wiretap, but can instead establish "John Doe" roving taps. The authorization of roving surveillance was designed in part as a response to new technologies such as cellular telephones, e-mail, and other means of rapid communication.

Although Title II requires warrants for searches and record seizures in terrorism investigations, it does not require the government to notify those being searched and indeed requires officials to keep their searches secret. Because these searches are performed without the knowledge of property owners, the Federal Bureau of Investigation (FBI) calls them "sneak and peek" searches. While warrants for access to records require the authorization of a judge, an order to obtain records may be granted *ex parte*, and warrants may not disclose the reason for the search. These sneak and peek warrants have since been used in drug cases and other ordinary criminal matters.[4]

Title III attempts to cut off funds to terrorist organizations by strengthening banking rules against international money laundering. It requires banks and other financial institutions to file reports with the federal government about transactions in excess of $10,000, and prohibits financial institutions from notifying customers when they report suspicious activity to the government. It also expands U.S. jurisdiction over financial crimes committed outside of the United States.

Title IV enhances the power of the attorney general and federal immigration authorities to prohibit people affiliated with terrorist organizations from entering the country. Critics note that the law does not provide for any judicial oversight of the "terrorist" designation of people or groups. Title IV also requires the attorney general to detain aliens engaged in activities that endanger national security. After these aliens have been held for six months, the attorney general must determine whether they still represent a threat. However, so long as the attorney general reviews and recertifies the threat every six months, aliens may be held indefinitely.

Title V of the PATRIOT Act contains a highly controversial provision that greatly expands the authorized uses of National Security Letters (NSLs). An NSL is a form of administrative subpoena that was created by FISA in 1978. FISA authorized the federal government to use NSLs to request that an electronic communication service, such as a phone company, provide information about its subscribers and their activities. NSLs were to be used only against persons directly suspected of terrorist activity, and companies were not permitted to tell these persons that the government had accessed their records.

NSLs have always been controversial because unlike other warrants, they do not require judicial oversight and do not allow subjects to know that they are being monitored. However, Title V of the PATRIOT Act expands the number of federal agents who may authorize the use of NSLs. It also permits the use of NSLs against a far broader category of targets: persons whose information is "relevant to an authorized investigation to protect against international terrorism or clandestine intelligence activities."

Title VII of the PATRIOT Act allows federal and state law enforcement agencies to share more information with one another than they previously could, and to "make grants and enter into contracts" with nonprofit organizations to stop criminal activities that cross jurisdictional boundaries.

Almost six years after it was passed, the nation remains divided over the PATRIOT Act. Eight states and 396 cities and counties have passed resolutions condemning the law as a violation of civil liberties. At least one city has passed a law barring city employees from complying with federal investigations that would violate civil liberties, although some experts question the legality of such an ordinance. Surveys have reported that at least half of Americans are concerned that tactics used in fighting terrorism may violate civil liberties.

National Security Agency Wiretapping Controversy

The PATRIOT Act is not the only post-9/11 measure to have awakened concerns about civil liberties. In December 2005, the *New York Times* reported that the National Security Agency (NSA) was eavesdropping on telephone calls between people in the United States and associates in foreign nations.[5] Under an ongoing program, the NSA was monitoring certain calls without obtaining a FISA warrant either in advance or retroactively. Bush had secretly authorized the program, claiming that the Constitution afforded him broad, inherent powers that superseded legislation like FISA. He also cited a resolution passed by Congress shortly after 9/11 that authorized him to use force in combating terrorism.

In response to the revelation of the NSA program, the Bush administration has asserted that the FISA warrant requirement is slow and cumbersome and had been hindering terrorism investigations. Some administration officials have said that if the NSA program had been in effect in 2001, it might have caught some of the 9/11 hijackers and averted the attacks.[6] But critics of the program note that FISA permits the NSA to seek retroactive warrants up to three days after it conducts surveillance, so that no surveillance need be delayed by the warrant process. Indeed, U.S. District Court Judge Royce Lamberth, presiding judge of the FISA court from 1995 to 2002, has in recent public remarks vigorously defended the court's speed, efficiency, and responsiveness, including specifically on the morning of September 11, 2001.[7] Furthermore, and notwithstanding Lamberth's insistence that the FISA court is not a *pro forma* process, the warrants are obtainable; through 2004, the court had denied only five of the 18,766 warrants the government had requested.

Despite the president's sweeping legal assertions, on August 17, 2006, a U.S. District Court judge found the NSA wiretapping program to be illegal under FISA and unconstitutional under the First and Fourth amendments, and ordered warrants to be obtained for all wiretaps. The judge's ruling has been stayed pending appeal.[8] On January 17, 2007, Attorney General Alberto Gonzales announced that the special presidential authorization allowing the warrantless surveillance would not be renewed, and that all future surveillance of terrorism suspects would be subject to the approval of a FISA court. In August 2007, Congress enacted legislation, to remain in force for only six months, that legalized warrantless wiretaps of American citizens in terrorism cases. As Congress was debating whether and how to amend that legislation in the autumn of 2007, the Democratic majority supported provisions that would require court approval for a number of procedures used by the government, including the method for selecting those subjected to surveillance. A related matter involved the question of legal liability for U.S. corporations that have cooperated with the NSA by providing it with data, apparently including e-mail and telephone communications between persons in the United States, as well as between persons in the United States and others abroad. With lawsuits pending against major telecommunications firms, the Bush administration was trying to persuade Congress to provide them with immunity for their handling of customers' information.[9]

The Extraordinary Rendition Program

Extradition treaties between the United States and many foreign governments require U.S. officials to arrest and extradite individuals suspected of having committed crimes in other signatory nations, and for whom arrest warrants have been issued in those nations. This practice is known as rendition. However, since the mid-1990s, the United States has engaged in "extraordinary rendition": turning over suspected criminals or terrorists to foreign governments for interrogation, trial, or imprisonment, even if no specific warrants have been issued for their arrest. Human rights advocates allege that the practice may allow suspects to be tortured in the countries to which they are taken.

The Central Intelligence Agency (CIA) first used extraordinary rendition in cooperation with foreign governments that were trying to investigate and dismantle militant Islamist organizations, particularly al-Qaeda. The policy was deemed necessary because without it, terrorist suspects held in the United States were entitled to due process rights that the CIA feared could jeopardize intelligence sources. The CIA also believed that intelligence agencies in suspects' home countries would be more successful than American officials in obtaining information from them, because of their common language and culture. The administration of President Bill Clinton accordingly issued an order in 1995 that permitted the practice.

Since 9/11, the United States has continued to use extraordinary rendition in terrorism investigations that involve foreign-born suspects who are believed to have key information. The government does not release information about the identity of suspects rendered, the countries to which they are taken, or the conditions under which they are held. However, some cases do come to public attention.

On September 26, 2002, for instance, Canadian citizen Maher Arar was detained by U.S. officials at New York City's JFK Airport, where he was awaiting a connecting flight on his way home from a vacation. In early October, U.S. authorities transferred Arar, who was born in Syria but had lived in Canada since he was 17, to the custody of the Syrian government as a suspected terrorist. He had been under U.S. investigation due to his relationship with two individuals suspected of ties to al-Qaeda.

Arar later reported that the Syrians held him for 10 months in a windowless cell, where he was beaten and tortured in an attempt to make him confess to terrorist activities.[10] He said that under this pressure he did confess that he had worked with terrorists in Afghanistan.

Canadian officials were not informed of Arar's rendition until several days after the fact. When it did learn that he had been rendered, Canada issued a temporary travel advisory warning Canadians born in Iran, Iraq, Libya, Sudan, or Syria "to consider carefully whether they should attempt to enter the United States for any reason, including transit to or from third countries." In addition to the rendition, Canada expressed concern about a U.S. decision to photograph, fingerprint, and monitor travelers born in those countries regardless of their current citizenship. In November 2003 the Bush administration agreed to exempt Canadian travelers from these identification and monitoring regulations, although they are still in effect for those without Canadian citizenship.[11]

After prolonged negotiations between the Canadian government and Syria, Arar was released and returned to Canada in October 2003. He was never charged with a crime. He has since sued the U.S. government, alleging that it was aware of Syria's policy of torture and that it deported him in violation of U.S. law and treaty obligations with Canada. Attorney General Gonzales responded that the United States had received assurances from Syria that Arar would not be tortured.

The U.S. government has also been accused of holding and torturing foreign nationals in its own secret prisons in violation of international law. According to one lawsuit filed by the American Civil Liberties Union (ACLU), the CIA in January 2004 took custody of German citizen Khaled El-Masri, who had been arrested by the government of Macedonia while he was vacationing in that country. The CIA took him to Afghanistan, where it held him for four months in a prison known as the "Salt Pit." While in custody, El-Masri alleges that he was beaten, threatened, and denied communication with a lawyer or his family. When he and other prisoners began a hunger strike to protest the conditions of their detention, he was force-fed and medicated under the supervision of American doctors. It is suspected that El-Masri was detained because his name was similar to that of terrorism suspect Khaled Al-Masri. He was warned as a condition of his release not to discuss his detention.[12]

In May 2006 a U.S. District Court ruled that El-Masri could not sue the CIA and the U.S. government for information about the extraordinary rendition program or for compensation for his detention. The court stated that El-Masri's lawsuit could jeopardize national security by forcing the government to disclose information about antiterrorism strategies.

In September 2006, President Bush publicly acknowledged for the first time that the CIA had operated secret prisons abroad. Some commentators have also alleged that the U.S. operates secret prisons aboard naval ships.[13] However, the president denied that torture had been used in American-run facilities, saying American agents used "alternative" interrogation methods to gather information from suspected terrorists. While these tactics were "tough," the president said, they were also "safe and lawful and necessary." State Department and administration officials said no detainees were being held in secret prisons at that time, but maintained that the CIA still had the authority to detain and question suspects in the manner described.

In response to President Bush's revelation, members of Congress began discussing new legislation to govern the use of military tribunals for terrorism suspects. Senator Carl Levin, a Michigan Democrat who became the chairman of the Senate Armed Services Committee in January 2007, promised a full investigation into the extraordinary rendition program and alleged abuses by the CIA. The European Parliament conducted an investigation of its own and found that many European Union member states had assisted in the capture and extraordinary rendition of suspects by the United States.[14]

Guantanamo Bay Detainment Camp

On November 13, 2001, President Bush issued an order authorizing the capture and detention of suspected al-Qaeda terrorists by military forces,[15] and in 2002, the U.S. military opened a prison and interrogation center at the Guantanamo Bay Naval Base in Cuba. Today the prison holds people suspected by the executive branch and the armed forces of being operatives of al-Qaeda or the Taliban, and most of them were captured by the United States or its allies on the battlefield in Afghanistan or Iraq. Both the status of these detainees and their treatment in detention are highly controversial in the United States and abroad.

A total of 775 detainees (or "enemy combatants") have been held at Guantanamo Bay, although approximately one-third have now been released. They include citizens of Pakistan, Saudi Arabia, China, the United Kingdom, and 30 other countries. In the 2001 order, President Bush specified the conditions under which the detainees would be held, calling for humane treatment, the free exercise of religion, and medical treatment, but excluding the right to challenge their detention or appeal the decisions of military tribunals in U.S. courts.

The stated reason for holding the prisoners is to interrogate them about ongoing terrorist activities. In the beginning, the Defense Department maintained that enemy combatants were not entitled to the protections of the Geneva Conventions,[16] and that the government was authorized to interrogate them using techniques that would otherwise be banned. Officials have issued several sets of orders approving interrogation techniques for use at Guantanamo Bay. In December 2002, Defense Secretary Donald Rumsfeld authorized a set of interrogation guidelines for Guantanamo that had been suggested in an action memo from William J. Haynes II, the Pentagon's general counsel. Among the approved techniques were: the use of physical "stress positions"; 20-hour interrogations; removal of clothing; using a detainee's phobias (such as fear of dogs) to induce stress; deception to make the detainee believe the interrogator was from a country with a reputation for torture; the use of falsified documents and reports; isolation for up to 30 days; and sensory deprivation.[17]

Under pressure from civilian and military attorneys, led by Navy General Counsel Alberto Mora, the Defense Department in January 2003 agreed to rescind orders for these techniques. In April 2003 new interrogation guidelines were released, eliminating some of the harsher measures approved in 2002. However, former prisoners and visitors to Guantanamo Bay have alleged that inmates have been drugged, beaten, electrocuted, and denied food and water. One FBI agent who witnessed interrogations told the *New York Times*, "On a couple of occasions, I entered interview rooms to find a detainee chained hand and foot in a fetal position to the floor, with no chair, food or water. Most times they had urinated or defecated on themselves and had been left there for 18, 24 hours or more."[18] The government has denied these claims.

In October 2005, President Bush signed the Detainee Treatment Act of 2005, which limited the interrogation techniques allowed at Guantanamo Bay and other American military detention facilities to those identified in the Army Field Manual.

Some legal experts are also concerned about the status of the Guantanamo detainees under international and U.S. law. The U.S. government at the time of their capture maintained that detainees did not have the same due process rights accorded to prisoners of war, in keeping with the executive order. In particular, the government argued that because Guantanamo Bay is in Cuba rather than in the United States, U.S. courts did not have jurisdiction to consider the legality of their detention. Amnesty International has expressed the views of many human rights advocates in asserting that as a result, the detainees are "held in effect in a legal black hole, many without access to any court, legal counsel or family visits."

The legality of the detainees' status has been the subject of numerous lawsuits, most of which have been decided against the Bush administration. In 2004, *Rasul v. Bush* challenged the U.S. government's practice of denying Guantanamo detainees the ability to file habeas corpus petitions in federal court. The Supreme Court ruled that because the United States has "complete jurisdiction" over the base, detainees may file habeas corpus petitions in American courts to challenge the validity of their detention.[19]

In response, the Defense Department in July 2004 announced the creation of Combatant Status Review Tribunals, in which detainees could contest their status as enemy combatants. The detainees would be allowed to view all unclassified evidence against them and to argue before military officials that they had been improperly designated and should be released. In February

2005, a federal judge ruled that the combatants were entitled to consult with legal counsel and to view all of the evidence against them in order to mount a defense.[20]

The Supreme Court dealt another blow to the Bush administration in *Hamdan v. Rumsfeld* (2006). In this case the court held that special military commissions set up to try detainees, which were separate from the review tribunals, "violate both the [Uniform Code of Military Justice] and the four Geneva Conventions."[21] The court found the administration's plan for the commissions inadequate, since it deviated from normal courtroom procedure—without explicit approval from Congress—by admitting evidence kept secret from defendants, allowing testimony gained through torture, and submitting appeals to the executive branch rather than to an appellate court. As a result of the decision, in July 2006 the Bush administration was forced to reverse its policy regarding the Geneva Conventions and state that all detainees at Guantanamo and in U.S. military custody elsewhere were now entitled to Article 3 Geneva protections.

On October 17, 2006, President Bush signed the Military Commissions Act to "facilitate bringing to justice terrorists and other unlawful enemy combatants through full and fair trials by military commissions." The act authorizes the president to create commissions according to the rules set forth in *Hamdan*. It has been criticized for denying habeas corpus rights to enemy combatants or aliens awaiting status determinations, and for allowing the government to detain them indefinitely without trial. However, the act does create a stronger legal basis for the military trials and limits the commissions' use to non–U.S. citizens.

American Citizens Held as Enemy Combatants

The enemy combatants held at Guantanamo Bay are foreign nationals. But in April 2002, officials at Guantanamo learned that Yaser Esam Hamdi, an enemy combatant captured while fighting for the Taliban in Afghanistan, was actually a U.S. citizen. Upon this discovery Hamdi was transferred to a military prison in Virginia, where he was held for questioning without access to a lawyer until December 2003. The government maintained the right to detain him indefinitely as an enemy combatant and filed no charges against him. In June 2002 Hamdi's family filed a habeas corpus petition and asked a federal judge to order the government to charge Hamdi or release him.

In the June 2004 ruling *Hamdi v. Rumsfeld*, the Supreme Court ordered the government to provide Hamdi with access to counsel and the opportunity to review and rebut the evidence against him. However, Justice Sandra Day O'Connor, writing for the court, also said that the rights of the accused must be balanced against the security interests of the nation as a whole. Requiring an ordinary criminal trial for Hamdi would impede the government's ability to maintain national security, while denying him the right to challenge his classification as an enemy combatant would grant him too little protection. O'Conner argued that Hamdi must have his case heard by an impartial, properly constituted tribunal, but that the tribunal could be run without some of the normal procedural protections afforded in a criminal court, such as a ban on hearsay evidence, and with the burden of proof on the defendant rather than the government.

In October 2004, the government announced that it had agreed to release Hamdi on the condition that he renounce his U.S. citizenship and move to Saudi Arabia, where the Saudi government would monitor his movements. (He had been born in the United States to Saudi parents, and the family had moved to Saudi Arabia when he was a child.) Hamdi also relinquished his right to sue the government over his detention.

Although *Hamdi* pertained specifically to citizen-detainees, the case had significant implications for the treatment of all alleged enemy combatants, including foreign nationals. Based on the holdings of *Hamdi* and *Rasul*, the U.S. government has conceded the right of all detainees to consult with legal counsel and to challenge their status as enemy combatants before impartial tribunals.

Another American citizen captured in Afghanistan, John Walker Lindh, was treated differently. Because he was immediately identified as an American, Lindh was detained at a Marine

Corps base in Afghanistan and questioned about his affiliations with the Taliban and al-Qaeda. He signed a confession, but later alleged that his request for an attorney had been denied and that he had been coerced into waiving his right to remain silent. Attorney General John Ashcroft announced that Lindh would be tried in the United States on charges of conspiracy to commit murder and conspiracy to commit terrorism. Because his confession would likely be excluded under U.S. law as the result of coercion, the government offered Lindh a plea bargain in return for his cooperation. He is currently serving a 20-year federal prison sentence.

Jose Padilla, an American citizen accused of being a terrorist, was arrested at a Chicago airport in May 2002 and held on a material witness warrant in connection with 9/11. Padilla challenged the warrant, and on June 9, 2002—two days before a judge was scheduled to rule on his challenge—President Bush ordered Defense Secretary Rumsfeld to detain him as an enemy combatant. The government alleged that Padilla had intelligence about future attacks on the United States and posed a continuing threat to national security. He was moved to a South Carolina military prison, where his attorney and family were denied access to him.

Padilla's attorney filed a habeas corpus petition naming Rumsfeld as the respondent. On December 18, 2003, the U.S. 2nd Circuit Court of Appeals in New York City found the habeas petition valid and ruled that "the President lacked inherent constitutional authority as Commander-in-Chief to detain American citizens on American soil outside a zone of combat." The court ordered Padilla released from military prison within 30 days, whereupon the government could choose to try him in civilian court.[22] The appeals court agreed to stay the release order pending a Supreme Court challenge.

After a series of procedural appeals that bounced Padilla's case through the federal court system for nearly two years, in September 2005 a three-judge panel of the U.S. 4th Circuit Court of Appeals in Richmond, Virginia, ruled that President Bush did indeed have the authority to detain Padilla without charges, holding that such detention during wartime is vital to national security.[23] The federal government moved Padilla to civilian custody and indicted him in November 2005 on charges of conspiracy, but not terrorism-related offenses. The move effectively averted a Supreme Court review of the Richmond court's judgment. On April 2, 2006, the Supreme Court formally declined Padilla's appeal, which had dealt with his military confinement, but Chief Justice John G. Roberts Jr. noted that the court would monitor the civilian trial to ensure that he received the protections "guaranteed to all federal criminal defendants."

Padilla alleges that he was tortured while in detention, and his lawyers have asked to present evidence of this to his jury. In November 2006, the Justice Department filed a petition to block them from doing so. Padilla's lawyers have also asked the judge in his case to dismiss the charges against him due to the severity of the abuse they say he suffered in detention. These efforts have been rejected by the courts, and in August 2007 he was convicted by a federal jury on conspiracy charges. Sentencing was scheduled to take place in December 2007.

Immigration

Because many of the 9/11 terrorists entered America legally, the government has since sought to tighten control of the nation's borders. The PATRIOT Act and other laws have provided funding to this end, and in March 2003, immigration fell under the jurisdiction of the new Homeland Security Department.

In addition, federal immigration authorities have been granted new power to detain illegal immigrants who cannot be returned to their countries of origin. Any who enter the United States illegally or commit crimes on U.S. soil, but who are stateless or whose home countries will not take them back, can be detained indefinitely. More than 3,000 people are now being held indefinitely by the immigration service.

Title IV of the PATRIOT Act requires the attorney general to monitor the activity of foreigners who enter the United States on student visas, as some experts have noted that student visas could easily be exploited by potential terrorists. Hani Hanjour, a 9/11 hijacker, had used a student visa to enter the country. However, increased scrutiny of visa applicants has created a hardship for many foreign students enrolled in American universities, especially those from "high-risk" nations.[24]

The immigration provisions of the PATRIOT Act have also affected some refugees seeking asylum from countries associated with terrorism. Under current law, asylum-seeking immigrants may be detained or deported if they have ever provided "material support" to terrorist organizations. However, the law makes no distinction between voluntary and coerced support. Some refugees seeking asylum in the United States—including those from Colombia, Burma, and other nations—have been denied entry because the terrorist groups in their home countries extorted money from them.[25]

The Transportation Security Administration

Before 9/11, airport security in the United States was a private enterprise. It was handled by companies under contract with government agencies that operated individual airports, companies that owned airport terminals, or individual airlines operating their own terminals. Security procedures were largely standardized, with metal detectors and other measures common to all major airports and carriers. Passengers were required to submit to searches of their persons and property as a condition of buying their tickets and boarding their flights.

After the 9/11 hijackers succeeded in bringing weapons aboard four commercial passenger jets, many critics of the decentralized American system charged that private companies were not doing enough to protect the nation from the threat of airline hijacking. They argued that because air travel constitutes interstate commerce and affects national security, the federal government should control airport security.

On November 19, 2001, President Bush signed the Aviation and Transportation Security Act, which authorized the

Transportation Department to federalize airport security. The department created the Transportation Security Administration (TSA), which oversees security for highways, railways, mass transit, ports, and domestic airports. In 2003, the TSA was placed under the new Homeland Security Department.

The TSA, which today employs more than 40,000 screeners, has been criticized by air travelers and civil liberties groups alike. Many of the complaints have developed into lawsuits concerning privacy issues, but they have been largely unsuccessful. While the Fourth Amendment generally protects Americans from searches of their persons or property without warrants, the courts have historically granted wider latitude to government agents participating in a systematic law enforcement program designed to prevent terrorism and other crimes.

In *United States v. Skipwith* (1973), the U.S. 5th Circuit Court of Appeals in New Orleans, Louisiana, held that people preparing to board planes, "like those seeking entrance into the country, are subject to a search based on mere or unsupported suspicion."[26] Random searches are allowed under certain circumstances, and law enforcement officials are given the benefit of the doubt in identifying probable cause for any specific search in light of their specialized training.[27] Airport screening has additionally been found constitutional because in most cases, passengers have the opportunity to refuse a search by refusing to fly. Passengers imply their consent to be searched when they attempt to fly, and that consent may not be revoked once passengers have presented themselves for boarding.[28]

Although security agents have broad authority to search passengers and profiling is permitted, U.S. law does not permit race or ethnicity to be the sole basis of the profile that triggers a search. Nonetheless, since its inception the TSA has been plagued by accusations that its screeners single out passengers who appear to be of Arab descent or Muslim faith.

In response, the TSA has implemented "racially neutral profiling," which targets passengers who behave suspiciously, for instance by paying cash for airline tickets, buying one-way tickets, or appearing agitated at security checkpoints. Passengers are also now subject to random additional searches based on their ticket numbers. Yet other critics charge that terrorists can adapt to behavior-based searches, and that random searches waste resources on passengers who are unlikely to be terrorists.

A no-fly list of suspected terrorists had been in use prior to 9/11, but it was greatly expanded following the attacks. While the list had 16 names on September 11, 2001, the CBS news program *60 Minutes* has claimed that a March 2006 copy had 44,000 names. Since 2001, there have been hundreds of false identifications in which individuals are delayed or prevented from flying because their names are similar to those on the list. Following a lawsuit brought by the ACLU in 2004, the government agreed to release details of how the list was compiled and used.

Some experts protest that many of the TSA's procedures amount to "security theater,"[29] designed to make passengers feel safer without actually enhancing security. For example, after Richard Reid attempted in December 2001 to blow up a jet with a bomb concealed in his shoes, the TSA began inspecting shoes at airport terminal checkpoints. In August 2006, in response to reports that terrorists planned to blow up planes using liquid explosives, passengers were forbidden to bring liquids or gels aboard planes. TSA officials and their defenders say these measures prevent terrorists from using known methods of attack and deter potential terrorists by creating an environment in which they are likely to be caught.

Some state and local law enforcement agencies have implemented their own search policies in response to threats against transportation infrastructure. In July 2005, after the London subway was bombed, the New York City Police Department began randomly searching bags carried by passengers entering the city's subway system. Yet because the police eschewed profiling, some argued that the searches would be ineffectual, while other critics charged that they violated the Fourth Amendment. A federal judge ruled in December 2005 that the searches were lawful,[30] and in October 2006 the Massachusetts Bay Transit Authority announced that it intended to introduce a similar program.

These practices have been compared both favorably and unfavorably to the system used by the Israeli national airline, which candidly applies enhanced scrutiny to Arabs and foreign nationals. Although many revile ethnic profiling, even some critics of the technique acknowledge that Israel has effectively prevented hijackings. Proponents of profiling have argued that prohibitions against it should be relaxed to make the American system more efficient.

Counterterrorism Efforts in Other Western Democracies

Other Western democracies have also changed their laws in the wake of 9/11. The British government has outlawed the "glorification" of terrorism and authorized the indefinite detention and deportation of terrorism suspects. Italy, the Netherlands, and France have authorized increased surveillance and wiretapping, and Germany is considering legislation that would permit the government to have greater access to individuals' financial records.[31]

In the United States and elsewhere, many have expressed horror at revelations of abuse in American-run prisons abroad. Yet several European nations are quietly exploring policies of extraordinary rendition and deportation to countries where torture is practiced. Canada has tightened its immigration policies and increased domestic surveillance, both in cooperation with the U.S. government and on its own. Everywhere, it seems, democratic nations grapple with the tension between preserving cherished liberties and protecting themselves from the very real threat of terrorism.

Conclusion

As this report is written, the core institutions of American democracy continue to grapple with the issues raised by the Bush administration's counterterrorism agenda, especially the assertion of enhanced authority by the executive branch. While administration actions have met with skepticism from different quarters, the most significant pushback has come from the press and the judiciary. The press continues to ask probing questions about the consequences of antiterrorism policies, publicize acts of injustice against individuals or groups, and assess the effectiveness of administration efforts. For its part, the judiciary has forced the government to adjust or even reverse course on some aspects of counterterrorism policy, while at the same time validating other initiatives. By contrast, Congress, though at times sharply critical of administration policy, has been reluctant to challenge the president on national security issues.

Yet even now, six years after 9/11, the impact of the administration's policies on the civil liberties of Americans remains unclear. This is due in part to attempts by the administration to limit public knowledge of its actions on national security grounds. At the same time, the proposition that, as some critics have said, counterterrorism policies are placing fundamental freedoms in jeopardy and leading to massive violations of civil liberties seems to be an overstatement of current conditions, especially when viewed in historical context. Constitutional protection of civil liberties, including the rights of immigrants, is proving much more resilient than in past periods of conflict. Despite a high degree of political polarization, critics of administration policies have been free to express their views in the media, on the internet, and through many public protests. Civil libertarians and other critics have not been subject to prosecution, surveillance, or witch hunts. Indeed, careful scrutiny of civil liberties in today's United States reveals how much the country has changed since earlier times of war or crisis.

In assessing America's performance since 9/11, we must also keep in mind the dramatically new nature of the challenge that America and other democracies are facing in the rise of Islamist terrorism. Even if we put aside the American case, it is clear that the new breed of terrorist—committed, as he is, to the mass murder of civilians—is forcing democratic societies around the world to consider adjustments in both the law and the techniques of national security. Throughout Europe, democratic governments have responded to the terrorist threat by tightening antiterrorism laws, expanding the surveillance powers of the state, adding restrictions to the asylum and immigration process, and enabling the deportation of immigrants who, through action or word, seem to support terrorism. While it will take some time to establish the proper relationship between security and liberty in an age of terrorism, current trends suggest that the United States and other democracies will successfully meet the challenge.

Endnotes

1. See the Racketeer Influenced and Corrupt Organizations Act, commonly referred to as the RICO Act or RICO, *U.S. Code* 18 §§ 1961 1968.

2. Reporters Committee for Freedom of the Press, "Questions for Attorney General John Ashcroft on the USA PATRIOT Act and its Effect on the News Media," August 20, 2003, http://www. rcfp.org/news/documents/20030820ashcroft.html.

3. University of Illinois Library Research Center, "Public Libraries and Civil Liberties: A Profession Divided," http://lrc.lis.uiuc. edu/web/PLCL.html.

4. "'Sneak-and-Peek' Law Helps More Than War on Terror," FOX News, August 15, 2005, http://www.foxnews.com/ story/0,2933,165799,00.html.

5. James Risen and Eric Lichtblau, "Bush Lets U.S. Spy on Callers Without Courts," *New York Times*, December 16, 2005.

6. Michael V. Hayden, "What American Intelligence and Especially the NSA Have Been Doing to Defend the Nation" (address to the National Press Club, Washington, DC, January 23, 2006).

7. Walter Pincus, "Judge Discusses Details of Work On Secret Court," *Washington Post*, June 26, 2007.

8. *American Civil Liberties Union et al. v. National Security Agency et al.* (2006), http://www.aclu.org/images/nsaspying/ asset_upload_file689_26477.pdf.

9. Dan Eggen, "Lawsuits May Illuminate Methods of Spy Program," *Washington Post*, August 14, 2007; Dan Eggen, "White House Fights Democratic Changes to Surveillance Act," *Washington Post*, October 11, 2007.

10. "Arar Says He Was Tortured in Syria," CBC News, October 30, 2003, http://www.cbc.ca/news/story/2003/10/30/arar_031030.html; "Maher Arar: Timeline," CBC News, January 26, 2007, http:// www.cbc.ca/news/background/arar/.

11. Elise Labott, "Canada Lifts Travel Advisory on U.S.," CNN. com, November 7, 2002, http://archives.cnn.com/2002/TRAVEL/ NEWS/11/07/canada.us.travel/.

12. American Civil Liberties Union, "Statement: Khaled El-Masri," http://www.aclu.org/safefree/extraordinaryrendition/22201res20051206. html.

13. "Speech of Michael Posner to the American Bar Association Center for Human Rights" (Human Rights First, Salt Lake City, UT, February 14, 2005), http://www.humanrightsfirst. org/us_law/commentary/posner_aba_0205.pdf.

14. Temporary Committee on the Alleged Use of European Countries by the CIA for the
Transportation and Illegal Detention of Prisoners, *Report on the Alleged Use of European Countries by the CIA for the Transportation and Illegal Detention of Prisoners* (European Parliament, January 30, 2007), http://www.europarl.europa.eu/comparl/ tempcom/tdip/final_report_en.pdf.

15. White House, "President Issues Military Order: Detention, Treatment, and Trial of Certain Non-Citizens in the War Against Terrorism," news release, November 13, 2001, http://www.white-house.gov/news/releases/2001/11/20011113-27.html.

16. See "Geneva Convention Relative to the Treatment of Prisoners of War" (Third Geneva Convention) and "Geneva Convention Relative to the Protection of Civilian Persons in Time of War" (Fourth Geneva Convention), August 12, 1949, available at http://www.ohchr.org/english/law/.

17. "Counter-Resistance Techniques," action memo from William J. Haynes II Counsel to Secretary of Defense, December 2, 2002, available at http://slate.com/features/whatistorture/ LegalMemos.html.

18. Anthony Lewis, "Guantanamo's Long Shadow," *New York Times*, June 21, 2005.

19. *Rasul v. Bush*, 542 U.S. 466 (2004).

20. Carol D. Leonnig, "Judge Rules Detainee Tribunals Illegal," *Washington Post*, February 1, 2005.

21. *Hamdan v. Rumsfeld*, 126 S. Ct. 2749 (2006).

22. *Padilla v. Rumsfeld*, 352 F.3d 695 (2d Cir. 2003).

23. "Timeline: Enemy Combatant?" CBS News, http://www.cbsnews. com/elements/2006/04/04/in_depth_us/timeline1469944_0_main.shtml.

24. Stephen Yale-Loehr, Demetrios G. Papademetriou, and Betsy Cooper, *Secure Borders, Open Doors: Visa Procedures in the Post–September 11 Era* (Washington, DC: Migration Policy Institute, 2005), http://www.migrationpolicy.org/pubs/visa_report.pdf.
25. Human Rights First, "Refugees at Risk Under Sweeping 'Terrorism' Bar," http://www.humanrightsfirst.org/asylum/asylum_refugee.asp.
26. *United States v. Skipwith*, 482 F.2d 1276 (5th Cir. 1973).
27. See *United States v. Davis*, 458 F.2d 819, 821 (D.C. Cir. 1972): "Conduct innocent in the eyes of the untrained may carry entirely different messages to the experienced or trained observer."
28. See *United States v. Herzbrun*, 723 F.2d 773 (11th Cir. 1984), and *United States v. Pulido-Baquerizo*, 800 F.2d 899, 902 (9th Cir. 1986).
29. Bruce Schneier, "Last Week's Terrorism Arrests," Schneier on Security, August 13, 2006, http://www.schneier.com/blog/archives/2006/08/terrorism_secur.html.
30. *McWade v. Kelly*, No. 05 6754 CV (2d Cir. 2006): "That decision is best left to those with 'a unique understanding of, and responsibility for, limited public resources, including a finite number of police officers.' Accordingly, we ought not conduct a 'searching examination of effectiveness.' Instead, we need only determine whether the Program is 'a reasonably effective means of addressing' the government interest in deterring and detecting a terrorist attack on the subway system."
31. Katrin Bennhold, "Europe, Too, Takes Harder Line In Handling Terrorism Suspects," *International Herald Tribune*, April 17, 2006.

Rule of Law: Criminal Justice and Property Rights

The rule of law requires that laws be adopted in accordance with established procedures, that they be made known to the public, and that they be enforced consistently and even-handedly. The rule of law is intended to ensure that a government exercises its authority fairly, and it is crucial to securing liberty and justice for the people of any nation.

No country is perfect in this respect, but overall and as compared to other countries, the United States conforms to the rule of law. In America, those accused of breaking the law have the right to fair, speedy trials, and convicted criminals are protected by rules intended to ensure that they are treated humanely. Civil courts exist to remedy breaches of administrative and civil law and to enforce private contracts, and courts are generally considered fair and impartial (judges tend to fare better in public opinion polls than do members of Congress). Both the federal and state constitutions protect property rights. Federal law protects women, racial and ethnic minorities, and other historically oppressed groups from governmental discrimination and in some cases from discrimination by private actors as well.

U.S. law is derived from four sources: the Constitution, statutes passed by legislative bodies, administrative decisions

27

by executive agencies, and common law based on the English legal tradition. The United States also divides the responsibility for enforcing the law among the federal, state, and local governments.

The U.S. Constitution is the "supreme law of the land" and establishes the authority of the federal Congress and the president to make laws and treaties. Federal and state judges are bound by the Constitution, and no state law may be passed in contravention of federal law or the federal Constitution.

The U.S. Congress has the power to pass laws for certain constitutionally limited purposes, such as regulating interstate commerce and protecting the rights of citizens from state power. Additionally, Congress may authorize the creation of executive branch agencies, which establish legally enforceable regulations and administrative rules. Federal laws and rules are published in the United States Code and the Code of Federal Regulations.

The rule of law must be evaluated in two distinct realms: criminal and civil.

American criminal law defines acts that are deemed to threaten the safety and security of society and punishes those who commit them. Murder, rape, and robbery are covered by criminal law because they are considered threats to the entire society, not merely to the individual victims, and they are among the most serious of crimes. Offenses such as reckless driving and selling marijuana are also believed to threaten society as a whole, and are categorized as criminal.

Civil law is used to settle disputes arising either among individuals or between individuals and governments. Civil law also governs the political process by which lawmakers are chosen and laws are made.

In the United States, most criminal and civil law is made and enforced by state and local governments. Each state retains a degree of sovereignty, with its own constitution, legislature, and legal codes, and states have wide powers to legislate matters not preempted by the federal Constitution or federal laws. The various states generally have similar laws on crimes such as rape and murder, but the treatment of lesser crimes and misdemeanors varies widely from state to state. States also establish their own laws governing the right to hold and dispose of property, the regulation of consumer products and services, business and corporate law, torts, and other civil matters. In short, the rights and responsibilities of citizens are not entirely uniform across the country.

Critics of the American system tend not to allege that the rule of law is stronger in other countries. Rather, they protest the ways in which they believe America fails to live up to its own ideals as expressed in its Constitution, its laws, and the rulings of its courts. Some critics cite disparities in the law's treatment of racial and other minorities as evidence of continuing institutional prejudice. Others note unequal access to high-quality (and high-cost) lawyers. They argue that overburdened courts and overcrowded jails and prisons result in the substandard treatment of suspected and convicted criminals. Many find fault in laws that severely punish nonviolent drug offenders, or object to recent legal and administrative decisions that have limited the rights of individuals to hold and use their property.

Criminal Justice

Incarceration. Today more than 7 out of every 1,000 residents of the United States are in jail or prison,[1] giving America the highest reported incarceration rate in the world. More than 5.6 million people in the United States, or one of every 37 residents, have spent time behind bars.

Other countries with comparable rates of incarceration include Russia, Belarus, and Bermuda. However, some experts suggest that actual rates of incarceration in more repressive countries are higher than reported. Cuba, for example, reports a rate of only 4 in 1,000,[2] but keeps lists of prisoners secret, making this number impossible to verify. Most Western European nations report incarceration rates of between 0.5 and 1.5 per 1,000 residents.

The rate of incarceration in the United States has risen steeply in the last 20 years, from 1.39 per 1,000 residents in 1980 to a high of 7.35 per 1,000 residents in 2005. Critics accuse the

United States of using incarceration to deal with social problems, such as drug use, that many countries handle through treatment programs and other less drastic means. However, the U.S. system's defenders note that crime has declined sharply as prison sentences have increased; incarceration, they argue, is an effective way to reduce crime.[3]

Rates of incarceration in the United States are not uniform across all segments of the population. Women are incarcerated at one-ninth the rate of men, although the rate of incarceration for women is rising more rapidly than the rate for men. Six of every 10 prison inmates is a member of a racial or ethnic minority. A black male in the United States has a 1 in 3 chance of being imprisoned at some point in his lifetime, while a white male has only a 1 in 17 chance of going to prison.

The United States is one of only a handful of countries that bar prisoners from voting. Furthermore, people convicted of felonies in most U.S. jurisdictions are stripped permanently of their right to vote in local, state, and federal elections. Because of this, some critics argue that inequalities in the justice system contribute to political inequality by disenfranchising large groups of people, primarily minority men. At any one time, more than 4 million Americans—or 1 in 50 adult citizens—are ineligible to vote due to a past criminal conviction. Of those, 1.4 million are black men, making up 14 percent of the nation's black male population.[4] Recently, however, following years of advocacy by civil liberties and prisoner rights organizations, a number of states have restored voting rights and other civil rights to former prisoners.

Capital Punishment. Federal law permits the imposition of the death penalty for certain violent crimes and treason. Capital punishment is legal in 38 states as well. Since colonial times, about 13,000 people have been executed in the country.

The death penalty was widely used in the United States until the twentieth century, when it began to be considered inhumane. In *Furman v. Georgia* (1972), the U.S. Supreme Court suspended use of the death penalty, ruling that because of the variation in state laws and the wide discretion given to judges and juries in its application, capital punishment was "arbitrary and capricious" and therefore unconstitutional under the Eighth and Fourteenth Amendments. In a series of cases in 1976, the court reversed itself and permitted use of the death penalty for specified crimes and with appropriate procedures.

Death penalty cases are now conducted using bifurcated trials in which juries must first determine defendants' guilt or innocence and then, in a second stage, consider mitigating and aggravating circumstances in deciding whether to recommend a death sentence.[5] Since 1976, more than 1,050 death sentences have been carried out. Some 3,370 people are currently on death row nationwide, although only about 10 percent of death-row inmates are ever executed.

The United States is unusual among democracies in permitting capital punishment. Most European and Latin American states have abolished the death penalty, although Guatemala, many Caribbean nations, and some African and Asian democracies retain it. In undemocratic countries the death penalty is common but not universal. In 2005 at least 80 percent of executions recorded worldwide took place in China, which reported executing 1,770 people (Amnesty International estimates that the actual number of Chinese executions might have been as high as 8,000).[6] Iran reported 94 executions in 2005, and Saudi Arabia at least 86, while the United States executed 60 people.

U.S. courts have proscribed capital punishment for criminals with a diminished mental capacity. In 2002, the Supreme Court ruled in *Atkins v. Virginia* that executing mentally retarded criminals violated the Eighth Amendment's prohibition on cruel and unusual punishment. In the ruling, the court affirmed that the Eighth Amendment should be interpreted in light of the "evolving standards of decency that mark the progress of a maturing society." The justices cited the fact that a growing number of state legislatures had banned execution of the mentally retarded as evidence of a shift in the national consensus on the matter.

In the 2005 case *Roper v. Simmons*, the Supreme Court again used the "evolving standards of decency" test to limit the use of the death penalty, holding that capital punishment could only be imposed on defendants who were at least 18 years old at the time of their crimes. Here the court cited sociological and scientific evidence suggesting that juveniles' incomplete brain development mitigates their responsibility for their actions. Despite this evidence, minors may still be tried as adults for certain crimes, and 41 states allow life sentences without the possibility of parole for minors. In 2005, Amnesty International and Human Rights Watch found that at least 2,225 American children were serving sentences of life without parole.[7]

Opinion polls have consistently found that a substantial majority of Americans want to retain the death penalty. However, critics cite the abolition of the death penalty by other democracies as evidence that prevailing moral standards now preclude execution as a punishment.

Death penalty opponents also argue that courts are not able to determine guilt to the degree of certitude that would justify execution. Between 1973 and 2005, 122 people in 25 states were released from death row after new evidence or new testing of old evidence revealed that they were innocent of the crimes for which they had been sentenced.[8] In 2006, Virginia Governor Mark Warner authorized the testing of DNA evidence in the case of Roger Keith Coleman, who was executed by the state in 1992. The evidence confirmed Coleman's guilt, and indeed no other case of wrongful execution has ever been proven in the United States. Nonetheless, the Coleman case may have set a precedent for the posthumous testing of evidence in other capital cases, and opponents of the death penalty say this could one day expose wrongful executions.

Some 42 percent of all death-row inmates are black men, and scholars have debated whether this reflects discrimination. In the 1987 case *McCleskey v. Kemp*, convicted murderer Warren McCleskey argued, ultimately without success, that Georgia's use of the death penalty constituted impermissible race discrimination under the Eighth and Fourteenth Amendments.

McCleskey relied on a study—led by University of Iowa professor David Baldus—on capital sentencing in Georgia in the 1980s, which found that prosecutors sought the death penalty in 70 percent of cases where a black defendant was accused of murdering a white victim, but in only 15 percent of cases where a white defendant was accused of murdering a black victim.[9]

In another study by Baldus and his colleagues, blacks in Philadelphia were found to be sentenced to death at four times the rate of nonblack defendants convicted of similar crimes. More than 89 percent of prisoners sent to death row in Philadelphia since 1976 have been people of color.[10] Similar reports have found significant sentencing disparities in other states. In *Saldano v. Texas* in 2000, the Supreme Court found that an expert witness had recommended the death penalty to a jury based on a calculus that included the defendant's race; the court overturned the death sentence in that case.

However, other studies have shown that black defendants in capital cases are no more likely to receive the death penalty than are whites. A 2004 article by John Blume, Theodore Eisenberg, and Martin T. Well argued that because of the reluctance to impose death sentences in cases of black-on-black crime, blacks convicted of murder are actually less likely than white defendants to end up on death row.[11] Similarly, after adjusting data to account for the circumstances of each crime, such as level of brutality or premeditation, a 2006 RAND Corporation study of 652 federal cases involving capital offenses found that federal prosecutors were no more likely to seek the death penalty for black defendants than for whites.[12]

Several states have placed formal or de facto moratoriums on capital punishment until concerns about bias and wrongful convictions can be resolved. Maryland declared a moratorium on capital punishment between 2002 and 2004 pending the completion of a study on racial and geographic disparities in sentencing. Although the report found significant disparities, Republican governor Robert Ehrlich lifted the moratorium in 2004, and two prisoners have since been executed. New Jersey, which allows capital punishment but has not carried out an execution since 1963, passed a legislative measure halting capital punishment in January 2006. The most discussed moratorium, though, was declared in 2000 by Illinois governor George H. Ryan. Between the reinstatement of Illinois' death penalty in 1977 and 2000, the state executed 12 people but freed 13 from death row because of new evidence. Ryan, a Republican, said he could not support a system that was "so fraught with error and has come so close to the ultimate nightmare, the state's taking of innocent life."[13] Before leaving office in 2003, he emptied the state's death row in a historic mass commutation.

Fairness in Sentencing. Punishments for the most serious crimes, such as rape and murder, are generally similar across jurisdictional lines. However, sentences for less severe crimes vary widely by jurisdiction. To ensure fairness, federal and state governments have implemented guidelines that mandate sentence ranges based on the crime and the mitigating or aggravating circumstances. The guidelines are meant to protect defendants from sentences influenced by their (or judges') personal characteristics, and from other potentially discriminatory judgments.

However, sentencing guidelines have been challenged in recent years, and the Supreme Court has limited them in several cases. Many of these rulings have reduced the sentencing authority of judges by stressing defendants' right to have the facts of their cases decided by juries.

In the 2000 case *Apprendi v. New Jersey*, the Supreme Court invalidated a statute that allowed judges to exceed the legislatively determined maximum sentence if they found that a crime had been committed because of racial bias. The court said that allowing judges to consider bias as an aggravating factor violated defendants' Sixth Amendment right to a trial by jury. In *Blakely v. Washington* (2004), the Supreme Court ruled that giving judges the power to increase sentences based on their own determinations of facts not presented to a jury violated the defendant's due process rights. Defendant Robert Blakely had pleaded guilty to murdering his wife. During the sentencing phase of his trial, the judge had determined that Blakely acted with "deliberate cruelty," an aggravating factor that significantly increased the mandatory minimum sentence for his crime. The Supreme Court's ruling in the case invalidated most state sentencing guidelines that gave judges the discretion to increase sentences based on aggravating factors. Two subsequent decisions by the high court in 2005, *United States v. Booker* and *United States v. Fanfan*, overturned mandatory federal sentencing guidelines on the same Sixth Amendment grounds cited in *Blakely* and *Apprendi*.

Some 55 percent of all federal prisoners and more than 21 percent of inmates in state prisons are incarcerated for drug crimes.[14] Although the percentage has declined, the absolute numbers of drug offenders in prison has risen steadily in recent years. This is due both to an increase in criminal prosecutions and to longer prison sentences for inmates convicted of drug crimes.

As of 2002, the average sentence for a federal inmate convicted of a drug-related felony (where the drug crime was the most serious offense for which the defendant was convicted) was 76 months, while overall the average felony sentence was 58.4 months.[15] More than 80 percent of the increase in the federal prison population between 1985 and 1995 was due to drug convictions.[16] The number of prisoners incarcerated for nonviolent crimes is now larger than the combined populations of Alaska and Wyoming.[17]

Most drug sentences under both federal and state law are based on legislatively determined guidelines that recommend minimum sentences based on the type of drug in question, the weight or amount of the drug entered into evidence, and the prosecutor's assessment of the defendant's intent to distribute or traffic the drug.

Even the form of the drug a defendant is convicted of possessing can affect his or her sentence. Notably, under current federal law, a person convicted of possessing five grams of crack cocaine would be subject to a five-year minimum sentence, while a defendant would have to be convicted of possessing at least 500 grams of powder cocaine in order to trigger the same sentence. Harsh sentences for the possession of crack cocaine were enacted during the 1980s in an effort to stem what the federal government and many urban community leaders believed was an epidemic linked to violent crime and unrest. However, the measures disproportionately affected poor and black defendants, since wealthier white drug users tended to use powder cocaine, leading to charges of racial bias. The Senate is currently considering a bipartisan bill that would bring the penalties for the two forms of cocaine closer together, although a significant gap would remain.[18] Black Americans represent 13 percent of the U.S. population but account for 37 percent of those arrested on drug charges, 53 percent of those convicted of such charges, and 67 percent of people imprisoned for drug crimes.[19]

More than 90 percent of prisoners are eventually released into society. However, the rate of re-arrest for criminal offenders is 67.5 percent in the three years following release.[20] Frustrated by this recidivism, states in the 1990s began passing laws aimed at habitual offenders, known colloquially as "three strikes and you're out" laws. Washington State passed the first such law by referendum in 1993. The measure mandated that any criminal convicted of a "most serious offense" three times be sentenced to life in prison without the possibility of parole. By 2004, the federal government and 26 states had passed similar laws.

Some "three strikes" laws have had unforeseen results. California's law, for instance, applies to any third felony conviction, even if it is nonviolent. In 1995, California felon Kevin Weber was sentenced to 26 years in prison for stealing four chocolate-chip cookies.[21] Defendants in the state may also be convicted of two "third strikes" in a single case, resulting in two consecutive life sentences.

Police Methods. According to federal statistics, the racial breakdown of those arrested nationwide does not correspond to the racial breakdown of the general population. Black Americans in particular are arrested in disproportionate numbers. In 2005, blacks made up 12.8 percent of the U.S. population, but 27.8 percent of those arrested.[22]

With this disparity in mind, some police departments informally include race in the set of characteristics, or profile, that officers use to help distinguish likely law-breakers from the general population. Opponents of racial profiling argue that it creates a vicious circle, with heightened police scrutiny of certain groups reinforcing the racial disparity in arrest and conviction figures. Critics have also refuted the notion that racial profiling always targets likely criminals. When San Diego released statistics on traffic stops in 2000, it was found that blacks and Hispanics had a 10 percent chance of being searched, while whites had a 3 percent chance. However, 13 percent of both whites and blacks were found to have had contraband, while Hispanics were found to have contraband only 5 percent of the time.[23]

The most notorious recent case of alleged racial profiling began in 1986, when the Drug Enforcement Administration (DEA) began a program known as "Operation Pipeline." As part of the program, some 27,000 law enforcement officials were trained to recognize what the DEA termed "key characteristics, or indicators, that are shared by drug traffickers."[24] Although the DEA maintained that "the program does not advocate such profiling by race or ethnic background," studies of police officers who received the training found that they were significantly more likely to stop minority drivers than white drivers. For example, a study of police behavior in Maryland between 1995 and 1999 found that African Americans constituted 63 percent of the motorists searched by state police on Interstate 95, even though only 18 percent of motorists on the highway were black.[25]

In the late 1990s, events in New Jersey began to reverse the widespread use of racial profiling. State troopers there were alleged to be detaining black motorists based on their race alone, and many troopers testified that their supervisors had ordered them to engage in racial profiling. A federal lawsuit on Fourteenth Amendment grounds ended with the placement of a federal monitor in the state police department and a consent decree in which the state police agreed not to detain individuals based on race unless they matched descriptions of specific criminal suspects.[26] Since then, other states and municipalities have adopted bans on profiling, and President George W. Bush has spoken out against the practice.

In 2005, approximately 7,000 of America's 18,000 police departments used tasers or stun guns, up from 1,000 in 2001. Reports that these weapons have led to approximately 160 deaths since 2000 have raised questions about their safety and the situations in which they should be used. In notable cases, stun guns have been used against handcuffed suspects and children who have committed minor offenses. Proponents of stun guns argue that they save lives, as they provide police officers with an alternative to lethal force. Critics have called for greater regulation of the weapons, with detailed reporting and monitoring procedures.[27]

The use of police lineups has also received increased scrutiny in recent years. After several exonerations of inmates following DNA testing, a number of states began to change lineup procedures in the 1990s. Witnesses were shown each person individually, rather than as part of a group, with the reasoning that the witness could more objectively and accurately identify a suspect alone than in comparison to other individuals. However, subsequent studies have shown that the new lineups lead to more inaccurate identifications than the old system, and no uniform system of lineups is currently in place in the United States.

Legal Services for Indigent Defendants. The Sixth Amendment guarantees the right of each defendant in a criminal prosecution "to have the assistance of counsel for his defense." Since 1938 the Supreme Court has held that the right to counsel in federal proceedings applies to all defendants. Many states have extended this right to misdemeanor cases and to appeals, although federal jurisprudence does not require it. Under federal law, all defendants also have the right to have an attorney present during any custodial interrogation by police, and evidence collected from interrogations during which that right was denied is generally inadmissible in court.

States and localities historically called upon attorneys to represent indigent defendants *pro bono* and enacted a patchwork of laws to help ensure that counsel was available to them. While some legal-aid organizations were present in large cities, in most venues the provision of free and low-cost legal assistance was inadequate. In 1963, however, the Supreme Court unanimously ruled in *Gideon v. Wainwright* that the Sixth and Fourteenth Amendments required state courts to provide lawyers at no cost to defendants in criminal cases.

That decision sparked the creation of government-funded programs to provide legal counsel to indigent defendants in most jurisdictions. Some smaller jurisdictions pay private criminal defense attorneys to represent indigent defendants on a case-by-case basis. Others provide legal services through private, non-profit legal-aid offices, which contract with the courts to accept cases. Many larger jurisdictions provide legal services through public defender's offices, which employ full-time attorneys at the expense of the government.[28]

Although the right to counsel in the United States is far stronger than in most other countries, some say the government has not done enough to protect the rights of criminal defendants. Attorneys and advocates for the poor complain that representation for the indigent is systematically underfunded and constitutionally inadequate. The American Bar Association has set standards for appropriate caseloads for criminal defense attorneys, but public defenders' caseloads frequently exceed the recommendations. In many jurisdictions, public defenders and prosecutors receive equal pay, but in others the pay for public defenders lags far behind compensation for prosecutors. Public defenders frequently complain that their resources—such as access to forensic testing, investigators, administrative support staff, and expert witnesses—are not comparable to those of prosecutors.

In 2005, the Louisiana Supreme Court ruled in *State v. Citizen* that a judge should "prohibit the State from going forward with prosecution" unless "adequate funds become available to provide [for the] constitutionally protected right to counsel."

Louisiana and other states have since allocated more resources to criminal defense. In 2005 Texas passed the Fair Defense Act, which created a task force to study the need for indigent-defense reform. As cases challenging the adequacy of criminal defense counsel make their way through state and federal courts, states may be compelled to devote more resources to reforming legal defense services.

Prison Conditions. Prisons in the United States are operated both by the federal government and by individual state governments. For less serious crimes, offenders may be sentenced to short terms in local jails—which also hold defendants awaiting trial—or to alternative forms of punishment such as community service, probation, or restitution.

Conditions in American prisons are better than those in most other nations. In the United States and other industrialized democracies, prisoners are guaranteed adequate housing, nutrition, exercise, and medical care. Inmates have the right to practice their religions, to send and receive mail, to use exercise facilities, and to be free from unnecessary intrusions on their dignity and privacy. Many prisons also offer educational, work, and other opportunities that are designed both to keep inmates occupied and to train them to play productive roles in society when they are released. Coerced prison labor, common in some other countries, is prohibited in the United States. American prisoners have access to legal information to assist in their appeals, and to procedures for filing grievances about prison conditions.

However, the Prison Litigation Reform Act, passed in 1996, curtailed the courts' authority in responding to prisoners' complaints amid a perceived excess of cases—in 1993 these suits made up 23 percent of all civil filings in federal court. The act ordered that prisoners exhaust all administrative remedies available before filing in federal court, and mandated that all federal court orders in response to complaints would expire after two years.

Many American prisons are now overcrowded, as more criminals are sentenced to longer terms and prison construction fails to keep pace with demand. In 2005, state prisons nationwide housed between 101 and 116 percent of the prisoner capacity for which they were originally designed. Federal prisons operated at 131 percent of capacity.[29]

Although prison conditions in the United States are generally superior to conditions in many other countries, human rights advocates often criticize the system for failing to live up to standards prescribed by U.S. law. In particular, violence in prisons, which has been linked in several studies to overcrowding, is commonplace.

More than 20 percent of all prison and jail inmates report having been sexually assaulted by a fellow inmate or guard.[30] In 2004, the Bureau of Justice Statistics reported 8,210 allegations of staff or inmate sexual violence. Many advocates for prison reform note that additional assaults may go unreported because of fear of reprisal, shame, or mistrust of prison staff. Although America generally treats rape as a serious crime, some experts assert that the public has become desensitized to prison rape.[31] In September 2003, Congress passed the Prison Rape Elimination Act, which called for an in-depth survey of sexual violence in state and federal prisons. Congress in 2005 established the National Prison Rape Elimination Commission to monitor prison conditions.

Prisoners frequently complain that they receive inadequate nutrition and medical treatment. The Supreme Court set the standard for prison medical care in *Estelle v. Gamble* (1976), finding that "deliberate indifference by prison personnel to a prisoner's serious illness or injury constitutes cruel and unusual punishment contravening the Eighth Amendment." State courts have held this decision to require diagnosis and treatment of major medical conditions by qualified medical personnel. Nonetheless, medical care continues to be a frequent subject of prisoner lawsuits.

Because some of their illnesses cause them to become disruptive or threatening, the mentally ill are often imprisoned. One in six prisoners in the United States has a diagnosed mental illness, and there are three times as many mentally-ill people in prisons as in hospitals. Human Rights Watch reported in 2003 that prisons are ill-equipped to treat mental illness, and that additional funding is necessary to ensure the proper treatment of inmates.[32]

RICO. The Racketeer Influenced and Corrupt Organizations Act (RICO), passed in 1970 as part of a larger crime bill, was designed to prosecute individuals to whom no specific crime could be attributed, but who headed an organization that engaged in illegal acts. Any individual found to be operating an organization guilty of a "pattern of racketeering activity," such as extortion, bribery, homicide, or drug dealing, could be prosecuted under the act.[33] Throughout the 1970s, RICO was primarily used against the Mafia, its intended target.

In the 1980s, however, the use of RICO increased as prosecutors and litigants were attracted by a clause that tripled damages in civil cases for anyone found to have been injured as a result of violations of the act. The broad interpretation of "racketeering activity" allowed prosecutors to use the act in cases involving corporate mail and wire fraud that were unrelated to organized crime in the traditional sense. A 1988 Supreme Court decision in *H.J. Inc. v. Northwestern Bell Telephone Co.* found that RICO need not apply only to Mafia cases, but could be used against legitimate corporations or businesspeople. From the 1980s onward, RICO has been applied to white-collar criminals, abortion protesters, and corrupt politicians. A RICO case brought against a business employing illegal immigrants is currently in the federal courts. Civil libertarians have objected to the expansive employment of the act, saying it has been stretched far beyond its intended scope.

Property Rights

The Constitution's Fifth Amendment protects the right to own and use private property, stating, "No person shall…be deprived of life, liberty, or property, without due process of law; nor shall private property be taken for public use, without just compensation." Property rights are also protected by precedent inherited from English common law and by state and federal laws that govern the use of private property.

Property rights are generally well respected in the United States. In most circumstances, property owners may use, sell, and develop their property without fear of government interference. However, the government may tax property to provide funding for public programs, and in limited cases it can compel the sale of private property or circumscribe the purposes for which the property may be used.

Property Takings. Under common law in America, the state retains an inherent power to exercise eminent domain, the right to expropriate private property without the owner's consent, either for the government's own use or for delegation to a third party who will develop it for public use. Common law systems in the United Kingdom, Australia, South Africa, Canada, and other countries also retain this right, which has historically been used to provide public amenities such as roads, bridges, and military installations.

However, in a controversial 2005 ruling, *Kelo v. City of New London,* the Supreme Court extended the government's right to take private property for public use. Suzette Kelo, a homeowner in New London, Connecticut, was notified by her city in 2000 that the area in which she lived had been declared economically depressed, and that the city would be buying her home and the homes of 115 of her neighbors as part of a comprehensive revitalization plan. The homes would be razed to make way for a resort, a park, and various new residential and commercial buildings. Kelo and several of her neighbors sued the city, arguing that the plan misused eminent domain because the seized property would benefit private developers rather than the general public. Under the provisions of the *Williams County v. Hamilton Bank* ruling in 1984, the plaintiff in a property-taking case must exhaust all other avenues of redress before appealing to the federal courts. After making its way through the Connecticut courts, Kelo's case reached the Supreme Court in 2005.

On June 23, 2005, the Supreme Court ruled, 5–4, in favor of the city, finding that economic development for a public purpose—in this case, to revitalize the city and broaden its tax base—met the public-use standard. The court said local governments should be afforded wide latitude in seizing property because land-use decisions are best made at the local level by individual communities. Justice John Paul Stevens wrote for the majority, "The city has carefully formulated a development plan that it believes will provide appreciable benefits to the community, including, but not limited to, new jobs and increased tax revenue."

In a dissent, Justice Sandra Day O'Connor argued that the plain meaning of "public use" included only uses of land by public entities or for amenities open to the public. She wrote, "Any property may now be taken for the benefit of another private party, but the fallout from this decision will not be random. The beneficiaries are likely to be those citizens with disproportionate influence and power in the political process, including large corporations and development firms."

Immediately after the decision, opinion polls found overwhelming opposition to the use of eminent domain for private development.[34] Representatives of the National Association for the Advancement of Colored People (NAACP) testified before Congress about the historical use of eminent domain to evict racial and ethnic minority homeowners from their property in the name of urban renewal, and predicted that *Kelo* would have a disparate impact on African Americans.[35]

The court's decision applied only to the rights of property owners under the federal Constitution and left open the possibility that both state and federal laws could limit the use of eminent domain. Eight states—Arkansas, Florida, Illinois, Kentucky, Maine, Montana, South Carolina, and Washington—already prohibited the use of eminent domain for economic development, except to eliminate blight. Since the decision, 35 state legislatures have passed laws or constitutional amendments to limit the use of *Kelo*-style takings. And in November 2005, the U.S. House of Representatives passed a bill that would prevent the federal government from using eminent domain for private development as well as deny federal economic development funds to state and local governments that used eminent domain for such purposes. However, the bill was placed on hold in the Senate in December 2006, effectively halting its legislative progress.[36]

Regulatory Takings. Federal and state governments in the United States may also limit otherwise lawful uses of private property for zoning, environmental protection, public accommodation, and other reasons. These limitations can substantially burden landowners by prohibiting some profitable uses of their land.

For example, the Federal Water Pollution Control Act and the Clean Water Act prohibit the development of federally designated "wetlands" in ways that would jeopardize animal or plant habitats. If an entire piece of property is classified as wetland, the law prohibits any development of it. In 2005 and 2006, the court heard two cases, *Carabell v. U.S. Army Corps of Engineers* and *Rapanos v. United States*, which challenged the extent of federal power under the Clean Water Act. The cases sought to establish whether tributaries close to wetlands, but not part of the navigable waters to which the law refers, are under federal jurisdiction. A divided court found that the water on the property in question needed to have a "significant nexus" with a navigable body of water, but failed to provide a clear definition of the term, leaving the lower courts to make decisions on a case-by-case basis.[37]

In some cases, local authorities have rezoned land from commercial to residential use, or prohibited particular types of business from operating in specific areas. Owners who buy land with the intention of developing it in a way that is subsequently prohibited by regulation can lose much of their investment. These losses are therefore sometimes called "partial" or "regulatory takings." Partial takings often occur as a result of the Endangered Species Act, under which it is illegal to kill or harm any plant or animal listed as endangered. Private property that is identified as the habitat of an endangered species can be subject to development restrictions. Development is banned in large sections of forest in the Pacific Northwest due to the act.

In 1992, the Supreme Court ruled in *Lucas v. South Carolina Coastal Council* that the state was not required to compensate a landowner whose anticipated property development had been barred by state environmental protection law. The decision distinguished between takings, which deprive a landowner of the entire value of a piece of property by transferring ownership to another party, and regulations, which merely deprive the owner of part of the expected value of his or her property by precluding some of its valuable uses. To be eligible for compensation, the court said, the taking must render the property valueless, which environmental regulations do not do.

While *Lucas* held that the Constitution does not *require* federal and state governments to compensate owners for the regulatory devaluation of their land, states may pass laws offering such compensation. Opponents of such measures say this amounts to paying landowners to obey the law and could undermine environmental protection efforts. States have responded in various ways. A 2004 Oregon law mandated that landowners be reimbursed for regulatory takings, and Arizona voters approved a November 2006 referendum to the same effect. However, voters in California, Washington, and Idaho rejected similar initiatives that month.[38]

Taxation. Residents of the United States are subject to a variety of taxes on their property, expenditures, and importantly, income. The federal government gained the power to tax individual income in 1913 with the passage of the Sixteenth Amendment. Today the United States has a graduated, progressive income-tax system, wherein wealthy taxpayers shoulder a greater proportion of the tax burden than poorer taxpayers. Federal income-tax rates range from zero to 35 percent. Each individual's overall income-tax payments depend on his or her income, family status, spending, and eligibility for a variety of tax breaks and credits.

The federal government also taxes the estates of deceased persons before their assets may be passed on to their heirs. In recent years this estate tax has grown controversial and its status has become complex. Today, the rate of the tax ranges from 18 to 55 percent of an estate's value, but the first $2 million is exempt from taxation. However, the exempt portion of the tax is scheduled to rise to $3.5 million in 2009. The tax itself is scheduled to expire in 2010, and then to return at a higher rate with fewer exemptions in 2011. This confusing state of affairs—with its bizarre incentives to die or to hope for death in particular years—has led to agitation for congressional action.

Opponents of the estate tax, which they pejoratively call the "death tax," believe that it unduly burdens heirs and supersedes the wishes of decedents. They note that inheritors of family-owned businesses such as farms or stores, the value of which is tied up in nonliquid assets, are sometimes forced to sell off the businesses to pay the tax.

Proponents of the estate tax argue that it helps to prevent the perpetuation of class distinctions through inherited wealth. They argue that current exemptions protect family farms and small businesses, and that lowering or repealing the tax would only benefit wealthy families who seek to avoid paying their share.

Consumer Products and Services Regulations. Most states have laws designed to protect consumers from dangerous products and low-quality services. These measures include mandated health and safety inspections of businesses, labeling requirements for consumer products, and occupational-licensure requirements for certain professions.

While many of these laws enjoy wide support, some analysts argue that they restrict commerce and increase prices. Most local governments, for example, impose building codes and zoning restrictions on business owners to ensure that buildings are safe and businesses do not disturb the communities around them. However, the rules limit some freedoms and impose costs on owners.

Since the mid-1980s, some states and localities have banned smoking in many businesses. The first smoking bans applied to offices and other nonpublic workplaces, but since 1993, the District of Columbia and 21 states have banned smoking in most bars, restaurants, and other workplaces open to the public. These laws are intended to protect customers and staff from the danger of environmental tobacco smoke. However, some argue that property owners should be able to decide whether to allow a legal activity such as smoking on their premises.

State and local governments require licenses for professions ranging from medicine to hair braiding and fortune telling. These licenses can be expensive and difficult to obtain. Courts have ruled that states may regulate certain professions, but that these laws must be enforced fairly. The Supreme Court's 1976 decision in *New Orleans v. Dukes*, for example, held that a state could not prevent new street vendors from operating if it allowed existing vendors to continue. Recently courts and legislatures have eliminated or relaxed requirements for licensure in cosmetology, coffin selling, weed control, sign hanging, and interior design.[39]

Under the Commerce Clause of the Constitution, the federal government is empowered to regulate products and services that are provided across state lines. However, these regulations often require states to permit the free movement of goods. For instance, in 2005 the Supreme Court overturned statutes in New York and Michigan that forbade direct shipments from out-of-state wineries to consumers. The court held that states may not treat interstate commerce in alcohol differently from intrastate commerce.[40]

The federal government has traditionally controlled certain forms of interstate travel, including air travel. In recent years, however, it has deregulated air travel to spur innovation and efficiency. Since 1969, the government has moved from directly allocating takeoff and landing rights to overseeing self-regulation by the commercial airline industry, and then to allowing the private ownership of transferable property rights in airport slots.[41] In the aftermath of this deregulation, which was completed in 1985, prices have fallen and available flights have dramatically expanded. A 1996 report by the U.S. General Accounting Office (now the Government Accountability Office) found that between 1976 and 1990, passenger fares had declined about 30 percent in inflation-adjusted dollars, and the number of miles flown had grown and was continuing to grow.

Some experts compare the federal government's deregulation of air travel to its management of the airwaves used for television and radio broadcasts and wireless communication. The government asserts that the airwaves are publicly owned, but issues licenses to private companies for their use. Since 1943, the Federal Communications Commission (FCC) has issued analog broadcast licenses to television and radio stations and required them to broadcast content of public interest. The FCC also has the authority to revoke licenses or levy fines against media outlets that broadcast content it considers indecent or inappropriate.

Until 1994, the FCC allocated commercial spectrum—a range of frequencies designated for commercial use—based on its view of the "best public use." Since then, however, the FCC has awarded licenses to the highest bidders in competitive auctions. This change has allowed wireless technology to proliferate and has catalyzed the creation of several new digital media outlets.[42]

Copyright and Intellectual Property. The U.S. Constitution grants Congress the power "to promote the progress of science and useful arts, by securing for limited times to authors and inventors the exclusive right to their respective writings and discoveries." The result has been a system of federal copyrights and patents that guarantees inventors and those who generate intellectual property the exclusive rights to sell, license, and use their creations during a specified term.

U.S. courts have found that because copyright is intended to encourage the production of creative works, the public's interest in gaining access to those works may supersede the interests of their creators. These rulings have been formalized into a system of "fair use" laws which allow some copyrighted materials to be used in related or derivative works. For example, under the Copyright Act of 1976, an author may copy portions of another author's work without permission in order to critique the work or make a related argument. Additionally, the owner of a copy of a copyrighted work may make copies for his or her personal use, such as a backup copy of a compact disc (CD).

Digital reproduction has made the enforcement of copyrights more difficult. To protect themselves, many producers of digital video discs (DVDs) and CDs now incorporate digital-rights management (DRM) technology that prevents the unauthorized copying of movies and songs. In 1998, Congress passed the Digital Millennium Copyright Act, which criminalized the production and distribution of technology designed to circumvent DRM and increased penalties for internet copyright infringement. The law has prevented the sale of some technologies, such as specially designed DVD-copying machines, and critics say it has also chilled the legitimate use of copyrighted materials.

In 2005, the Supreme Court ruled in *Metro-Goldwyn-Mayer Studios Inc. v. Grokster* that an online service that allowed users to download unlicensed copies of copyrighted materials could be sued for inducing copyright infringement. The ruling caused several online file-sharing services to either close or alter their business practices to discourage the sharing of copyrighted materials.

Also debated is the matter of what information may be copyrighted. The Database and Collections of Information Misappropriation Act, now pending in Congress, would permit the copyrighting of aggregated factual data, such as databases of names and addresses. This measure would make it easier for the creators of databases to earn money. However, by preventing the copying of such aggregations, the measure would also restrict the use of publicly available information.

Rights of Gays, Lesbians, and Sexual Minorities

Federal law does not prohibit discrimination on the basis of sexual orientation. However, an executive order bars the federal government from such discrimination in hiring. In addition, 17 states, the District of Columbia, and more than 180 cities and localities prohibit discrimination by sexual orientation in private employment.

Battles are underway in many states to determine whether the right to marry should be extended to same-sex couples. Same-sex marriages or similar civil contracts are currently recognized in 20 countries and eight U.S. states, though in most cases civil unions, and not marriage, have been sanctioned. Twenty-six states have passed constitutional amendments that explicitly ban recognition of same-sex partnerships, and 43 states, including some of those that allow same-sex civil unions, define marriage by statute as a union between a man and a woman. The 1996 Defense of Marriage Act forbids the federal government from recognizing same-sex or polygamous marriages and allows states where such marriages are illegal to decline to recognize same-sex marriages performed in other states.

Endnotes

1. Bureau of Justice Statistics, "Prison and Jail Inmates at Midyear 2005," bulletin, May 2006, http://www.ojp.usdoj.gov/bjs/pub/pdf/pjim05.pdf.
2. International Centre for Prison Studies, "World Prison Brief," King's College, University of London, http://www.kcl.ac.uk/depsta/rel/icps/worldbrief/world_brief.html.
3. Dan Seligman, "Lock 'Em Up," *Forbes*, May 23, 2005.
4. Brandon Rottinghouse, *Incarceration and Enfranchisement: International Practices, Impact and Recommendations for Reform* (Washington, D.C.: International Foundation for Election Systems, 2003).
5. See *Woodson v. North Carolina*, 428 U.S. 280 (1976); *Roberts v. Louisiana*, 428 U.S. 325 (1976); *Gregg v. Georgia*, 428 U.S. 153 (1976); *Jurek v. Texas*, 428 U.S. 262 (1976); and *Proffitt v. Florida*, 428 U.S. 242 (1976).
6. Amnesty International, "Death Penalty Developments in 2005," April 20, 2006, http://web.amnesty.org/library/Index/ENG ACT500052006?open&of=ENG-CHN.
7. Human Rights Watch and Amnesty International, *The Rest of Their Lives: Life Without Parole for Child Offenders in the United States*, October 12, 2005, http://hrw.org/reports/2005/us1005/.
8. Death Penalty Information Center, "Innocence: List of Those Freed From Death Row," http://www.deathpenaltyinfo.org/article.php?scid=6&did=110.
9. David C. Baldus, Charles Pulaski, and George Woodworth, "Comparative Review of Death Sentences: An Empirical Study of the Georgia Experience," *Journal of Criminal Law and Criminology* 74, no. 3 (1983): 661–753.
10. Baldus, Pulaski, and Woodworth, *Equal Justice and the Death Penalty: A Legal and Empirical Analysis* (Northeastern University Press, 1990).
11. John Blume, Theodore Eisenberg, and Martin T. Well, "Explaining Death Row's Population and Racial Composition," *Journal of Empirical Legal Studies* 1, no. 1 (2004): 165–207.

12. RAND Corporation, "RAND Study Finds No Evidence of Racial Bias in Federal Prosecutors' Decisions to Seek Death Penalty from 1995 to 2000," news release, July 17, 2006, http://www.rand.org/news/press.06/07.17.html.

13. Office of the Governor of the State of Illinois, "Governor Ryan Declares Moratorium on Executions, Will Appoint Commission to Review Capital Punishment System," news release, January 31, 2000, http://www.illinois.gov/PressReleases/ShowPressRelease.cfm?SubjectID=3&RecNum=359.

14. Bureau of Justice Statistics, "Prisoners in 2004," bulletin, October 2005, http://www.ojp.usdoj.gov/bjs/pub/pdf/p04.pdf.

15. Bureau of Justice Statistics, "Federal Criminal Case Processing, 2002: With Trends 1982–2002," January 2005, 12, Table 6, http://www.ojp.usdoj.gov/bjs/abstract/fccp02.htm.

16. Bureau of Justice Statistics, "Prisoners in 1996," bulletin, June 1997, http://www.ojp.usdoj.gov/bjs/pub/pdf/p96.pdf.

17. John Irwin, Vincent Schiraldi, and Jason Ziedenberg, *America's One Million Nonviolent Prisoners* (Washington, D.C.: Justice Policy Institute, 1999), 4.

18. *Drug Sentencing Reform Act of 2006*, S 3725, 109th Cong., 2nd sess.

19. Ira Glasser, "Drug Busts = Jim Crow," *Nation*, July 10, 2006; Milton Friedman, "There's No Justice in the War on Drugs," *New York Times*, January 11, 1998.

20. Bureau of Justice Statistics, "Reentry Trends in the United States," http://www.ojp.usdoj.gov/bjs/reentry/reentry.htm.

21. Ken Ellingwood, "Three-Time Loser Gets Life in Cookie Theft," *Los Angeles Times*, October 28, 1995.

22. Federal Bureau of Investigation, "Crime in the United States 2005," September 2006, http://www.fbi.gov/ucr/05cius/; U.S. Census Bureau, "Population Estimates by Race," http://www.census.gov/popest/estimates.php.

23. John Cloud, "What's Race Got to Do With It?" *Time*, July 22, 2001.

24. Drug Enforcement Administration, "Inside the DEA: Operations Pipeline and Convoy," http://www.dea.gov/programs/pipecon.htm.

25. John Knowles, Nicola Persico, and Petra Todd, "Racial Bias in Motor Vehicle Searches: Theory and Evidence," *Journal of Political Economy* 109, no.1 (2001).

26. New Jersey Division of Criminal Justice, "Eradicating Racial Profiling," attorney general directive, http://www.njdcj.org/agguide/directives/racial-profiling/racial-profiling.htm.

27. Amnesty International, *Excessive and Lethal Force? Amnesty International's Concerns About Deaths and Ill-treatment Involving Police Use of Tasers*, November 30, 2004.

28. Bureau of Justice Statistics, "Indigent Defense," selected findings, February1996, http://www.ojp.usdoj.gov/bjs/pub/pdf/id.pdf.

29. Norman Seabrook, "Prison Violence on the Rise," *USA Today Magazine*, September 2005.

30. C. Struckman-Johnson, "Sexual Coercion Rates in Seven Midwestern Prison Facilities for Men," *Prison Journal* 80, no. 4 (2000): 379–90.

31. Robert Weisberg and David Mills, "Why No One Really Cares About Prison Violence," *Slate*, October 1, 2003.

32. Human Rights Watch, "Ill-Equipped: U.S. Prisons and Offenders With Mental Illness," October 2003, http://www.hrw.org/reports/2003/usa1003/.

33. Ricoact.com LLC, "RICO in a Nutshell," http://www.ricoact.com/ricoact/nutshell.asp#intro.

34. See Gary J. Andres, "The Kelo Backlash," *Washington Times*, August 29, 2005; John Harwood, "Poll Shows Division on Court Pick," *Wall Street Journal*, July 15, 2005; Quinnipiac University, "Connecticut Voters Say 11–1 Stop Eminent Domain, Quinnipiac University Poll Finds; Saving Groton Sub Base Is High Priority," news release, July 28, 2005; Americans for Prosperity, "Public Opinion Poll on Eminent Domain," February 2006.

35. Senate Judiciary Committee, *The Kelo Decision: Investigating Takings of Homes and Other Private Property*, 109th Cong., 1st sess., 2005.

36. Property Rights Protection Act of 2005, HR 4128, 109th Cong., 2nd sess.; and *Private Property Rights Protection Act of 2006*, S 3873, 109th Cong., 2nd sess.

37. Linda Greenhouse, "Justices Divided on Protections Over Wetlands," *New York Times*, June 20, 2006.
38. Kevin E. McCarthy, "Referenda and Initiatives on Eminent Domain in Other States," Connecticut Office of Legislative Research, November 17, 2006, http://www.cga.ct.gov/2006/rpt/2006-R-0706.htm.
39. See Institute for Justice for a list of cases: http://ij.org/economic_liberty/index.html.
40. See *Granholm v. Heald* (2005).
41. Itai Sened and William H. Riker, "Common Property and Private Property: The Case of Air Slots," *Journal of Theoretical Politics* 8, no. 4 (1996): 427–47.
42. Federal Communications Commission, "About Auctions," http://wireless.fcc.gov/auctions/default.htm?job=about_auctions.

Immigration:
Despite Challenges,
a Source of Strength

Immigration is integral to the American national identity. Before they became "Americans," the nation's first citizens were English, Scottish, Irish, Welsh, Dutch, or German. Notwithstanding recurring waves of anti-immigrant sentiment, and intense controversy over policies aimed at managing the flow of immigrants, the United States largely prides itself on being a "nation of immigrants." Most Americans consider the diverse population and pool of talent attracted by the country's unique freedoms and opportunities to be crucial to its economic, political, and cultural achievements. Vital to the country's ongoing allure as a destination for immigrants from every part of the world is its policy of assimilation, which contrasts with the approach taken by most European democracies and many other countries.

Immigration is a political issue that often stokes powerful emotions. All Americans regularly experience the effects of immigration policy as it influences the labor market, the cost of consumer goods, the ethnic composition of neighborhoods and school districts, popular culture, and national security efforts. Pundits and politicians routinely exploit the presence of immigrants in America, particularly during times of economic, political, or military uncertainty.

Indeed, the September 11, 2001, terrorist attacks on the United States have drawn increased attention to the relationship between immigration and national security, and terrorism concerns have driven many of the changes in immigration and especially visa policy over the last six years. These changes are often seen to disproportionately affect the freedoms enjoyed by residents from predominantly Muslim countries, most of whom are in the United States legally. Also at play, however, is the dilemma presented by the roughly 12 million immigrants currently living in the country illegally—a figure that has quadrupled over the past two decades. Most of these men and women seek to integrate themselves and their families into American society through hard work and education, as earlier waves of immigrants, legal and illegal, have done. In addition to simmering concern about the cultural implications of their assimilation, the ubiquity and status of millions of undocumented workers and their families presents a bracing rebuke to Americans' desire to establish a secure homeland in a period of anxiety about terrorist threats and heightened appreciation for the rule of law. The presence of these workers ranks as the single most important factor behind an increasingly contentious immigration debate

In June 2007, a bipartisan congressional initiative to modernize decades-old immigration laws, backed by President George W. Bush and key cabinet members, collapsed in the face of a determined opposition that, while including liberals and Democrats, was animated largely by conservative Republicans. "The American people understand the status quo is unacceptable when it comes to our immigration laws," said President Bush after a critical procedural vote killed the proposal in the Senate. "A lot of us worked hard to see if we couldn't find a common ground—it didn't work."[1]

Other immigration controversies at present include the matter of whether the United States will provide a haven to refugees from Iraq, in particular those whose families have been endangered by their service to the American armed forces or civilian organizations. Between October 2006 and August 2007, only 719 Iraqi refugees were admitted to the United States—an embarrassing abdication of national responsibility for men and women who have allied themselves with the American effort in Iraq.[2] In addition to the ever-present discussion about the differences in treatment given to migrants arriving by boat from Cuba versus those from Haiti (and other locations in the Western Hemisphere), there is disquiet about the failure of the executive branch to provide entry to refugees from North Korea, despite a 2004 law requiring that it be done.[3]

In assessing the effect of U.S. immigration policy on the freedom enjoyed by today's American, it is important to consider that while the Universal Declaration of Human Rights guarantees everyone the "right to seek and to enjoy in other countries asylum from persecution,"[4] no international human rights law or treaty guarantees noncitizens the absolute right to enter and remain indefinitely in a country.[5] Furthermore, while the U.S. Constitution does not give foreigners the right to enter the country, it does guarantee their right to fair and equal treatment once they arrive, including protection from discrimination based on race or national origin and from arbitrary decisions by the government.[6] How welcoming the United States is to new arrivals depends, as ever, on a mix of personal, cultural, economic, and security considerations, and is the subject of everlasting discussion in our society. The national debate, like this chapter, largely omits explicit reference to the two portions of the population that are not of immigrant origin: the Native Americans who resided here before Europeans arrived, and those involuntary migrants who came from Africa as slaves. Descendants of these communities, along with successor generations of purposeful immigrants, make up important parts of the American social fabric that continues to attract newcomers.

Early Immigration Policy

America's founding fathers opposed massive, unrestricted immigration,[7] but they largely agreed that immigration would be essential to building the new nation and expanding it westward. Early American entrepreneurs advertised overseas for immigrant laborers to work the new country's farms, mines, factories, and mills. Congress played a role as well, actively helping Polish exiles to settle in Illinois and Michigan in 1834, and passing the Homestead Act in 1862 to draw additional settlers with cheap land grants.[8]

As the nineteenth century advanced, however, nativists gained strength and succeeded in tightening immigration policies. The first cohesive, politically influential nativists were the Know-Nothings, a movement with primarily Protestant membership that opposed the mass influx of Irish and German Catholics in the 1840s and 1850s. Its formal expression in the American Party was short-lived; though it won 21 percent of the national vote in the presidential election of 1856, with former president Millard Fillmore as its standard-bearer, the party disappeared by the following election.

Race soon replaced religion as the driving force behind nativism, with attention turning from European to Chinese immigrants. By 1870, more than 60,000 Chinese had entered the country and—following the completion of the Union Central Pacific Railroad—approximately 10,000 of them had entered the California labor market. This alarmed Western laborers and contributed to a widespread fear of Chinese encroachment on American society.[9] The "Chinese issue" reached the Senate floor as a result of political concerns that illegal or nonnaturalized Chinese immigrants might commit election fraud, to the benefit of the Democratic Party.[10] The national immigration debate in the late nineteenth century thus revolved around the same issues that would animate U.S. immigration policy for the next 125 years: jobs, culture, and politics.

The discussion in Congress led to the Chinese Exclusion Act of 1882, the first significant reversal of the country's historical openness to immigration. The new law prohibited the entry of both skilled and unskilled Chinese laborers and imposed burdensome paperwork requirements on many Chinese who had already arrived.[11] A series of subsequent acts expanded Chinese exclusion and made it permanent in 1902. In 1892, every Chinese person already living in the United States became an illegal resident "unless he or she could demonstrate otherwise."[12]

While Chinese immigrants were perceived as the greater cultural threat in the years between 1850 and 1910, the number of immigrants from Asia was dwarfed by the wave of immigrants who arrived from more and more parts of Europe, and by the vast numbers arriving overall. From 1881 to 1890, for example, a total of 4,735,484 immigrants arrived from Europe while just 69,942 came from Asia. Between 1900 and 1910, a massive 8,795,386 immigrants from all nations arrived in the United States—roughly four times the number that had entered in each of the decades between 1850 and 1880, and more than 11.5 percent of the country's population at the start of that decade.[13]

The turn of the century saw a spike in immigration from Southern and Eastern Europe. The newcomers' languages, religions, and cultures differed from those of earlier Northern European and British immigrants, galvanizing anti-immigrant forces. The result would be two decades of intensifying restrictions on immigration.

Overriding a veto by President Woodrow Wilson, Congress in 1917 established a literacy test for all immigrants and an "Asiatic Barred Zone" that further restricted immigration from Asia.[14] The Red Scare that followed Russia's Bolshevik Revolution inspired the Immigration Act of 1918, which for the first time allowed aliens to be deported because of their ideological beliefs or membership in certain organizations. A bombing traced to anarchists in 1919 provoked the Justice Department to compile lists of thousands of suspected radicals and their affiliations, and to conduct massive raids that resulted in the arrests of more than 10,000 people. Setting a precedent for some of the actions taken after the September 11, 2001, (or 9/11) terrorist attacks, the government's effort to root out alleged foreign and leftist subversives compromised the due process rights of many and led to the deportation of hundreds of people.

World War I temporarily slowed immigration. In its aftermath, though, Congress passed the 1921 Quota Act, sometimes referred to as the "Emergency Quota Act" or the "Johnson Act." This law established an overall quota of 358,000 immigrants per year and set quotas for particular nations of origin as well. The 1924 Immigration Act, or Johnson-Reid Act, tightened these restrictions further and made the system permanent and preferential.

The new limits imposed in 1924 significantly favored immigrants from Northern and Western Europe. Quotas for these countries were cut by only 29 percent, whereas quotas for Southern and Eastern Europe were cut by 87 percent. Italy's quota alone was slashed from 42,057 to 3,845 persons.[15] The 1924 act also prohibited all immigration from Asia, including Japan for the first time. On the other hand, all Western Hemisphere countries were excluded from the quota system because the U.S. government did not want to estrange its neighbors, and because the U.S. economy depended on Mexican agricultural labor.[16]

The 1924 act marked the peak of nativist influence on federal immigration policy. It reflected postwar concerns about job competition, the fear that immigrants' willingness to work for lower wages would reduce living standards, and—especially for American Protestants—the fear that immigrants from Southern and Eastern Europe, most of them Roman Catholic, Orthodox Christian, or Jewish, threatened American values.[17] Congressional support for the bill was nearly unanimous; only six senators cast dissenting votes. The number of immigrants from Europe fell sharply, while immigration from the New World grew from 8.6 percent of the total in 1910 to 45.1 percent in 1924, with the clear majority of those coming from Canada and Mexico.[18]

During the Great Depression, President Herbert Hoover stepped up immigration controls administratively, and the number of migrants fell significantly. The first net outflow of migrants occurred in 1934, when roughly 10,000 more people left the country than entered, leaving large portions of most quotas unfilled.[19] Even the number of Mexican immigrants dropped markedly, as there were fewer low-level jobs available.

World War II brought strict policies governing "enemy aliens," including the notorious internment of nearly 120,000 Japanese and Japanese Americans in "relocation centers." Nonetheless, immigration policy was liberalized during the 1940s in important ways, with the repeal of Chinese exclusion laws in 1943 and the extension of naturalization and full-quota immigration rights to other Asian groups.

The United States had long been a haven to political refugees and failed revolutionaries. The Displaced Persons Acts of 1948 and 1950, however, introduced the first formally articulated U.S. policies for admitting those fleeing persecution. Refugee policy has come to represent one of the most generous aspects of immigration in America and, at the same time, provides a clear example of the ties between immigration and foreign policy considerations. By the 1940s, racist and economic motivations for restrictionism were outweighed by concerns about the political loyalties of the American population and, for some, a need for immigration policy to support foreign policy. Mindful of the country's past failure to give refuge to Jews fleeing Nazi oppression and a new obligation to welcome those whom the U.S. government was encouraging to leave oppressive Communist societies, U.S. leaders began a dramatic shift away from restrictionism in the 1950s that would culminate in the abolition of the old national quotas in 1965. The 1953 Refugee Relief Act (RRA) authorized the admission of 214,000 refugees from European and especially Communist-dominated countries, outside of the national-origins quota system. Other refugee legislation (for example, the Refugee Escapee Act of 1957, the Fair Share Law of 1960, and subsequent legislation prompted by the Vietnam War in the 1970s and 1980s) admitted 29,000 Hungarians after the unsuccessful 1956 Hungarian revolution, 700,000 Cubans after leftist guerrillas toppled President Fulgencio Batista's government in 1959, and more than 400,000 Southeast Asians after the fall of South Vietnam and Cambodia to Communist forces in 1975.[20]

The shift toward a more open immigration policy arguably began with President Harry Truman's 1952 veto of the McCarran-Walter Act, which prescribed a rigid and ethnically biased national quota system that clearly contradicted the country's international campaign for freedom and against Communist oppression. Congress overrode Truman's veto, however, partly to ensure the enactment of the bill's domestic security provisions. McCarran-Walter authorized the deportation of any alien who engaged or had purpose to engage in activities prejudicial to the public interest or subversive to national security.[21]

The most fundamental change occurred when President Lyndon Johnson signed the Hart-Celler Immigration Act in 1965, making family reunification—and not national origin—the cornerstone of U.S. immigration policy. The 1965 law was the product of both foreign policy concerns—competition with the Soviet Union and the decolonization of Asia and Africa—and the civil rights movement in the United States. It allocated 170,000 visas to the Eastern Hemisphere, with a ceiling of 20,000 per country, and 120,000 to the Western Hemisphere, with no per-country limit. However, a seven-category preferential system for visa admissions gave priority not to nationality, but to relatives of U.S. citizens and individuals with needed skills and abilities. McCarran-Walter had introduced similar preferences for U.S. relations and job skills, but only within the strict national quotas.[22]

Supporters of the 1965 Act, which the Senate approved in a vote of 76 to 18, did not anticipate drastic changes to the existing pattern of immigration. The bill was intended to eliminate discrimination among immigrants, not to encourage all races to immigrate; few Asians and Africans were expected to arrive because, according to one of the bill's sponsors, the family-ties and job-skills provisions would "hold the numbers down."[23]

In a dramatic illustration of the law of unintended consequences, the 1965 Immigration Act catalyzed an era of mass immigration and a fundamental demographic overhaul. The prioritization of family reunification caused the number of nonquota immigrants to skyrocket. Three times as many legal immigrants crossed U.S. borders between 1965 and 1995 as during the 30 years before, and unprecedented numbers came from Asia and Latin America. Within five years of the bill's passage, 27,859 immigrants entered the country from India alone.[24] An amendment passed in 1976 extended the 20,000 per-country ceiling and the preference system to Western Hemisphere countries, and another passed in 1978 merged the separate hemispheric ceilings into one worldwide limit of 290,000 visas.[25]

Meanwhile, a new debate over immigration policy was fueled by heightened job competition amid stagflation and recession in the late 1970s; the Mariel boatlift crisis of 1980, in which some 124,000 undocumented Cuban migrants entered the United States in 25 overcrowded vessels;[26] and a continuing influx of Haitians. In 1981, the Select Commission on Immigration and Refugee Policy identified undocumented (illegal) immigration as the country's primary immigration problem.[27]

The 1986 Immigration Reform and Control Act (IRCA) was primarily designed to reverse the sharp increase in the number of immigrants entering the country illegally. It was the product of deep congressional divisions, however, and it effectively expanded both legal and illegal immigration.

On the one hand, the law established penalties for employers who "knowingly" hired, recruited, or referred aliens who were not authorized to work in the United States. It also strengthened U.S. border controls, through improved technology and a 50 percent increase in Border Patrol staff. On the other hand, IRCA established a Visa Waiver Pilot Program that enabled the admission of certain nonimmigrant foreigners without visas for educational, business, and other purposes (a system now notorious for allowing the entry of some of the 9/11 hijackers), and authorized a new classification for seasonal agricultural workers (SAW). In a provision that continues to generate controversy, the law also legalized all aliens who had resided in the United States unlawfully since before January 1, 1982.

Controlling America's Borders: The Ongoing Debate

The restrictive provisions of the 1986 law proved to be largely ineffective, and with the exception of a few recent enforcement measures, they remain so today. Despite a series of hikes in the number of Border Patrol agents and funding for improved technology, the border has remained largely permeable. Moreover, many of these border control efforts have encouraged immigrants to seek alternative points of entry that are more dangerous for them to cross and harder for the government to police.[28] Since 1986 the government has passed a host of laws to stem illegal immigration—from the so-called Kennebunkport Order in the early 1990s, which authorized the Coast Guard to forcibly repatriate more than 20,000 Haitians,[29] to the 1996 Illegal Immigration Reform and Immigrant Responsibility Act, which streamlined the deportation process and devoted still more resources to securing the border. Yet the number of illegal immigrants in the United States has continued to increase, from an estimated 3 million in 1986 to some 12 million in 2006. Many perceive this population to be a source of competition for native-born workers, an affront to the rule of law, and—since 9/11—a threat to national security, but policymakers struggle to agree on a remedy. It remains unclear how the country can control its borders without damaging the economy, violating the rights of legal immigrants, and fundamentally contradicting the nation's historical commitment to offering American freedoms and opportunity to newcomers. As the U.S. government continues to grapple with this vexing dilemma, the heightened attention is leaving a sizable, hardworking part of the population increasingly vulnerable.

The congressional debate over two immigration bills—one supported by the House and another backed by the Senate and President George W. Bush—during the run-up to the 2006 midterm elections hinged on many of the same issues addressed 20 years earlier: border security and workplace enforcement, a temporary-worker program, and legalization of undocumented immigrants (usually characterized by its opponents as amnesty).[30]

In keeping with the consistent emphasis on border security, the only piece of immigration legislation that was passed in 2006 was the Secure Fence Act, which called for two layers of new fencing along 700 miles of the 2,000-mile U.S.-Mexico border. The fence has generated considerable controversy. For many Americans it clashes with the country's history of open doors and freedom-based ideals; for others it represents a necessary precaution against external threats.[31] Generally speaking, however, lawmakers of every political stripe tend to agree on the need to protect national security, and those who appear to differ expose themselves to criticism. Therefore, the number of Border Patrol agents on the U.S.-Mexican border has tripled over the last two decades; since 9/11 it has increased by roughly 15 percent. In 2005, Congress granted the secretary of the Homeland Security Department the authority to waive any law that stood in the way of border security.[32] In the same year, the department launched the Secure Border Initiative, a "comprehensive, multi-year plan to secure America's borders and reduce illegal migration" through increased numbers of Border Patrol agents and procedural and technological improvements.[33]

Workplace enforcement, like border security, is supported across much of the political spectrum. The 2006 House and Senate bills both would have required employers to verify their workers' legal status through a national database of Social Security or work-identification numbers, and would have imposed criminal penalties on those who hire unauthorized workers. Still, attempts to control illegal immigration by monitoring the workplace remain highly sensitive. Unauthorized immigrants are estimated to make up nearly 5 percent of the nation's workforce, and perhaps as much as 70 percent of the seasonal agricultural workforce;[34] both parties hesitate to upset the economy by attempting to send them home.[35]

Only about 66,000 unskilled immigrants are permitted to enter the country legally to seek work each year. Businesses seeking unskilled labor say that native-born Americans will not take such jobs and that 66,000 is not enough. They also object to being tasked with worker verification, saying it amounts to a law enforcement function.[36] On the other hand, the workplace is the most likely place to identify those who enter the country legally but overstay their visas. That group makes up an estimated 40 percent of the country's 12 million illegal immigrants.[37]

Under current law, companies are required to review two forms of government-issued identification to verify employees' legality. Employers are likely to take immigrant workers at their word, however, because the alternative is to hire American-born workers who would demand higher pay. The government, for its part, has been inclined to look the other way because such wage hikes would raise the cost of living for everyone. Workplace enforcement has thus been infrequent at best, and declined further in the aftermath of 9/11 as the government diverted its resources to fighting terrorism. The *Washington Post* reported that the government scaled back workplace enforcement operations by 95 percent between 1999 and 2003, while the number of employers prosecuted each year for unlawfully hiring immigrants dropped from 182 to four.[38]

U.S. policymakers and especially the Republican Party have been sharply divided on whether immigration reform should include a guest-worker program and a path toward citizenship for illegal aliens. The 2006 House and Senate bills largely reflected the two approaches to this issue. The House version represented the "enforcement first" camp, which supports—in addition to the border fence and increased penalties for employers of illegal immigrants—making it a crime to assist illegal immigrants and raising illegal immigration from a civil violation to a felony. An "earned citizenship" approach, supported by the 2006 Senate bill, would have instituted a guest-worker program and a path to citizenship for many illegal immigrants already living in the country.

Various proposed guest-worker programs would allow businesses to give temporary work visas to resident illegal immigrants or new migrants if the employers can document that American workers will not take the jobs they are seeking to fill.

The president and many Democrats insist that such a program would provide a legal way to fill these jobs while encouraging the undocumented to "come out of the shadows" and helping to win Mexico's cooperation in securing the southern border.[39] Current temporary-worker programs admit only 250,000 to 300,000 individuals annually, with most slots reserved for highly skilled, specialized workers.[40]

Opponents argue that guest-worker programs would only aggravate the current problem of immigrants taking jobs from low-skilled American workers and depressing wages. Labor economist George Borjas has lent support to this point of view. Backing his arguments is a recent report from the Center for Immigration Studies, which asserts that only 9 percent of the net increase in jobs for adults between March 2000 and March 2005 went to people born in the United States.[41] Moreover, immigrants make up more than 40 percent of adults in the labor force without high school diplomas, as opposed to 15 percent of the total adult workforce.[42] However, other economists have conducted studies showing that native-born Americans with less education are not significantly harmed by immigration. David Card, an influential member of this camp, argues that the price paid by native workers is small and that, overall, immigrants stimulate the economy by diversifying the skill set within it.[43]

Advocates of the enforcement-first approach see any plan that offers guest-worker status or eventual citizenship to illegal immigrants as tantamount to amnesty. They point specifically to IRCA's legalization of between two and three million undocumented workers in 1986, arguing that any repetition of that move would only perpetuate the problem.

The guest-worker program and the possibility of a path to citizenship for illegal immigrants again proved to be the most controversial provisions when a revised immigration reform bill reached the floor of Congress, now controlled by the Democrats, in 2007. The 2007 bill would have allowed the legalization of illegal immigrants who paid a series of significant fines and fulfilled other requirements. It also marked a departure from the 2006 debate with the introduction of a new points-based system that could fundamentally shift the criteria of immigration from family relations to job skills, education, and English-language proficiency. President Bush and some senators saw the proposed system as an effective means of tying immigration policy to long-term economic growth, but others argued that points-based systems, such as those employed by Canada and the United Kingdom, contradict the United States' long-standing tradition of social mobility and undermine its very identity as a land of opportunity.

In the aftermath of the latest legislation's defeat in June 2007, the administration pledged to enhance its enforcement of existing sanctions on illegal workers and their employers, though the funding that would have facilitated greater diligence in this regard was lost with the collapse of the bill. In one aspect of this enforcement effort, the Social Security Administration collaborated with the Homeland Security Department to warn employers that discrepancies in Social Security records would oblige them to fire the workers in question or face prosecution. By the end of the summer, a federal judge had ordered a halt to this program, based on a lawsuit citing a December report by the Social Security Administration inspector general that said 17.8 million of the agency's 435 million records contained errors that could result in doubts about a worker's legal status.[44] Meanwhile, efforts are multiplying in localities across the country to enact rules restricting access to public services for residents without documentation, and the courts are being asked to rule on whether it is the proper function of these governments to enforce immigration laws.[45]

The debate over how to control American borders has been tied tightly to national security interests since 9/11 and to economic concerns for a good deal longer. All of the current discourse over illegal immigration, however, appears to underestimate the extent to which today's immigrants—both legal and illegal—compose contemporary American society and contribute to the country's strength.

Assimilating American Immigrants

In a July 2006 interview, Representative Tom Tancredo, a Colorado Republican, presidential hopeful, and one of the strongest advocates for an enforcement-first approach, decried the rise of multiculturalism in America and declared, "We're losing sight of who we are."[46]

Tancredo takes a harder line than most, but he is not alone in believing that immigration threatens American culture and identity. Never before in the history of the United States has immigration been so dominated by a single region and, indeed, by a single country. Some 58 percent of all immigrants who arrived between 2000 and 2005 were from Latin America.[47] An estimated 42 million ethnic Latinos live in America today, making up about 14 percent of the U.S. population, and more than a third are younger than 18. The vast majority of U.S. Latinos are of Mexican origin or descent.[48] As of late 2005, 10.8 million Mexican immigrants were living in the United States, making up 31 percent of the immigrant population and almost six times the combined total for China, Taiwan, and Hong Kong. Moreover, Mexicans account for a clear majority of the illegal immigrant population.

These unprecedented levels, coupled with the fact that Latino immigrants have tended to concentrate regionally (Mexicans in Southern California and Texas and Cubans in Miami, for instance), have helped spark a national debate over whether today's immigrants are assimilating into American culture as well as into the national economy.

Such concerns are fueled, to some extent, by the wage gap between Mexicans and natives and between Mexicans and other immigrant groups. At $22,300, the average annual income of Mexican immigrants is currently half that of native-born workers.[49] While immigrants are slightly more likely than natives to have an advanced degree, in 2005 about 30 percent of all immigrants aged 18 and over in the labor force—a group in which Mexicans make up a clear majority—did not have high school diplomas.[50] Poverty rates among Mexicans are therefore higher, and while noncitizen, first-generation immigrants do not qualify for public assistance, their U.S.-born children do. Immigrants' use of public services has been a long-standing source of concern for nativists seeking more restrictive immigration policies. California's Proposition 187, although struck down soon after its easy passage in a 1994 referendum, made "illegal immigrants ineligible for public social services, public health care services (unless emergency under federal law), and public school education at elementary, secondary, and post secondary levels."[51] Federal welfare reform legislation that passed in 1996 authorized states to prevent legal immigrants who arrived after the law's date of enactment from receiving "means tested" public benefits—such as food stamps, Supplemental Security Income, Temporary Assistance for Needy Families, Medicaid, and the State Children's Health Insurance Program—for at least five years. Furthermore, those immigrants who enter under the family unification provision of immigration law are often barred from receiving means-tested benefits because the sponsor's income is transferred to the immigrant until he or she establishes a work history of roughly 10 years, which often makes the immigrant's income too high to qualify.[52]

Refugees are eligible for more public benefits after arriving than other immigrants and are much more likely to use them. Studies by the Urban Institute and the Migration Policy Institute have otherwise found that immigrants' use of most public benefits has declined significantly since the 1996 reforms and is substantially lower than that of U.S. citizens.[53]

Public education remains the exception to this broader trend and is central to the issue of assimilation. The children of immigrants now account for 19.2 percent of the total school-age population in the United States,[54] and about a third of these children have parents who lack high school educations.[55] In California, 55 percent of all students are the children of immigrants, and in Texas the figure is 25 percent.[56] Especially in these states with the largest immigrant populations, the debate over assimilation has played out in battles between advocates of bilingual education and those who support "English immersion" programs.

A successful 1998 California ballot initiative, Proposition 227, marked one of the first significant victories for the latter. The law requires all California public schools to teach "limited English proficient" (LEP) students in special classes that are conducted almost entirely in English, eliminating bilingual classes in most cases and shortening the amount of time LEP students spend in special classes before moving into regular classes.[57]

Public funding for immigrant education and English-language learning is complicated by the fact that 75 percent of the country's immigrant population is concentrated in a handful of states: California, New York, Texas, Florida, Illinois, and New Jersey.[58] At the same time, recent growth rates have been most dramatic in states with little prior experience in educating immigrant children, such as Kansas, Georgia, Oregon, and North Carolina.[59] The No Child Left Behind (NCLB) Act, an education reform initiative proposed by the Bush administration and passed with broad bipartisan support in 2001, replaced the Bilingual Education Act (BEA), or Title VII, with the English Language Acquisition Act. The change amounted to a major overhaul of the priorities and kinds of language programs supported by federal funds. Since 1968, the BEA had reserved a significant share of funding for language programs that employed students' native languages in instruction, fostering the autonomous development of bilingual language programs in many districts; a 1974 Supreme Court ruling went even further, requiring schools to provide special instruction to non-English-speaking students.[60] The new NCLB-linked legislation focuses exclusively on English-language skills and makes English-language proficiency a critical part of the state learning standards on which NCLB as a whole is centered. The former federal Office of Bilingual Education and Minority Languages Affairs (OBEMLA) is now the Office of English Language Acquisition, Language Enhancement, and Academic Achievement for Limited-English-Proficient Students. Rather than being administered by the federal government through a competitive grant system, funding is now distributed through formulaic grants by the states based on the number of English-language learners and immigrant students in each district, giving state education agencies much greater control over funding decisions.[61]

The Emergency Immigrant Education Program (EIEP) was established in 1984 to help state educational agencies serve the influx of immigrant children in their schools. As of 1999, the Department of Education identified the purpose of the program as the provision of "high-quality instruction to immigrant children and youth…to help [them] make the transition into American society and meet the same challenging State performance standards expected of all."[62] NCLB changed the criterion for EIEP funding from the overall number of immigrants to high growth in the immigrant population. As a result, the number of immigrants who qualified in California fell from 206,000 to 133,000 the year after NCLB was passed, while funding per student fell from $153 to $67.[63]

Public schools have not been the only battleground in the struggle over language in America. An "English Only" movement has promoted legislation that would restrict or prohibit the use of languages other than English by government agencies and, in some cases, by private businesses. This movement gained momentum in the early 1980s, and 16 states now have such laws. Critics of English-only laws, such as the American Civil Liberties Union, argue that they violate the Equal Protection Clause of the Fourteenth Amendment and could result in non-English speakers being deprived of critical services.[64] Advocates of these laws believe that knowledge of the English language is essential to productive membership in American society, and say the laws will ensure that immigrants learn it. They also argue that English is an important unifier of the country's diverse population.

In May 2006, the U.S. Senate voted 63 to 34 vote to designate English as the national language. While the measure stopped short of the "official language" status sought by English-only advocates, it did say that no one has "a right, entitlement or claim to have the government of the United States or any of its officials or representatives act, communicate, perform or provide services or provide materials in any language other than English."[65]

Meanwhile, evidence suggests that many immigrants have the desire but lack the means to learn English. A study by the New York Immigration Coalition found that, as of 2002, one million immigrants in New York State were in need of English classes but there were seats for only 50,000.[66] According to the Arizona Department of Education in 2004, 5,009 adults were on waiting lists for English classes and 5,686 more were turned away.[67]

Latino immigrants' frequent trips home to their native countries and adherence to the Spanish language are cited as evidence that they are diverging from the assimilationist path of previous immigrant groups. Some say Latinos have been slow to assimilate because native-born Americans discriminate against them, while others argue that Latino immigrants and their children are simply less committed to assimilation than their European predecessors.

However, studies indicate that today's immigrants, including Spanish speakers, are no exception to the generational pattern. Typically, first-generation immigrants make some progress in learning the new language, but speak mostly in their native tongue. The second generation is typically bilingual, and the third generation speaks English exclusively. A study conducted by a team at the State University of New York at Albany found that 72 percent of third-or-later-generation Latino students spoke English exclusively.[68] One study notes some evidence of a decline in education among the grandchildren of Mexican immigrants specifically. But other studies show that Latino immigrants and their children, including Mexicans, have done much to close the educational and economic gaps between themselves and native-born whites, and that their progress is just as rapid as that of earlier generations of immigrants.[69] Importantly, one study notes that generational assimilation today may be less visible than it was in the past. While the earlier wave of European immigration largely came to a halt with the restrictionist policies of the 1920s, today's immigrant population is in a constant state of replenishment, so that "each generation is a mix of cohorts and each cohort has a mix of generations."[70]

Intermarriage rates, often cited as a measurement of assimilation, may be the wild card among current trends. While interracial and interethnic marriage rates began to rise in the 1970s and continued to grow through the 1980s, a 2007 study published in the *American Sociological Review* found that intermarriage rates began to decline in the 1990s, particularly between whites and Asians or Latinos; the latter two immigrant groups have traditionally had the highest intermarriage rates with whites. The study maintains that the growth in the immigrant population in the 1990s, especially among these two groups, has led "more native-born Asian Americans and Latinos to marry their foreign-born counterparts."[71] Interracial marriages involving African Americans significantly increased during the 1990s, although the rates remained far behind those of other minorities.[72]

It is worth noting that non-Latino immigrant groups consistently outperform natives in each generation. They arrive in the United States with a lower high-school drop out rate than that of natives, and these rates fall farther below the native average in each subsequent generation.[73] Highly skilled immigrants are increasingly visible in medicine, computer science, and engineering, and they make key contributions to the country's knowledge-driven economy. Immigrants as a whole have made up 46 percent of the growth in the U.S. labor force since 2000,[74] and refugees and immigrants, both legal and undocumented, are estimated to contribute a net surplus of nearly $30 billion to the U.S. economy each year.[75]

Moreover, the rapid pace at which immigrants are opening new businesses has made immigrant communities an essential source of neighborhood and city revitalization. A February 2007 study by the Center for an Urban Future found that the number of businesses opened and the job growth experienced in immigrant-dominated neighborhoods from 1994 to 2004 in the New York City region far exceeded the corresponding figures for the city as a whole.[76] Census results dating as far back as 1880 reveal that immigrants are more likely to be self-employed than native-born residents.[77] The 2007 study showed that, in

New York, the number of self-employed foreign-born individuals grew by 53 percent between 1990 and 2000, while the self-employed number for the native-born decreased by 7 percent. More generally, the study found that more businesses are being started by foreign-born than native-born entrepreneurs in major cities nationwide.[78] Beyond providing essential services, immigrants are thus driving growth in a range of sectors including restaurants and food, real estate, and health care, while also helping to boost tax revenues and create jobs.

Muslim Immigration Since 9/11

The 9/11 attacks greatly intensified Americans' awareness of the link between immigration and national security, and it is not surprising that immigration policy has since been employed in the larger effort to prevent further attacks. At the same time, it is important to recognize the extent to which the national security issue has also been used to galvanize bipartisan support for broader and otherwise highly contentious immigration legislation. In an effort to revive the 2007 revised immigration reform bill after it was shelved yet again by a clearly divided Senate, Commerce Secretary Carlos Gutierrez said, "This is a national security bill. We are fixing a national security problem."[79]

Whether the government's new security-related immigration measures are essential or effective has been a matter of intense national debate, as have the measures' implications for the rights of immigrants. It is indisputable that most Muslims in the United States are immigrants, many fairly recent, and that they have come under heightened scrutiny from law enforcement agencies and others. Anxiety, hostility, and bias regarding Arab and Muslim immigrants is not inconsiderable in the population at large. A 2006 Gallup survey found that one-third of Americans believe Muslim Americans sympathize with al-Qaeda, and 39 percent think Muslims should be required to carry a special identification card. The survey also found that only 49 percent of Americans consider Muslim Americans to be loyal to the United States.[80]

In the immediate aftermath of the 9/11 attacks, Attorney General John Ashcroft authorized the detention of foreign citizens indefinitely and without congressional or judicial oversight "in the event of an emergency or other extraordinary circumstance." Soon thereafter the Immigration and Naturalization Service (INS) was empowered to override an immigration judge's order allowing an individual's release.[81] By early November 2001, some 1,147 primarily Arab and Muslim noncitizens had been arrested, 60 percent of them on immigration charges.[82] Many were held for long periods and in solitary confinement before they were charged. The Justice Department conducted closed immigration proceedings for many detainees and would not disclose their identities or whereabouts.

A task force report published in August 2007 by the Chicago Council on Global Affairs notes that since 9/11 "more than 80,000 Arab and Muslim nonnational residents of the U.S. have been required to undergo fingerprinting and registration, 8,000 have been identified for questioning, approximately 5,000 have been arrested or detained, and at least 400 have been criminally charged in terrorism-related investigations," although the report also says these estimates are considered low by many in the Muslim American community.[83] The inspector general of the Justice Department has reported that between 2001 and 2005, many cases that had been attributed to antiterrorism efforts in fact involved crimes such as drug trafficking or marriage fraud.[84]

The 9/11 attacks have not fundamentally changed who may enter the United States, nor have they fundamentally altered U.S. immigration law. They have, however, made the visa process much more security conscious and led to new, mandatory procedures for applicants from Muslim-majority countries.[85] The State Department slowed the process for granting visas to men aged 16 to 45 from specific Arab and Muslim countries by roughly 20 days.[86] Heightened security procedures in the first two years after 9/11 caused a greater number of visa applications to be rejected. The Department of Agriculture in February 2002 abruptly discontinued its sponsorship of the J-1 visa waiver program, which had allowed citizens of certain countries to come to the United States for limited tourism or business stays without obtaining a visa. The number of Muslims granted permission to live in the United States through the Diversity Immigrant Visa Program—a congressionally mandated program that allocates a certain number of resident visas to eligible persons from countries with low immigration rates—decreased by almost 14 percent by April 2002 as a result of prolonged security checks. The issuance of student visas became particularly complicated with the establishment of the Student and Exchange Visitor Information System in 2003. This system requires colleges and universities to provide consular officers overseas with electronic notification of all nonimmigrant visa applicants' acceptance as students.

Because some of the 9/11 terrorists were in the United States on expired visas, the government is also paying closer attention to visa overstays. In November 2001, the INS began an initiative in San Diego to arrest students who had violated the terms of their student visas. The program was geared particularly toward nationals of Iran, Iraq, Sudan, Pakistan, Libya, Saudi Arabia, Afghanistan, and Yemen.[87] The Alien Absconder Initiative—launched at the end of 2001 by the INS and the Justice Department and now operated by the Homeland Security Department—had by 2003 provided local law enforcement agencies with the names of 314,000 immigrants with orders for deportation or removal; the initiative allows law enforcement to enter information about civil immigration violations into the National Crime Information Center database. Thousands of men from "countries in which there has been al-Qaeda terrorist presence or activity" were designated as "priority absconders" in January 2002.[88]

Implemented on the one-year anniversary of the attacks, the U.S. National Security Entry-Exit Registration System requires male nationals of certain countries—Afghanistan, Algeria, Bahrain, Bangladesh, Egypt, Eritrea, Indonesia, Iran, Jordan, Kuwait, Libya, Lebanon, Morocco, North Korea, Oman, Pakistan, Qatar, Somalia, Saudi Arabia, Sudan, Syria, Tunisia, United Arab Emirates, and Yemen—to register with the Bureau of Citizenship and Immigration Services at specified points of entry and departure. Amnesty International reports that by the end of the program's first year, 177,260 men and boys were registered and 13,799 men were placed in deportation proceedings, but not one was charged with "terrorism."[89] Re-registration was required annually until December 2003. In effect, the program restricts the airports that nationals of these countries can fly into and out of, and requires that after receiving their boarding passes, participants present themselves to the U.S. Customs and Border Protection office. Another measure, the US VISIT program, requires that visitors from almost every country be fingerprinted and photographed each time they leave or return to the United States.

All of these measures have been controversial. A study by the Migration Policy Institute argues that by basing such requirements on national origin rather than intelligence-driven criteria, the government is violating the Fifth Amendment guarantee of equal protection.[90]

There is no doubt that these policies should be scrutinized, both to assess their utility in combating terrorism and for their civil liberties implications. The reality, however, is that national origin has always played some role in U.S. immigration policy, and that the United States has often expected its immigration policies to serve its perceived national security needs. During times of national security crisis, this formula has always affected the rights and treatment of various immigrant groups to some extent.

A survey released in May 2007 by the Pew Research Center for the People and the Press found that a majority of Muslim Americans—53 percent—believe it has become more difficult to be a Muslim in the United States since the 9/11 attacks, and that "most also believe the government 'singles out' Muslims for increased surveillance and monitoring."[91] However, the Pew survey more generally found that Muslim Americans are highly assimilated into American society, especially as reflected in income and education levels. In fact, the average salary of immigrants from Muslim countries is roughly 20 percent higher than that of other U.S. residents, and a larger percentage of Muslims have graduate degrees.[92] Moreover, according to the

Pew survey findings, fully 71 percent of Muslim Americans feel that "most people who want to get ahead in the U.S. can make it if they are willing to work hard."[93]

While the number of anti-Islamic hate crimes spiked in 2001 to a high of 481 "incidents" as recorded by the U.S. Federal Bureau of Investigation, the number had dropped significantly to 128 by 2005. To help put these figures in context, it may be worth noting that the number of reported incidents against Jews was 1,043 in 2001 and 848 in 2005.[94]

After a sharp post-9/11 decline in the number of immigrants from Muslim countries (the figure dropped by more than a third in 2003),[95] nearly 96,000 people from Muslim countries became legal permanent U.S. residents in 2005—more than in any single year in the previous two decades.[96] Some 40,000 of these people had arrived in the country the same year. Notwithstanding clear reservations about U.S. policy in the Middle East and some frustration with America's new security measures, large numbers of Muslims continue to come seeking political freedom and economic opportunity, just as other immigrants have done since the country's founding.

Conclusion

Since 1965, the United States has had a relatively liberal immigration policy that prioritizes family reunification and permanently resettles a greater number of refugees each year than any other country in the world.[97] Unlike in a number of European countries, where the right to family reunification was first implemented only in 2005 in compliance with a new European Union directive, a large number of refugees and an estimated 60 percent of all legal immigrants reunite with family members in the United States.[98] In 2006, for example, 63 percent of the grants of lawful permanent residence in the United States were based on family relations with a U.S. citizen or permanent legal resident.[99]

Furthermore, the REAL ID Act of 2005 eliminated the annual cap of 10,000 asylum seekers permitted to change status to legal permanent residence in the United States, while a number of European countries have tightened their asylum systems in the last few years. In 2003, right-wing parties and candidates campaigned on anti-asylum platforms in Denmark, Austria, Switzerland, and the United Kingdom. Austria may have implemented the most stringent rules, deporting most asylum seekers whose cases were being appealed and refusing to accept asylum applications at land borders.[100] Sweden remains an exception, and is a highly sought destination for refugees; it took in 9,000 Iraqis in 2006—almost half of the entire 22,000 seeking asylum in the industrialized world.

The different approaches to the asylum issue in Europe and the United States reflect a more general divergence in the roles immigrants play and the sentiments they arouse in each society. Despite the prevalence of immigrant-dominated neighborhoods, ethnic enclaves, and clear socioeconomic gaps in the United States, American immigrants are largely assimilated into the national culture, and especially the national economy. This is not the case in many European countries. The socioeconomic differences between immigrants and natives are often more profound in Europe, with immigrants experiencing far higher levels of unemployment than their counterparts in the United States. These conditions generate higher levels of resentment among native-born residents, politicians, and the immigrants themselves.[101]

Still, in the aftermath of 9/11 and a series of subsequent terrorist attacks and plots in the United Kingdom, Germany, and Spain, the United States and Europe are confronting many of the same challenges. The immigration policies of the European Union and its member states, like those of the United States, are being reshaped around the need to provide secure borders, prevent future attacks, maintain the rule of law, attract skilled labor, ensure economic growth, and preserve national cultures and identities. Each country has weighed these often conflicting priorities for itself. For example, recent changes to immigration law in Germany, where significant terrorist plots have been detected, established vague criteria for deportation and require that all immigrants undergo a check by the country's security service before being granted citizenship. Recruitment of foreign workers has been halted altogether. The United Kingdom, on the other hand, launched a revamped highly-skilled-migrants program in 2003.

In the United States, many of the fundamental dilemmas that have confronted lawmakers for the last two years have also been major obstacles in the past, and they are likely to persist. Questions of amnesty, the benefits and liabilities of guest-worker programs, points systems versus family unity, and a legitimate path to citizenship will continue to incite passions and divide Americans. While advocates of the latest immigration reform proposal voice serious concerns about some of its content, they recognize the extent to which immigration legislation has always been and will continue to be a matter of political compromise. And even with the right legislation, enforcement is uncertain. Nevertheless, a recent study by the Pew Research Center for the People and the Press shows that most Americans—a full 63 percent, with nearly identical portions of Republicans, Democrats, and independents—support providing a way for current illegal residents to gain legal citizenship under certain conditions, specifically by passing background checks, paying fines, and holding jobs.[102]

The U.S. government may not be obligated by any international treaty to make this happen, but a failure to do so would contradict the inclination of almost two-thirds of Americans across the political spectrum and clash with the country's history of thriving on diversity and the American promise of opportunity. The reality is that most of today's illegal immigrants just want to provide better opportunities for their families, and that as they do so, they are also enriching American culture and helping to maintain the country's economic strength. The government owes it to the country's significant immigrant population—and to the American democratic tradition—to push through a revised immigration policy that acknowledges this reality and makes the immigrant contribution legitimate. In fact, immigration reform provides a rare chance to advance both national security objectives and the freedoms enjoyed by many Americans. Our elected national leaders should seize the opportunity.

Endnotes

1. Michael Sandler, "Immigration Bill Appears Doomed After Cloture Vote Fails in Senate," *Congressional Quarterly*, June 28, 2007.
2. Associated Press, "U.S. Admits More Iraqi Refugees," *Los Angeles Times*, September 5, 2007, http://www.latimes.com/news/nationworld/world/la-fg-refugees5sep05,1,2837949.story?coll=la-headlines-world.
3. *North Korean Human Rights Act of 2004*, Public Law 108-333, enacted October 18, 2004. On March 1, 2007, the State Department's special envoy for North Korean human rights, Jay Lefkowitz, testified to a congressional committee that only 30 such refugees from North Korea had been admitted to the United States at that point. House Committee on Foreign Affairs, Subcommittee on Asia, the Pacific, and the Global Environment, *North Korean Human Rights: An Update*, 110th Cong., 1st sess., 2007.
4. United Nations Office of the High Commissioner of Human Rights, *Universal Declaration of Human Rights*, GA Resolution 217 A (III), December 10, 1948, http://www.unhchr.ch/udhr/lang/eng.htm.
5. Alison Parker, "Inalienable Rights: Can Human-Rights Law Help to End U.S. Mistreatment of Noncitizens?" *American Prospect* 15, no. 10 (October 2004), also available at http://hrw.org/english/docs/2004/10/01/usdom10493.htm.
6. American Civil Liberties Union (ACLU), "The Rights of Immigrants—ACLU Position Paper," September 8, 2000, http://aclu.org/immigrants/gen/11713pub20000908.html.
7. Today's anti-immigrant groups frequently invoke this point in making their cases for tighter controls. See, for example, Americans for Immigration Control, "A Brief History of Immigration: From the Discovery and Settlement of the United States to the Destructive Flood of Immigration Today, " http://www.immigrationcontrol.com/short_history.htm.
8. Ibid.

9. The 1870 census recorded more than 60,000 Chinese, with nearly three-quarters living in California; most were men. Roger Daniels, *Guarding the Golden Door: American Immigration Policy and Immigrants Since 1882* (New York: Hill and Wang, 2004), 12.

10. Ibid., 12–14.

11. Ibid., 19; "The People's Vote: 100 Documents That Shaped America—Chinese Exclusion Act," *U.S. News and World Report*, http://www.usnews.com/usnews/documents/docpages/document_page47.htm.

12. Daniels, *Guarding the Golden Door*, 21.

13. Federation for American Immigration Reform (FAIR), "U.S. Immigration History," http://www.fairus.org/site/PageServer?pagename=research_research9c29.

14. Center for Immigration Studies, *Three Decades of Mass Immigration: The Legacy of the 1965 Immigration Act* (Washington, DC: Center for Immigration Studies, September 1995), http://www.cis.org/articles/1995/back395.html.

15. "Immigration Act of 1924," http://www.historicaldocuments.com/ImmigrationActof1924.htm.

16. Ibid.

17. Daniels, *Guarding the Golden Door*, 49.

18. Ibid., 51.

19. Ibid., 60.

20. The figure for Cuban refugees represents the cumulative number who entered the country prior to 1980, when a second influx began under new legislation. The number for Southeast Asians refers exclusively to those who arrived prior to 1980. Daniels, *Guarding the Golden Door*, 194–203.

21. Alicia J. Campi, *The McCarran-Walter Act: A Contradictory Legacy on Race, Quotas, and Ideology* (Washington, DC: American Immigration Law Foundation, 2004), http://www.ailf.org/ipc/policy_reports_2004_mccarranwalter.asp.

22. Ibid.; Center for Immigration Studies, *Three Decades of Mass Immigration*.

23. Ibid.

24. Ibid.

25. FAIR, "U.S. Immigration History."
26. GlobalSecurity.org, "Mariel Boatlift," http://www.globalsecurity.org/military/ops/mariel-boatlift.htm.
27. Daniels, *Guarding the Golden Door*, 220.
28. Betsy Cooper, *Reforming Immigration: A Strong Security, Pro-Immigrant Policy for Democrats* (Washington, DC: Truman National Security Project, April 2006), http://www.trumanproject.org/trumanpaper4.html.
29. ACLU, "The Rights of Immigrants."
30. Romano L. Mazzoli and Alan K. Simpson, "Enacting Immigration Reform, Again," *Washington Post*, September 15, 2006.
31. Peter Skerry, "How Not to Build a Fence," *Foreign Policy* (September/October 2006), http://www.foreignpolicy.com/story/cms.php?story_id=3557.
32. Ibid.
33. Department of Homeland Security, "DHS Announces Long-Term Border and Immigration Strategy," news release, November 2, 2005, http://www.dhs.gov/dhspublic/interapp/press_release/press_release_0795.xml.
34. Steve Inskeep and Jennifer Ludden, "Feds Stand Down on Immigration Crackdown," *Morning Edition*, NPR, September 4, 2007, http://www.npr.org/templates/story/story.php?storyId=14149812.
35. S. Mitra Kalita and Krissah Williams, "Help Wanted as Immigration Faces Overhaul," *Washington Post*, March 27, 2006; Mazzoli and Simpson, "Enacting Immigration Reform, Again."
36. Mazzoli and Simpson, "Enacting Immigration Reform, Again."
37. Spencer S. Hsu and Kari Lydersen, "Illegal Hiring Is Rarely Penalized," *Washington Post*, June 19, 2006.
38. Ibid.
39. See Siobhan Gorman, "Reframing the Debate," *National Journal*, March 2, 2002.
40. Cooper, *Reforming Immigration*; Daniels, *Guarding the Golden Door*, 142–143.

41. Ron Scherer, "Immigration Debate Crux: Jobs Impact," *Christian Science Monitor*, March 30, 2006, http://www.csmonitor.com/2006/0330/p01s01-ussc.html.
42. Steven A. Camarota, *Immigrants at Mid-Decade: A Snapshot of America's Foreign-Born Population in 2005* (Washington, DC: Center for Immigration Studies, December 2005), http://www.cis.org/articles/2005/back1405.html.
43. Roger Lowenstein, "The Immigration Equation," *New York Times Magazine*, July 9, 2006, http://www.nytimes.com/2006/07/09/magazine/09IMM.html?ex=1310097600&en=45962e550ceea8df&ei=5088&partner=rssnyt&emc=rss.
44. Julia Preston, "Social Security Warns of Logjam From Immigration Ruling," *New York Times*, September 7, 2007.
45. See, for instance, Claudia Lauer, "Ban Could Deny Illegal Immigrants Service," *Los Angeles Times*, July 14, 2007; and Sarah Karush, "2 Virginia Counties OK Immigration Crackdown," Associated Press, August 25, 2007.
46. See Robert McMahon, "Tancredo: Tough Immigration Reform Essential to Maintain U.S. Identity," Council on Foreign Relations, July 24, 2006, http://www.cfr.org/publication/11141/tancredo.html.
47. Camarota, *Immigrants at Mid-Decade*, 9–10.
48. "The Wrong Side of History; Immigration," *Economist*, July 13, 2006.
49. Lowenstein, "The Immigration Equation."
50. Camarota, *Immigrants at Mid-Decade*, 11.
51. Daniels, *Guarding the Golden Door*, 243.
52. Michael Fix, "Immigrants' Costs and Contributions: The Effects of Reform" (Migration Policy Institute, testimony prepared for the U.S. House Committee on Ways and Means, July 26, 2006), http://www.migrationpolicy.org/pubs/FixTestimony072606.pdf.
53. Ibid.
54. Camarota, *Immigrants at Mid-Decade*, 25.
55. Urban Institute, "Beyond Bilingual Education: Immigrant Students and the No Child Left Behind Act," December 7, 2004, http://www.urban.org/publications/900764.html.

56. Pia Orrenius, "Immigrant Assimilation: Is the U.S. Still a Melting Pot?" Federal Reserve Bank of Dallas, January 2004, http://www.dallasfed.org/research/indepth/2004/id0401a.html.
57. California Secretary of State, "Proposition 227: Analysis by Legislative Analyst," http://primary98.ss.ca.gov/VoterGuide/Propositions/227analysis.htm.
58. Urban Institute, "Beyond Bilingual Education."
59. "Section G: Programs for English Language Learners (Title III)," in *ESEA Implementation Guide* (Washington, DC: Small Axe Educational Communications, 2003), http://www.humnet.ucla.edu/humnet/linguistics/people/grads/macswan/Title%20III,%20No%20Child%20Left%20Behind%20Act.pdf.
60. Ibid.
61. James Crawford, "The Bilingual Education Act (1968–2002)," Spring 2002, http://ourworld.compuserve.com/homepages/JWCRAWFORD/T7obit.htm.
62. Department of Education, "Emergency Immigrant Education Program," *Federal Register* 66, no. 7 (January 10, 2001).
63. Urban Institute, "Beyond Bilingual Education."
64. ACLU, "Briefing Paper Number 6: English Only," http://www.lectlaw.com/files/con09.htm.
65. Carl Hulse, "Senate Passes a Bill That Favors English," *New York Times*, May 19, 2006.
66. Suzanne Sataline, "Immigrants' First Stop: The Line for English Classes," *Christian Science Monitor*, August 27, 2002.
67. Daniel Gonzalez, "Immigrants Jam English Classes," *The Arizona Republic*, July 26, 2005.
68. Rachel Swarns, "Children of Hispanic Immigrants Continue to Favor English, Study of Census Finds," *New York Times*, December 8, 2004.
69. See, for example, James P. Smith, "Assimilation Across Latino Generations," *American Economic Review* 93, no. 2 (May 2003), http://www.aeaweb.org/articles/issue_detail.php?journal=AER&volume=93&issue=2&issue_date=May%202003; Roger Waldinger and Renee Reichl, "Today's Second Generation: Getting Ahead or Falling Behind?" in *Securing the Future: The US Immigrant Integration Policy Agenda*, ed. Michael E. Fix (Washington, DC: Migration Policy Institute, forth-

coming 2006); Mary C. Waters and Tomas R. Jimenez, "Assessing Immigrant Assimilation: New Empirical and Theoretical Challenges," *Annual Review of Sociology* 31 (2005).
70. Waters and Jimenez, "Assessing Immigrant Assimilation," 121.
71. *Newswise,* "Immigration Slows Rate of Racial and Ethnic Intermarriages," February 6, 2007, http://www.newswise.com/articles/view/527129/.
72. Ibid.
73. Orrenius, "Immigrant Assimilation."
74. Fix, "Immigrants' Costs and Contributions."
75. USA for UNHCR, "Educational Resources—Games—Fact or Fiction," http://www.usaforunhcr.org/usaforunhcr/dynamic.cfm?ID=73.
76. See Center for an Urban Future, *A World of Opportunity: Understanding and Tapping the Potential Economic Potential of Immigrant Entrepreneurs* (New York: Center for an Urban Future, February 2007), http://www.nycfuture.org/content/about/immigrant_entrepreneurs_media.cfm.
77. Kerry Miller, "The Impact of Immigrant Entrepreneurs," *Business Week,* February 6, 2007, http://www.businessweek.com/smallbiz/content/feb2007/sb20070206_487251.htm?link_position=link1.
78. Bart Jones, "Immigrants Driving Growth: Neighborhoods Dominated by Ethnic Groups See Rise in New Businesses, Helping to Revitalize Areas," *Newsday* (New York), February 7, 2007, http://www.newsday.com/business/ny-nyimmig075083713feb07,0,846096.story?coll=ny-business-print.
79. Robert Pear, "Security Is Focus of Revived Effort on Immigration," *New York Times,* June 13, 2007, http://www.nytimes.com/2007/06/14/washington/14immig.html?_r=1&hp&oref=slogin.
80. Farooq Kathwari, Lynn Martin, and Christopher B. Whitney, *Strengthening America: The Civic and Political Integration of Muslim Americans* (Chicago: Chicago Council on Global Affairs, 2007), 29–30.
81. Laura K. Donohue, "The British Traded Rights for Security, Too" *Washington Post,* April 6, 2003.

82. Robert Charles Hill and Donald Kerwin, "Public International Law: Immigration and Nationality Law," *International Lawyer* 36 (Summer 2002).
83. Kathwari, *Strengthening America*, 28.
84. Ibid., 29.
85. See Stephen Yale-Loehr, Demetrios G. Papademetriou, and Betsy Cooper, *Secure Borders, Open Doors: Visa Procedures in the Post–September 11 Era* (Washington, DC: Migration Policy Institute, 2005), http://www.migrationpolicy.org/pubs/visa_report.pdf#search=%22Secure%20Borders%20Open%20Doors%22.
86. Neil A. Lewis and Christopher Marquis, "Longer Visa Wait for Arabs; Stir Over U.S. Eavesdropping," *New York Times*, November 10, 2001.
87. Hill and Kerwin, "Immigration and Nationality Law."
88. Migration Policy Institute, "Chronology of Events Since September 11, 2001 Related to Immigration and National Security," Migration Information Source, May 1, 2003, http://www.migrationinformation.org/chronology.pdf#search=%22Chronology%20of%20Events%20Since%20September%2011%2C%202001%22.
89. Amnesty International, "'War on Terror' Human Rights Issues: Quarterly Bulletin for Members, Groups, Networks," January 30, 2004, http://www.amnestyusa.org/waronterror/bulletin/bulletin_jan2004.html.
90. Muzaffer A. Chishti, Doris Meissner, Demetrios G. Papademetriou, Jay Peterzell, Michael J. Wishnie, and Stephen W. Yale-Loehr, *America's Challenge: Domestic Security, Civil Liberties, and National Unity After September 11* (Washington, DC: Migration Policy Institute, 2003), 8, http://www.migrationpolicy.org/pubs/Americas_Challenges.pdf#search=%22America's%20Challenge%2C%20Migration%20Policy%20Institute%22.
91. Pew Research Center for the People and the Press, *Muslim Americans: Middle Class and Mostly Mainstream* (Washington, DC: Pew Research Center, May 22, 2007), http://pewresearch.org/assets/pdf/muslim-americans.pdf.

92. Andrea Elliott, "More Muslims Are Coming to U.S. After a Decline in the Wake of 9/11," *New York Times*, September 10, 2006.
93. Pew Research Center, *Muslim Americans*.
94. Federal Bureau of Investigation (FBI), *Hate Crime Statistics 2001* (Washington, DC: FBI, 2002); FBI, *Hate Crime Statistics 2005* (Washington, DC: FBI, 2006), http://www.fbi.gov/ucr/ucr.htm.
95. Migration Policy Institute, "Coming to America Two Years After September 11, 2001," news release, September 9, 2003, http://www.migrationpolicy.org/pubs/Immigration_Since_9-11.pdf.
96. Elliott, "More Muslims Are Coming to U.S."
97. USA for UNHCR, "Educational Resources—Games—Fact or Fiction."
98. Ibid.
99. Kelly Jefferys, *Annual Flow Report: U.S. Legal Permanent Residents 2006* (Washington, DC: Department of Homeland Security, Office of Immigration Statistics, March 2007), http://www.dhs.gov/xlibrary/assets/statistics/publications/IS-4496_LPRFlowReport_04vaccessible.pdf.
100. Michelle Berg, "Regional Summaries: Europe," in *World Refugee Survey 2004* (Washington, DC: U.S. Committee for Refugees, 2004), http://www.refugees.org/article.aspx?id=1162.
101. See the discussion of Muslims in Europe found in Kathwari, *Strengthening America*, 36.
102. Pew Research Center, *Mixed Views on Immigration Bill* (Washington, DC: Pew Research Center for the People and the Press, June 7, 2007), http://people-press.org/reports/display.php3?ReportID=335.

Racial Inequality: America's Achilles' Heel

s European societies grapple with problems posed by an influx of immigrants from the Middle East, North Africa, and Asia, the United States is often held up as a model of assimilation. But while America has proven relatively successful at the integration of immigrants of differing cultures, nationalities, and skin colors, it still confronts serious problems stemming from the unequal status of African Americans. If the United States can claim that it is uniquely welcoming to immigrants from around the world, it must also acknowledge that, as was the case at the founding of the republic, racial injustice is the Achilles' heel of American democracy. The continuing plight of black Americans is accentuated by the fact that the United States has become, in commentator Ben Wattenberg's phrase, the world's first multinational society. Instead of a simple black-white racial divide, there is today a divide between blacks and a constellation of groups that includes both whites and immigrants from Asia, Latin America, the Caribbean, Africa, and other parts of the world.

Moreover, the fact that America has truly become a "diverse" society has affected the debates over a series of social-policy issues that were once identified as pertaining almost exclusively to the status of African Americans. Among these are affirmative action, residential segregation, education, and the tension between assimilation and separateness. And while many observers object strongly to the application of lessons from the immigrant experience to the question of black advancement, the fact that nonwhite newcomers have made important strides toward participation in the American mainstream has affected and will continue to affect public opinion, government policy, and the intellectual debate over strategies to accelerate the pace of black progress.

While America's history of slavery and legal segregation is well known, it is important to note that the United States was unique in the size of its slave population, that population's geographical concentration, slavery's legal duration, the fact that slavery was ended through civil war, and the discrimination, humiliation, and violence to which blacks were subjected after slavery was abolished. Other societies maintained slaves, but no society has suffered a legacy of slavery that equals the American experience.

The United States is also unique with respect to the number and magnitude of the laws, policies, and enforcement and monitoring agencies that are meant principally to curb racial bias, enhance racial integration, and direct public attention to actions and policies deemed to have an unfair impact on African Americans or other minorities, most notably Hispanics. Likewise, America is unusual in the degree to which racial concerns and sensitivities permeate public life. Incidents in which the police kill or beat black suspects continue to spark national debates about the role of racial profiling or racial bias in the broader society. The proportion of minorities in the ranks of professional sports coaching is a perennial controversy, as are the use of race in legislative redistricting, the relationship between race and standardized tests used for university admissions, and the racial impact of environmental decisions.

The issues associated with immigration, especially immigration from Latin America and the Muslim world, are dealt with in other chapters in this volume. But as this study does focus on the state of freedom in the period after the September 11, 2001, terrorist attacks, it is worth stressing how little the developments of the past five years have influenced the core debates over American race relations and the status of African Americans. Indeed, the key racial problems facing the United States are remarkably similar to those which confronted the society a quarter century ago: continuing inequality, a level of poverty among blacks that is greater than that of any other group, uneasy relations between blacks and the police, and serious public disagreement over affirmative action, a central policy concern of the civil rights lobby.

Such recent developments as domestic terrorism and the debate over the country's immigration policies have, if anything, directed the public's attention away from these racial matters to questions including border control, the problem of illegal immigrants, the assimilation of Arab Americans, and bias against immigrants from Muslim countries. Yet even as race declines as a topic of discussion and ethnicity, language, and immigrant status move to a more prominent place on the American agenda, the laws, policies, and public attitudes that were shaped by the civil rights protests of an earlier era continue to play a key role in determining how the new controversies stemming from American diversity are resolved.

Civil Rights Law

The foundations of today's civil rights enforcement were set down in three laws adopted by Congress during the 1960s. Taken together, the laws make discrimination illegal in practically every aspect of public life.

The most significant of these laws is the Omnibus Civil Rights Act of 1964. More than any other statute or judicial decision, the Civil Rights Act put in place the core legal guarantees of equal rights for blacks, other minority groups, and women. In a sweeping fashion, it established federal authority over aspects of American life that had been governed by the states since the country's founding. And it established a precedent for similar civil rights laws on issues ranging from the rights of homosexuals, the rights of the disabled, the education of the mentally handicapped, and the sexual harassment of women in the workplace. The 1964 law bans discrimination on the basis of race, ethnic origin, or gender in a broad range of institutions and in public accommodations, education, and employment. The public accommodations provision of the law applies to sites including hotels, restaurants, and theaters. The act encourages the desegregation of schools and authorizes the attorney general to file suits to move the desegregation process along. The section dealing with job discrimination, Title VII, prohibits bias by employers and unions, and prohibits retaliation against workers who bring claims of bias to the relevant authorities.[1]

The second legislative pillar of civil rights protection is the Voting Rights Act of 1965. It was designed to eliminate practices that minimized black voter participation, which were widespread in the segregated South at the time. Thus the law banned literacy tests for prospective voters as well as the requirement to pay a poll tax before being allowed to vote. The act also extended the authority of the federal government into various aspects of the political process that were traditionally overseen by the states, at least in those states with a history of systematic racial discrimination. Important here was a provision that forced state and local officials in areas with a substantial black presence to seek the approval of the Justice Department before making changes in registration procedures, legislative district boundaries, or other factors that might influence the ability of minorities to participate in the political process or attain a measure of political power. The Voting Rights Act has been reauthorized on two subsequent occasions, most recently in 2006. During that reauthorization debate, some Republicans argued that the sections calling for Justice Department oversight of voting and redistricting procedures be dropped on the grounds that racial attitudes in Southern states had changed enough to render such supervision unnecessary. This argument was ultimately rejected, and the final bill included the provision for federal oversight.[2]

The third major piece of civil rights legislation is the federal Fair Housing Act. Passed in 1968, the law prohibits racial discrimination in the sale or rental of housing. Initially, single-family, owner-occupied homes were exempted from the legislation's coverage, but in subsequent years, practically all housing came under the jurisdiction of the law.[3]

The Fair Housing Act has relatively weak enforcement provisions. At the same time, a number of states have passed fair-housing laws with stricter enforcement mechanisms. Most states, in fact, have enacted their own versions of the more important federal civil rights measures, including those designed to combat discrimination in education and the workplace.

In addition to adopting laws against racial bias, the United States has established an impressive roster of commissions, agencies, and monitoring and enforcement mechanisms tasked with preventing discrimination, promoting affirmative action, or punishing bias crimes against minorities, women, and other "protected groups." The Equal Employment Opportunity Commission was established to assist in the enforcement of laws against discrimination in the workplace. The U.S. Commission on Civil Rights is an advisory body that conducts studies and hearings on issues including workplace bias, police conduct, and voter-suppression campaigns directed at minorities. There are, in addition, civil rights offices within each of the cabinet departments. The civil rights offices in the Department of Justice and the Department of Education have had considerable influence in shaping government policy and determining when the government will bring discrimination charges against an individual, corporation, labor union, or public entity. And just as most states (and many cities) have enacted their own versions of civil rights legislation, so the states have established their own versions of the civil rights enforcement units that exist at the federal level.

Hate Crimes

The United States has adopted an aggressive policy on prosecuting crimes that are motivated by racial hatred. The prosecution of bias crimes is largely undertaken by the states and not the federal government. Practically all states have adopted laws that include additional penalties for crimes in which racial bias (or bias against immigrant groups, women, or homosexuals) plays a role. There is also a federal law, the Hate Crimes Sentencing Enhancement Act of 1994, which directs the U.S. Sentencing Commission to add a sentencing enhancement of not less than three offense levels for violent crimes in which hate is deemed a major factor.[4] In certain egregious cases of bias, the federal government and state and local authorities will collaborate in the investigations. A good example of this kind of cooperation occurred in the response to the 1998 murder of James Byrd, a black man, by three white men in Jasper County, Texas. Although the crime was under the jurisdiction of local law enforcement officials, the forensic expertise and civil rights experience of the Federal Bureau of Investigation (FBI) and the Justice Department were crucial in bringing the case to a swift conclusion.[5]

Another major federal hate-crime law, the Hate Crime Statistics Act of 1990, requires the Justice Department to gather data on crimes that manifest bias based on race, ethnicity, or sexual orientation, and to publish an annual statistical report using material from state and local law enforcement agencies. A 1968 measure, adopted when resistance to desegregation remained strong in parts of the South, prohibits the use of force or intimidation against individuals or groups attempting to vote, enroll in a school, gain employment, or use public transportation or public accommodations. In addition, the Justice Department has the authority to intervene in criminal cases when there is evidence that a victim's civil rights have been violated. Under this power, the federal government has brought a number of cases against local law enforcement officials who have been accused of using abusive tactics against minority suspects or defendants.

The original impetus behind the special attention for hate crimes was the victimization of blacks. However, hate-crime statistics today reflect the increasing diversity of American society. While blacks rank as the largest group targeted, a substantial number of whites, Hispanics, Asians, homosexuals, and Jews were also listed as hate-crime victims in statistics published by the FBI for the year 2004. Blacks accounted for about one-third of reported hate crimes, Jews for some 12 percent, and male homosexuals for about 10 percent. Interestingly, relatively few hate crimes were directed at Muslims; these reflected about 2 percent of the total.[6]

An ongoing controversy involves racial profiling, or the use of race, especially by police, to identify possible criminal suspects. It includes a wide range of practices, including stopping and frisking African Americans at random or searching the cars of black or Hispanic motorists for illegal narcotics or stolen goods. In either case, what distinguishes racial profiling from normal police tactics is the use of race as the determining factor and the absence of strong additional evidence of criminal behavior. Many civil libertarians have accused local police departments of engaging in racial profiling, especially in drug cases. In response to highly publicized incidents involving the police and members of minority groups, a number of states have taken steps to curb the practice. And while the controversy over profiling originally emerged in relation to police treatment of blacks, the focus is now on the treatment of immigrants from the Middle East and South Asia.

Prosecuting Crimes of the Past

The federal government continues to pursue criminal cases involving murders and other serious crimes against blacks that were committed during the era of civil rights protest. Thus in 2005 Edgar Ray Killen was convicted of manslaughter for his part in the killing of three civil rights workers in Philadelphia, Mississippi, a case memorialized in the 1988 film *Mississippi Burning*. Killen was brought to justice 41 years after the crime was committed.[7]

A number of Southern states have revived investigations of crimes committed against blacks or civil rights advocates four or five decades ago. Some states have also established variants of the truth commissions that new democracies in Latin America, Africa, and Eastern Europe have used to set the historical record straight about past crimes or acts of repression in which the state was complicit. North Carolina formed a special commission in 2000 to investigate a race riot that occurred in 1898 in the city of Wilmington.[8] Some states have provided compensation to victims of acts of racial injustice. Florida gave compensation to the nine survivors of the 1923 Rosewood race riot—another incident that became the subject of a film—and set up a fund to provide university tuition assistance for descendants of the victims.[9]

Some African American activists have launched a movement to win financial reparations for the descendants of black slaves in the United States. Among other things, proponents point to congressional action that provided payments to Japanese American survivors of World War II internment as precedent for similar compensation for blacks. Attempts to gain congressional support for slavery reparations have never made much progress, and the effort largely collapsed in the wake of the 2001 terrorist attacks. At the same time, advocates of reparations have initiated lawsuits against corporations in the insurance, financial services, tobacco, and other industries, demanding reparations for their or their predecessor-companies' ties to slavery.[10]

Race and Poverty

Some black critics have expressed frustration at the resources devoted to finding and punishing the perpetrators of civil rights crimes and the commissions of inquiry into incidents like the Rosewood riot. They assert that by focusing on past wrong-doing, white society is giving itself sanction to ignore more pressing contemporary problems stemming from economic and social inequality. Among other things, they contend that a real commitment to equality would require a serious and expensive antipoverty program directed at black youth in inner cities.

However, the statistics on the level of poverty in black America tell a mixed story. One can find data that reinforce the views of optimists or confirm the bleakest conclusions of pessimists.

For the optimists, the figures show a substantial decline in poverty and a general improvement in other economic indicators over the past four and a half decades. In 1959, when the U.S. Census Bureau began publishing data on poverty, the poverty rate for African Americans stood at a huge 55.1 percent. The comparable figure for whites was 18.1 percent. By 1970, poverty for both blacks and whites had declined substantially due to a decade of uninterrupted growth and job creation in the industrial sector. For blacks, poverty stood at 33.5 percent—still high, but dramatically lower than 11 years earlier. The rate for whites was 9.9 percent, half the rate of 1959. By 1980, black poverty had again declined, but only by a modest amount, to 32.5 percent, whereas white poverty had actually risen to 10.2 percent. These relatively unimpressive figures came at the end of a decade notable for a substantial increase in oil prices and general economic stagnation. Poverty for blacks again dropped slightly by 1990, to 31.9 percent; for whites, the rate was 10.7 percent. By 2000, however, black poverty had registered another substantial decrease, to 22.5 percent; the rate for whites stood at 9.5 percent.[11]

These statistics demonstrate that for both whites and blacks, the 1960s were crucial in bringing down the rate of poverty in America. They also show that while the rate of decline in poverty has slowed considerably, the rate of decline for black poverty has exceeded that for whites, and blacks have continued to make progress despite the transition from an economy based on industrial production to one anchored in services, knowledge, and high technology.

That is the good news. The not-so-good news is that poverty for blacks remains far higher than for whites and indeed exceeds the rate for most immigrant groups, including groups that have come to America in substantial numbers only recently.

A similar racial gap can be found in America's unemployment statistics. Thus in 1980, the unemployment rate for whites was 6.3 percent while the rate for blacks was 14.3 percent. In 1990, the white rate was 4.8 percent; for blacks, unemployment stood at 11.4 percent. Eight years later, in the midst of a period of sustained growth, jobless rates for whites stood at 3.9 percent; for blacks the figure was 8.9 percent.[12] Finally, for the first quarter of 2006, the average monthly rate for whites was 4.1 percent, with a 9.2 percent rate for blacks.

In other words, as with the ratio for poverty rates, the black-white unemployment ratio has remained more or less steady since the Labor Department began to examine racial and ethnic subcategories. Whether the economy is robust or in recession, the rate of black unemployment remains at slightly more than twice the level for whites. An additional factor is the number of adults who have dropped out of the workforce and are not counted in jobless statistics. In this category, blacks are represented at a higher rate than other racial or ethnic groups.

The statistics for educational attainment are somewhat more positive. According to a Census Bureau report for 2003, school dropout rates by race and ethnicity were as follows: white, 7.9 percent; black, 12.2 percent; Asian, 1 percent; Hispanic, 24 percent. Likewise, the figures for college enrollment show that while blacks continue to lag, their enrollment level is high by historical standards. Of all students enrolled in college in 2003, 68 percent were white, 13 percent were black, 7 percent were Asian, and 10 percent were Hispanic.[13] This represents a major shift over the previous two decades. In 1983, white college enrollment was 86 percent of the total; for blacks, the figure was 10 percent, while 4 percent were in the "other races" (including Asian) category, and 4 percent were Hispanic.[14] Studies have also shown that a college degree has a greater impact on the future earnings of blacks than on earnings for whites or other groups. For example, a study conducted by the National Center for Educational Statistics showed that for blacks and whites aged 25–34 with undergraduate university degrees, the ratio of earnings was 1.06, or near parity. Put another way, in 2003 black college graduates earned $40,900 on average, while white college graduates earned $43,400. The comparable figure for Hispanics was $37,600.[15]

Likewise, studies have shown that blacks with undergraduate degrees have an employment rate that is roughly similar to that of their white counterparts. In 2004, black college graduates aged 25–34 had an unemployment rate of 3.2 percent, slightly above the 2.3 percent rate for whites.[16] At the same time, while black college graduation rates have increased substantially, they still lag significantly behind rates for whites. The percentage of blacks aged 25–29 who were university graduates stood at its highest level of 18.0 percent in 2002, a threefold rise from a figure of 6.7 percent in 1971. At the same time, the 2002 figure for whites in the same age cohort stood at 35.9 percent, about double the figure for blacks.[17]

As these statistics suggest, the clearest path to racial equality in America is through the schoolhouse door. Those who argue that the educational playing field is uneven point to the disproportionate representation of African Americans in community colleges and second-tier state universities, and to the small percentages of blacks in science, computer technology, business administration, and other cutting-edge disciplines. Again, however, the data show that the very act of enrolling in college and completing an undergraduate curriculum greatly enhances opportunities for blacks to attain a standard of living comparable to that of the rest of America.

While the promise of equality has become real for black college graduates, positive data can obscure the plight of inner-city blacks, especially the current generation of young men. The predicament of a substantial group of young men is not captured by higher education or unemployment statistics, since they have dropped out of high school and the workforce, or are serving time in prison.

Here some of the more positive statistical findings can be deceptive. While the overall school dropout rate for blacks nationally is not high by historical standards, in many inner cities it remains high for males, in some cases extraordinarily high. The outlook for these dropouts is bleak. Sixty-five percent of black high school dropouts in their twenties were not involved in the legal economy in 2000. By the time they reach their thirties, about 60 percent of black male dropouts have spent some time in jail. In 1995, 16 percent of black men in their twenties who were not enrolled in college were incarcerated. By 2004, the percentage for the same cohort was 21 percent. According to some research, on any given day there is a higher proportion of black men in their late twenties in jail (34 percent) than are employed (30 percent). Although they are only 13 percent of the overall population, blacks account for 41 percent of prison inmates serving sentences of more than one year.[18] There is also a significant gap between the academic performance of low-income black and Hispanic students in the public schools and their better-off white peers. The gap widens the longer students are in school. Some studies suggest that at the fourth grade level, the majority of black and Latino children are illiterate, while a substantial percentage of black and Latino twelfth graders function at an eighth grade level.

The relationship between black men and crime has for many years been a sensitive subject in the United States. In part, this is due to the unfortunate historical experience of African Americans. Prior to the civil rights revolution, the personnel of the criminal justice system were overwhelmingly—and in many parts of the South, entirely—white. Today, however, this is no longer the case. Blacks compose a substantial proportion of police, judges, and prosecutors in large cities. Court decisions have established that it is illegal to exclude blacks from juries on racial grounds. In most large cities, police have undertaken special training in managing racial and ethnic differences.

Nevertheless, the extraordinarily high black prison population has remained a matter of national controversy and a source of special pain for blacks themselves. Some critics believe that there are far too many Americans, and especially blacks, in prison for relatively minor and nonviolent drug offenses. At the same time, declines in violent crime in a number of large cities have paved the way for a revitalization of inner-city neighborhoods. While the dynamics of crime reduction are complex, one factor, many believe, is the large number of criminals who are in prison and off the streets.

Neighborhood Desegregation

Since the beginning of the modern civil rights era, school desegregation has been a central objective in the strategy for racial equality. Indeed, the landmark Supreme Court decision that desegregated the schools, *Brown v. Board of Education* (1954), is regarded as a galvanizing event in the drive for change. After *Brown*, civil rights advocates launched a broad-based campaign for school integration that included lawsuits and civil disobedience. Despite fierce and sometimes violent resistance in some communities, legal school segregation was effectively dismantled by the end of the 1960s.

The end of legal segregation has not, however, brought about the widespread school integration that civil rights advocates had hoped for. The principal reason is the persistently high level of neighborhood segregation. To be sure, studies conducted by the Census Bureau and the Brookings Institution indicate that racial isolation in major cities has continued to decline through the years. But the pace of change is slow; America has made much more progress in integrating the workplace, the media, universities, and the criminal justice system than it has in achieving neighborhoods that are racially mixed. Citing figures provided by the Census Bureau for the year 2000, Douglas Massey, a professor of sociology at Princeton University, writes that "while segregation has moved downward since 1980, indices remain extreme in the nation's largest urban black communities, especially in the Northeast and the Midwest." According to the Census Bureau, the most segregated cities are Detroit, Michigan; Newark, New Jersey; Milwaukee, Wisconsin; New York City; and Chicago, Illinois. Ironically, neighborhood segregation is less extreme in the big cities of the South.[19]

Massey, whose writings have been influential in the debate over residential segregation, contends that the failure to create conditions that facilitate housing integration has contributed to racial inequality by leading to high levels of school segregation. He cites a Harvard University study that indicates that racial isolation in the schools actually increased during the

1990s, and asserts that one-sixth of African American students attend schools that are 99 percent black. Massey writes, "Segregation inevitably concentrates poverty, social disorder, and poor health in dysfunctional schools that place African Americans, and increasingly Hispanics, at a severe competitive disadvantage in attempting to enter America's better colleges and universities."[20]

The causes of neighborhood segregation are difficult to pin down, although obviously the relatively low earnings of blacks and Hispanics is an important factor. Massey and advocacy organizations like the National Fair Housing Alliance (NFHA) contend that outright discrimination plays an important role in preventing blacks from leaving the inner city and moving to suburban neighborhoods. In a 2006 study, the NFHA contends that real-estate firms routinely use techniques that are illegal under fair housing laws to steer black applicants away from predominantly white neighborhoods, and to steer whites away from neighborhoods in which there is a substantial African American presence. Several studies that have made use of civil rights testers have also concluded that housing discrimination is commonplace.[21]

At the same time, a study by the Brookings Institution concludes that the minority presence in America's traditionally white suburbs rose by substantial numbers during the 1990s. The study showed that in 2000, 27 percent of major suburban populations belonged to minority groups, up from 19 percent in 1990. The study showed that about half of Hispanics and 39 percent of blacks lived in the suburbs.[22]

Affirmative Action

When the 1964 Civil Rights Act was enacted, most Americans were confident that major gains toward racial equality would automatically follow the dismantling of legal segregation. Indeed, major gains in employment, poverty reduction, and education were attained during the 1960s. Under conditions of near full employment, hundreds of thousands of black workers found jobs in the booming industrial sector. At the same time, universities made special efforts to enroll greater numbers of blacks and also provided financial assistance for minority students.

But this progress was accompanied by a series of developments that suggested that achieving racial equality would be a more complex and longer-term challenge than Americans had initially imagined. There was, to begin with, the discovery that racial prejudice and inequality were not limited to the South. Throughout the rest of the country, blacks faced many of the problems associated with legal segregation: job discrimination, inferior educational opportunities, and, especially, exclusion from white neighborhoods. Efforts to address these problems through demonstrations and civil disobedience—tactics that had proven effective in bringing down legal discrimination in the South—were ineffective in the other regions.

Another sign of the complexity of America's racial dynamic was the increase in single-parent families. This phenomenon was initially pointed out by Daniel Patrick Moynihan, at the time a domestic policy adviser in the administration of President Lyndon Johnson. The report in which Moynihan discussed the growth in female-headed families was bitterly attacked by black and white academics, and Moynihan was accused of "blaming the victim" in his paper. In fact, the problem that he identified became much more pronounced in subsequent years, with serious consequences for American race relations. Meanwhile, the reaction to Moynihan's findings was a disturbing sign of the difficulties impeding a frank discussion about the most effective strategies for achieving racial equality.

The combination of urban disorder, the problems faced by the black poor, and the realization that the elimination of legal barriers to equality would have a limited impact on the overall status of black Americans led policymakers and some academics to advocate a more aggressive approach. Two basic strategies were put forward to accelerate the integration of blacks into the educational and economic mainstream: the busing of school-children outside their neighborhoods to promote classroom integration, and affirmative action in the workplace and university admissions. Both concepts were implemented primarily through action taken by the federal government, and both have proven intensely controversial.

The thinking behind busing was that the integration of public education would be hampered in practice by the substantial degree of de facto housing segregation in most American communities. Although some advocates proposed wide-ranging desegregation plans that called for busing large numbers of blacks to predominantly white schools and whites to predominantly black schools, in practice the children who participated in busing plans were overwhelmingly black. Busing was instituted in a number of communities, often despite resistance from whites and the ambivalent attitudes of black parents.

It soon became clear, though, that desegregation schemes would have a limited impact in many large cities because few white children were enrolled in the public schools, and because of worries that busing plans were encouraging "white flight" to the suburbs. Civil rights advocates therefore proposed that busing schemes be expanded to embrace both urban and adjacent suburban school districts to ensure a sufficiently large pool of white students to make integration viable. In *Milliken v. Bradley* (1977), the Supreme Court ruled that these cross-district busing plans could not be imposed on suburban communities, thus thwarting the more ambitious aims of busing supporters.[23] Moreover, by preventing the government from compelling communities to accept cross-district busing, the court took an important step toward minimizing busing as a desegregation tool. With enrollment in big-city school districts increasingly dominated by black and Hispanic students, school integration diminished as a goal of civil rights policy. By the 1990s, many of the desegregation plans that incorporated busing had been abandoned.

Affirmative action, by contrast, has assumed a more or less permanent place in American civil rights policy. Initially, during the 1960s, it was regarded as a program to encourage private corporations and government units to voluntarily adopt measures to hire, train, and promote black workers. A key theory behind affirmative action was that an important source of inequality was institutional racism. This concept held that several centuries of racial discrimination had been internalized by corporations, universities, government agencies, and other institutions. To overcome this legacy, advocates urged policies that would, in effect, compel the hiring of qualified blacks and the admission of blacks to colleges, especially prestigious private universities.

The federal government thus began to pressure employers to hire and promote blacks, and where the percentage of black employees fell short of their presence in the local population, it took legal action to force companies or government entities to develop plans that would increase their minority workforces. One obstacle to the implementation of affirmative action plans was a provision in the 1964 Civil Rights Act that forbade "reverse discrimination," that is, the hiring of minorities over better-qualified whites. But the Supreme Court ruled in several cases that a certain degree of affirmative action did meet constitutional muster. Once the courts gave legitimacy to race-conscious remedies, federal initiatives to encourage the hiring of minorities mushroomed.

The government scrutinized not only the number of employees in a company as a whole, but often looked at the minority representation in separate units. It assessed the minority representation within the middle- and upper-management ranks, and would frequently order a company to devise a plan for the promotion of minorities or women. The government also scrutinized the qualifications or standards established by state entities—such as police and fire departments—and corporations, and required employers to justify any qualifications that seemed to have what was known as a "disparate impact" on minorities or women.

Although affirmative action was originally meant to accelerate the movement of blacks into the economic mainstream, the plans advanced by the government almost always applied to groups other than blacks that were also deemed to be the victims of discrimination: women, Hispanics, Asians, American

Indians, and various smaller indigenous groups. The lumping together of these various groups, including some that scored relatively well on indices of income, education, and wealth, had unintended and perverse consequences. For example, federal rules that called for a specified threshold of minority contractors were sometimes exploited by new Asian-owned companies that had had little or no experience with bias.

From the outset, affirmative action was viewed with skepticism by most whites. Opinion polls have generally shown that whites will support soft or voluntary affirmative action but oppose government-imposed plans that seem to favor minority hiring over whites or the lowering of employment or university admissions standards. Because of the emotional response and intense controversy affirmative action has generated, Congress has been generally unwilling to deal with the issue, either by giving affirmative action the validation of legislative approval or by voting to curb or eliminate the policy. The one major exception came in 1990, when Congress passed, and President George H. W. Bush signed, the Civil Rights Restoration Act, a measure that nullified several Supreme Court decisions which had limited the scope of affirmative action plans.[24]

By the 1990s, most private employers had instituted changes in their hiring and promotion policies to eliminate practices that the courts and enforcement agencies might deem discriminatory. At this point, civil rights advocates put forward a new rationale for policies to encourage or compel corporations and universities to introduce racially or ethnically based hiring and admissions policies. They contended that even if a corporation or university had eliminated overt bias from its policies, it should be obliged to consider race on diversity grounds, that is, on the grounds that major economic and educational institutions should roughly reflect the broader society's diverse racial and ethnic composition.

During the 1990s, affirmative action met with several major setbacks in the courts and the political arena. In two states, California and Washington, referendums to eliminate affirmative action in employment and university admissions were adopted by voters. Likewise, the Supreme Court, in *Adarand v. Pena* (1995), ruled that the federal government could not force affirmative action plans on private corporations on diversity grounds alone.[25]

More recently, the principal battles over affirmative action have focused on admissions to public universities. In 2003, the Supreme Court issued important decisions in two cases involving the University of Michigan. In *Grutter v. Bollinger*, the court ruled that race can be considered among other factors in the admissions process, while in *Gratz v. Bollinger* it ruled out affirmative action plans that seemed to set a strict numerical goal for minority admissions.[26] Partly as a response to the rulings, Michigan voters in November 2006 backed a referendum banning affirmative action in public education, contracting, and employment. Clearly, this will not be the final word on the issue. Given the contentious nature of race-based admissions programs, it is likely that affirmative action will come before the courts again in the relatively near future.

African Americans and American Politics

The example of Senator Barack Obama of Illinois illustrates both the impressive gains that African Americans have made in American political life and the limits of their acceptance as full participants. Although he is relatively young and is serving only his first term in the Senate, Obama has emerged as one of the most popular and sought-after figures in the Democratic Party, as well as a serious contender for his party's presidential nomination in 2008. At the same time, Obama is the only black member of the 100-seat Senate and only the third black senator in modern history. Likewise, only two African Americans have won election to a governorship: Douglas Wilder of Virginia in 1990 and Deval Patrick of Massachusetts in 2006.

There are a number of factors behind the difficulty blacks have encountered in winning statewide elections where the electorate is mostly white. Lingering prejudice may be part of the answer. Another factor is the ghettoized nature of black politics. While literally thousands of blacks have won election to the U.S. House of Representatives, city councils, and state legislatures, most represent districts in which black voters predominate, often by overwhelming margins. Black legislators are thus often perceived, fairly or not, as focused on the needs of blacks and favoring an agenda that is well to the left of the political mainstream. In the 109th Congress, there were 43 members of the Congressional Black Caucus, all of whom were Democrats and almost all of whom represented districts where minorities predominated.[27]

To a modest degree, the number of majority black districts has remained high due to the policy of racial gerrymandering, under which legislative districts are drawn so as to ensure that the majority of voters are black, or in some cases Hispanic. In some states, blacks' desire to ensure that certain congressional districts would remain secure for black candidates has led to the anomalous situation of African American Democrats joining with Republicans in the drawing of neighboring districts that would likely produce Republican victories. The Supreme Court has ruled against several of the more extreme racially drawn districts while allowing race or ethnicity to be taken into consideration in a modest way in other cases.

In the future, of course, the indicator of America's success at assimilating minorities into the political system will be the participation and representation of the entire constellation of nonwhite groups, and not just blacks. Although the Republican Party has long been accused of hostility to minority interests, the administration of President George W. Bush has included two African American secretaries of state, a Hispanic attorney general, and several Asian Americans in high positions, including two who were prominent in developing the administration's counterterrorism policy.

Conclusion

Aside from Supreme Court decisions on affirmative action, the past five years have been notable for the absence of major controversies that focus on the status of blacks in American society. They have also been notable for the public's generally upbeat appraisal of the state of race relations as measured in opinion surveys. According to a 2005 poll sponsored by the National Association for the Advancement of Colored People (NAACP), roughly two-thirds of Americans view relations between blacks and whites as positive, while only 29 percent saw relations as negative.[28]

Societies throughout the world are currently grappling with the challenges posed by racial, ethnic, or religious differences. Scholars who study democratic development have identified racial or ethnic division as an important obstacle to liberal democracy in many countries. The most murderous civil conflicts—in places like Chechnya, Iraq, and Sri Lanka—are fueled by sectarian or ethnic hatreds, while a number of European societies are experiencing a degree of social discord that is unprecedented in the postwar period due to tensions associated with the arrival of Muslim immigrants. Within this global context, the United States stands out for its ability to integrate, however incompletely, African Americans and nonwhite immigrants into the core of its social, cultural, and political life.

The American model of race relations may not be applicable to societies that lack this country's long history as a destination for immigrants. But fundamental principles that undergird America's approach to civil rights—resolute enforcement of anti-discrimination laws, assimilation, integration, full citizenship—have enabled the United States to emerge from a profound social revolution as a stronger nation.

The most pressing racial problems—inequality, poverty, the condition of the inner-city poor—will clearly not be resolved through traditional civil rights strategies. Even its most ardent advocates acknowledge that affirmative action cannot work effectively as an antipoverty program. The ultimate test for

America in the future lies in transforming the condition of the black poor.

How the United States is to meet this challenge is unclear. An interesting development in recent years has been the broadening of the debate over the causes of inequality and therefore the options for encouraging further black progress. The traditional liberal voices of civil rights advocacy have been joined by a new generation of black conservatives. On a policy level, conservatives have emphasized concepts like vouchers and school choice, by which children in failing inner-city schools are given the option of transferring to better-performing public schools or funds to help defray the cost of private-school tuition. Despite the concept's conservative pedigree, school choice has been embraced by a growing number of black parents who are frustrated with the state of public education in the cities. Liberals, by contrast, stress government initiatives to improve the public schools, arguing that school choice would benefit only a small minority of inner-city children.

Another set of critical voices has recently entered the discussion, consisting of prominent African Americans with generally liberal identifications who have become disturbed by the influence of popular culture on young blacks. Bill Cosby, the television personality; Juan Williams, a prominent columnist and commentator; and John McWhorter, the author of several important books on black culture, have been sharply critical of violent and misogynistic lyrics in hip-hop music, and of an inner-city youth culture that belittles the work ethic and success in school. They have also criticized African American political leaders for failing to speak out on the corrosive effects of current cultural trends.

The emergence of genuine intellectual diversity among those who will be shaping the debate over future strategies for achieving racial equality is something positive in itself. It offers hope that new methods for reducing poverty and inequality can be found, just as previous ideas that challenged the status quo once helped uproot the foundations of racism, legal discrimination, and second-class citizenship.

Endnotes

1. *Civil Rights Act of 1964*, Public Law 88-352, 88th Cong., 2nd sess. (July 1964), http://usinfo.state.gov/usa/infousa/laws/majorlaw/civilr19.htm.
2. *Voting Rights Act of 1965*, *U.S. Code* 42, § 1973–1973aa-6, amended in 1970, 1975, 1982, 2006.
3. *Civil Rights Act of 1968*, title VIII (Fair Housing Act), *U.S. Code* 42, §§ 3601 et seq., http://www.usdoj.gov/crt/housing/title8.htm.
4. *Hate Crime Sentencing Enhancement Act*, Public Law 103-322, title XXVIII, § 280003, 103rd Cong., 2nd sess. (September 1994).
5. U.S. Senate, "Section II: Pre-Existing Law and the Need for Expanded Jurisdiction," *Senate Report 107-147: The Local Law Enforcement*, 107th Cong., 2nd sess. (May 2002), http://thomas.loc.gov/cgi-bin/cpquery/1?&sid=TSOP1079w&hd_count=500&xform_type=0&maxdocs=500&variant=y&r_t=h&r_t=s&r_t=jc&refer=&r_n=sr147.107&db_id=107&item=1&&w_p=pre+existing+law+and+the+need+for+expanded+jurisdiction&attr=0&sel=TOC_6479&.
6. Federal Bureau of Investigation, *Hate Crime Statistics 2004* (Washington, D.C.: November 2005), http://www.fbi.gov/ucr/hc2004/tables/HateCrime2004.pdf.
7. Shaila Dewan, "Ex-Klan Figure in 1964 Killings Is Freed on Bond," *New York Times*, August 13, 2005.
8. Scott Marshall, "North Carolina Confronts Shameful History," *People's Weekly World* (National Edition), March 18, 2006.
9. Ibid.; Toonari, "Rosewood," *AfricanaOnline*, http://www.africanaonline.com/rosewood.htm.
10. Erin Texeira, "Slavery Reparations Gaining Momentum," *Seattle Post-Intelligencer*, July 10, 2006.
11. Carmen DeNavas-Walt, Bernadette D. Proctor, and Cheryl Hill Lee, *Income, Poverty, and Health Insurance Coverage in the United States: 2004* (U.S. Census Bureau, August 2005), Table B-1, 46–51, http://www.census.gov/prod/2005pubs/p60-229.pdf.

12. U.S. Census Bureau, "Employment Status of the Civilian Population: 1970 to 1998," *Statistical Abstract of the United States: 1999*, Table No. 651, http://www.census.gov/prod/99pubs/99statab/sec13.pdf.

13. Hyon B. Shin, *School Enrollment—Social and Economic Characteristics of Students: October 2003* (U.S. Census Bureau, May 2005), 7–9, http://www.census.gov/prod/2005pubs/p20-554.pdf.

14. Ibid., 9.

15. National Center for Education Statistics, *The Condition of Education 2005* (U.S. Department of Education, June 2005), 146, 148, http://nces.ed.gov/pubs2005/2005094.pdf.

16. Ibid., 150.

17. Ibid., 162.

18. Paige M. Harrison and Allen J. Beck, *Prisoners in 2004* (Bureau of Justice Statistics, October 2005), 8, http://www.ojp.usdoj.gov/bjs/pub/pdf/p04.pdf.

19. John Iceland, Daniel H. Weinberg, Erika Steinmetz, *Racial and Ethnic Residential Segregation in the United States: 1980–2000* (U.S. Census Bureau, August 2002), http://www.census.gov/hhes/www/housing/housing_patterns/papertoc.html.

20. Douglas S. Massey, "The Race Case," *American Prospect* 14, no. 3 (2003), http://www.prospect.org/print/V14/3/massey-d.html.

21. National Fair Housing Alliance, "Unequal Opportunity: Perpetuating Housing Segregation in America," *2006 Fair Housing Trends Report* (New York: 2006).

22. William H. Frey, *Melting Pot Suburbs: A Census 2000 Study of Suburban Diversity* (Washington, D.C.: Center on Urban & Metropolitan Policy, Brookings Institution, 2001), http://www.frey-demographer.org/reports/billf.pdf.

23. For more information on *Milliken v. Bradley*, see: http://www.law.cornell.edu/supct/html/historics/USSC_CR_0433_0267_ZS.html.

24. For more information on the Civil Rights Restoration Act, see: http://www.usdoj.gov/crt/grants_statutes/legalman.html.

25. For more information on *Adarand v. Pena*, see: http://supct.law.cornell.edu/supct/html/93-1841.ZS.html.

26. For more information on *Gratz v. Bollinger*, see: http://www.law.cornell.edu/supct/html/02-241.ZS.html.
27. Mildred L. Amer, *Black Members of the United States Congress: 1870–2005*, Congressional Research Service, http://www.senate.gov/reference/resources/pdf/RL30378.pdf.
28. Lydia Saad, "Americans Mostly Upbeat About Current Race Relations," Gallup Organization, news release, July 14, 2005, http://www.galluppoll.com/content/?ci=17314&pg=1.

The Press: Still Free and Independent

Since the establishment of the United States as an independent nation, the concepts of freedom of the press and freedom of expression have been upheld by both law and custom. The freedom enjoyed by the American media is protected by the U.S. Constitution; by numerous federal, state, and local laws; and by a strong judicial tradition. However, in the past five years this tradition has come under strain. Among other things, the security measures following the September 11, 2001, terrorist attacks and the consolidation of media ownership have presented journalists with new challenges in reporting the news.

Respect for freedom of the press in the United States is rooted first and foremost in the First Amendment of the Constitution. Although much First Amendment jurisprudence has pertained to freedom of speech in general and not to the press in particular, these cases have nonetheless been instrumental in establishing a legal tradition that supports media freedom.

In addition to such constitutional protections, the press benefits from numerous other safeguards, most of which have developed since the mid-twentieth century. These include laws establishing preferential access for the press to news conferences and courtrooms, freedom of information legislation, state shield laws, protection from police searches of newsrooms, and indirect government subsidies such as tax exemptions for media outlets.[1] The allowable grounds for prosecuting the media for libel or so-called hate speech are considerably narrower in America than in many European countries, and attempts to prevent the press from publishing (otherwise known as "prior restraint") are almost never upheld in court. In general, the print media are protected more fully than broadcast media, which are subject to a wider range of restrictions through the Federal Communications Commission (FCC).

However, legal protections for journalists have weakened in recent years. Access to official information has been circumscribed, and reporters' ability to cover both foreign and domestic events has been, at times, curtailed. Increased political polarization has affected coverage as both public and private media outlets have been accused of either liberal or conservative bias. And while many of these strains are direct consequences of 9/11, the aftermath of the terrorist attacks is not the only force influencing the culture and freedom of the American press. Efforts by the administration of President George W. Bush to control or influence news coverage have led to reduced professional privileges for journalists, and the long-term trend toward the consolidation of major media outlets in the hands of a few large corporate owners has tested the quality and diversity of news coverage. At the same time, technology-driven changes in the way people receive their news have affected coverage in ways both positive and negative.

The ongoing power of the media to deliver the news and inform the American public despite these handicaps is evidence that freedom of the press remains robust even in a more volatile age and under pressure from a more antagonistic government.

History and Legal Background

In the colonial era that predated the United States, freedom of speech was limited by prepublication censorship, licensing for printing presses, and laws intended to punish blasphemy and seditious libel. However, with the adoption of the U.S. Constitution in 1789 and the accompanying Bill of Rights in 1791, press freedom and freedom of speech received explicit legal protection. "Congress shall make no law," declares the First Amendment, "abridging the freedom of speech, or of the press."[2]

Two caveats should be noted. First, the amendment initially applied only to the legislative branch of the federal government. Although many states chose to enshrine the concept of press freedom in their own constitutions, not until *Gitlow v. New York* (1925) was it decided that under the Fourteenth Amendment, the First Amendment must also apply to the states and to other branches of government.

Second, from the beginning the First Amendment did not prevent either federal or state authorities from restricting speech that was considered seditious, libelous, defamatory, blasphemous, or obscene, or from prosecuting citizens and media outlets that contravened these laws, especially during wartime or periods of political turmoil or polarization. For example, the Sedition Act of 1798, although originally aimed at French citizens living in America who were critical of President John Adams, was used to punish the authors of a wide range of antigovernment writings. In the three years before it expired in 1801, more than 24 newspaper editors, all of whom were aligned with the president's opponents, were arrested and tried, and a number were fined or jailed.[3]

During World War I, Congress passed the Espionage Act of 1917, which was intended to prevent speech or writings that could cause sabotage or interfere with military operations. More than 2,000 people were convicted of violating the act during and immediately after the war. The law was amended in 1940 and 1970 but remains in force today.[4] Similarly, the Smith Act of 1940 criminalizes speech that advocates the overthrow of the government. This law has been used to suppress political dissent, particularly amid the vehemently anti-Communist atmosphere following World War II.[5]

The Supreme Court did not begin to interpret the First Amendment significantly or to adjudicate freedom of speech cases until the landmark case *Schenck v. United States* in 1919. In *Schenck*, the court articulated the important concept that speech had to present a "clear and present danger" for anyone to be prosecuted under laws designed to suppress it. This supplanted a more restrictive "bad tendency" doctrine that allowed the government to restrict speech that could lead to future lawbreaking.

Although *Schenck* introduced a comparatively liberal doctrine, it led to a number of convictions for sedition in the years between 1919 and 1968.[6] However, 50 years later, *Brandenburg v. Ohio* (1969) expanded protections for speech by establishing the "incitement" standard for sedition, which held that unless speech led to immediate danger or imminent lawless action it was protected under the First Amendment.[7]

"Prior restraint," referring to censorship that prevents speech from being published, was firmly rejected by the Supreme Court in the 1931 case *Near v. Minnesota* (1931). The court argued that it was better to prosecute offenses after the fact than to prevent publication. The ruling did allow exceptions on the grounds of "public decency" or "incitements to acts of violence and overthrow by force of orderly government,"[8] but the federal government has only rarely attempted to impose prior restraint. Exceptions have included cases in which the information slated for publication was believed to include vital state secrets, such as the 1971 "Pentagon Papers" case (*New York Times Co. v. United States*) and books and articles written by former employees of the Central Intelligence Agency (CIA). Even in these situations, though, the courts have argued that it is incumbent on the government to show why the press should not be allowed to publish.[9]

Defamation, libel, blasphemy, obscenity, and hate speech are not absolutely protected by the First Amendment and can be subject to prosecution. However, in recent decades a number of attempts at prosecution have been rejected by the Supreme Court, and the grounds on which these cases may be pursued are currently narrow. In *New York Times v. Sullivan* (1964), the Supreme Court ruled that public officials who sue for libel must prove "actual malice" on the part of their critics, and subsequent rulings have extended this to apply to all public figures.[10] In *Garrison v. Louisiana* (1964), the same court ruled that some criminal libel laws could be constitutional as long as actual malice was used as a test and truth could be used as a defense.

In the years following these two key decisions, a number of criminal libel laws were repealed or overturned in the states (there are no federal laws against libel or defamation), though most states have civil laws against libel. In the 17 states that retained criminal libel laws as of 2004, the statutes are rarely invoked.[11] The last conviction occurred in Kansas in July 2002, when a publisher and an editor were sentenced to fines and a year of unsupervised probation after publishing an article that falsely accused local politicians of residing outside the districts they represented.[12] Legal conditions in the United States are comparable to those in Western Europe, where all countries have civil libel laws and a number also have criminal libel provisions. However, Western European practices diverge noticeably from American law in that truth is less widely considered an absolute defense in libel cases.

U.S. law also offers far more protection for blasphemy and hate speech than the laws in most other democracies. Canada and practically every European country have laws against hate speech, and a number have laws prohibiting blasphemy as well. In some of these countries the laws are quite broad; in Denmark, for example, vaguely worded statutes effectively give the government great discretion in deciding whether to prosecute.[13] Although the U.S. Supreme Court has ruled that—subject to caveats—state and federal law may censor "obscenity," the court formally rejected the sort of blasphemy laws that exist in Europe in *Joseph Burstyn Inc. v. Wilson* (1952). And since *Brandenburg*, the court has protected many kinds of hate speech (and behavior) and has tended to reject laws that punish abusive, insulting, or offensive expression.

Historically, American journalists have also benefited from laws and jurisprudence that protect their access to official information and to governmental and judicial proceedings. In 1966, Congress passed the Freedom of Information Act (FOIA) with the explicit purpose of improving public access to government records. FOIA covers only federal agencies and exempts nine categories of information, including national security material, trade secrets, and privileged governmental communications.[14] A second federal law guaranteeing public access to government meetings, called the Sunshine Act, was passed in 1976. The Sunshine Act applies to the same agencies as FOIA and provides similar exemptions. All state and local governments have their own precedents or legislation mandating public access to most records, documents, meetings, legislative procedures, and lower-level court proceedings. Generally, the U.S. Supreme Court has reinforced these rules in the judicial arena. It has held that as a matter of First Amendment law, courtrooms should be open to the press unless there is convincing evidence that publicity would preclude a fair trial, and it has struck down many attempts to impose "gag orders" on the media.

Most journalists believe that their right to protect the identities of their confidential sources even in courts of law is a core professional privilege. However, legal recognition of this privilege has been inconsistent. The issue first came to public notice in the 1970s when the administration of President Richard M. Nixon subpoenaed nearly 200 journalists during his first two years in office. The Supreme Court addressed the matter in *Branzburg v. Hayes* (1972), a ruling that covered four separate cases involving three journalists who had been subpoenaed by grand juries. In a tight vote, the court rejected the journalists' claim that they need not reveal their sources when subpoenaed.[15] Some of the dissenting justices argued for an absolute journalistic privilege, while others said that a qualified version should exist based on a three-part test of relevance, alternative means, and compelling interest.[16]

Since then, lower federal courts have generally recognized the qualified privilege of source confidentiality based on this test. More than 30 states plus Washington, D.C., have shield laws designed to protect the right of source confidentiality, while courts in four other states without explicit shield laws have consistently ruled in favor of source confidentiality.[17] However, there is still no national standard for source protection. Even in jurisdictions with shield laws, some statutes do not cover non-confidential sources of information, while others do not consider freelancers to be journalists.[18]

In the decades since *Branzburg*, reporters have had the greatest success defending the confidentiality of their sources in civil cases and at the local and state levels. Because there is no federal shield law, reporters are most vulnerable to being subpoenaed by the federal court system. In response to a FOIA request made in 2006 by the Reporters Committee for Freedom of the Press (RCFP), the Justice Department reported that "approximately 65 requests for media subpoenas have been approved by the Attorney General since 2001." Unpublished author and freelancer Vanessa Leggett spent the second half of 2001 in jail after she refused to turn over research notes regarding a murder case to a federal grand jury.[19]

Journalists also argue that newsrooms should be protected from unannounced police searches accompanied by a warrant. However, the Supreme Court ruled in the 1978 case of *Zurcher v. Stanford Daily* that they are not. This decision proved so unpopular that in 1980 Congress passed the Privacy Protection Act, which guards newsrooms against such searches except in special circumstances.[20]

Governmental Control of Media Coverage

The Bush administration's desire to expand secrecy and executive privilege, as well as to limit or control media coverage, has led the federal government to issue narrower guidelines for interpreting FOIA, increase the amount of information that is classified, and in some cases threaten media outlets that publish stories based on leaks of such information. In addition, the government in recent years has taken a more aggressive stance toward journalists who decline to reveal their sources, bringing the issue of source confidentiality to the forefront of the press freedom debate. The Bush administration has also stepped up attempts to influence or "spin" the news through covert payments to columnists and the increased dissemination of officially produced news clips.

Classification of Information. In March 2003, a year and a half after 9/11, President Bush signed Executive Order 13292. Despite the tradition of open government established by FOIA and the Sunshine Act, this order considerably expanded government secrecy by giving the executive branch the power to delay the release of classified documents and reclassify previously released information, broadening the exceptions to declassification rules and lowering the standards under which material could be exempted from release.[21] The result, according to one source, was that the number of documents classified jumped from 8.7 million in 2001 to 14.2 million in 2005, an increase of about 60 percent in three years.[22] According to the *New York Times*, even decades-old information is being reclassified, and attempts to retrieve information under FOIA have become slower and more burdensome.[23] Although in the immediate aftermath of 9/11 journalists generally accepted some national security or war-related restrictions, many have since become concerned that the new rules are also restricting access to normal political and economic information.[24]

In March 2007 the House of Representatives passed a number of measures that, among other things, require government agencies to respond more promptly to FOIA requests, reverse a 2001 Bush decision that protected presidential records from public scrutiny, and increase protection for whistleblowers. These proposed laws have yet to be discussed in the Senate, and the White House has warned that they may be vetoed.

Despite the new restrictions on FOIA, reporters have been able to use leaks or still-permitted FOIA requests to obtain a number of important documents about the government's war on terrorism. These include memorandums outlining policies for the severe treatment of prisoners detained in Iraq, Afghanistan, and Guantanamo Bay, Cuba. Furthermore, the CIA in 2007 declassified thousands of files from the cold-war era that detailed agency discussions concerning assassinations, coup plots, and other embarrassing programs.

Crackdown on Leaked Information. Even as the amount of classified information has grown, the press has, on occasion, obtained highly sensitive information from government officials in the form of both sanctioned and unsanctioned leaks. Particularly in recent years, many journalists have been less willing to heed administration calls to withhold certain stories in the interest of a patriotic and united front against terrorism. Tensions have emerged between the Bush administration and media practitioners who have chosen to resume publishing exposés based on leaked classified documents.

In the past, journalists who received information legally were able to publish it without prosecution or reprisal. Yet as early as 2002, then-Attorney General John Ashcroft was promising to tighten existing laws against leaking, and some within the administration had called for leakers to be prosecuted under the Espionage Act when they were believed to have jeopardized national security. The act requires proof of intent to harm the United States or aid a foreign government and has therefore never been used to formally prosecute a journalist. But by 2006, at the behest of some conservative journalists, politicians, and government officials, it was increasingly used as a way to threaten reporters and media outlets that published stories based on leaked secrets.[25]

Most of these threats have been directed at the *New York Times*, due to a series of December 2005 stories revealing that the National Security Agency was tracking terrorism suspects by monitoring domestic telephone calls without a warrant. President Bush called the publication of this series a "shameful act," and then-Attorney General Alberto Gonzales suggested in a May 2006 ABC News interview that existing law permitted the administration to prosecute.[26] The *Washington Post*'s Dana Priest was also condemned by the administration for revealing the existence of secret CIA prisons in foreign countries; this story, also based on classified information, had been leaked by a CIA employee who was subsequently fired.

Ultimately, no legal action was taken against the reporters or newspapers who published these leaks, and leading newspapers continue to print probing stories on U.S. policies in Iraq and the war on terrorism generally. Even so, such incidents undoubtedly serve as fuel for the debate over the boundaries between investigative watchdog journalism and the media's responsibility not to undermine national security.

Confidentiality of Sources and Shield Laws. As discussed previously, American journalists have never had an absolute right to protect the confidentiality of their sources.[27] However, in recent years a number of high-profile cases involving major news outlets and key political players have drawn more serious attention to this issue.

The best-known incident occurred in the summer of 2005, when *New York Times* reporter Judith Miller was jailed for 85 days for refusing to turn over her notes or to testify before a federal grand jury in a case involving the possibly illegal disclosure of the identity of CIA employee Valerie Plame Wilson (usually called Valerie Plame). Miller, who did not directly cover the Plame story, eventually agreed to testify after being encouraged to do so by her source, I. Lewis "Scooter" Libby, the chief of staff to Vice President Dick Cheney. In the same case, *Time* magazine correspondent Matthew Cooper was threatened with jail for initially refusing to testify about his source, who was also Libby. Cooper similarly testified after Libby granted him a waiver.

In another major case, a federal judge held *Washington Post* reporter Walter Pincus in contempt for refusing to reveal his sources for articles about Wen Ho Lee, a former nuclear scientist charged with espionage. Lee had accused government officials of leaking his personnel files to the press and sued the government. Four other reporters were also cited for contempt in the case and escaped prosecution only when Lee settled out of court.

The Plame and Lee cases demonstrated that journalists have no clear right to protect their confidential sources. This became particularly evident when the Supreme Court refused to hear appeals from any of the news organizations involved. However, the ambiguity of the issue has also been demonstrated in lesser-known cases unrelated to national security issues. For example, in 2004 Rhode Island television reporter Jim Taricani was fined, charged with contempt of court, and sentenced to four months of house arrest for failing to reveal a source.[28] Separately, a judge in September 2006 jailed two *San Francisco Chronicle* journalists in a criminal case involving alleged steroid use by professional athletes, after the journalists published a story based on leaked grand jury testimony. The charges against the reporters were dropped in March 2007, when the source of the leak came forward.[29] In another case, freelancer and video blogger Josh Wolf was jailed in August 2006 after he refused to surrender a videotape of an anarchist demonstration to judicial authorities. Wolf was released in April 2007 after spending 226 days in jail, a U.S. record.[30]

In a positive step following the Miller case, members of Congress proposed legislation that would shield reporters from the compulsion to reveal confidential sources. The first of these proposals, a 2005 bill, would have granted reporters an almost complete guarantee of source confidentiality. However, in response to objections—some from lawmakers concerned about national security—this proposal was amended. The resulting "Free Flow of Information Act," a bipartisan measure introduced in the Senate in May 2006, offers no protection to reporters' nonconfidential notes, e-mails, drafts, and interviews. For confidential sources, it specifies that "public interest in the information provided (as determined by a judge) is critical to the protection the source will receive."[31] In other words, prosecutors or private lawyers must convince a judge that the harm caused by a leak outweighs the value of making the information public.

The proposed law therefore allocates considerable power to federal judges. Although it is not as strong as some journalists and press freedom organizations would like, it offers greater protection and clarity than the status quo. At the same time, some advocates of press freedom have raised questions as to whether the legislation might eventually lead to the licensing of journalists as a means of determining qualifications for coverage under the law. The bill continues to enjoy considerable bipartisan support, but it has so far made little progress.

Domestic Impediments to the Coverage of Sensitive Topics. In addition to heightened controls over access to information and threats against journalists who publish classified information, the media's physical ability to cover certain sensitive stories has been limited in the past five years, affecting both foreign and American journalists.

Initial coverage of the aftermath of Hurricane Katrina in August 2005 was sharply critical of the Bush administration's performance and spoke of widespread crime, looting, and mayhem. In response, the Federal Emergency Management Agency (FEMA)—the governmental agency responsible for dealing with the disaster—worked to restrict coverage. Camera crews and photographers were instructed to refrain from capturing images of dead bodies, and some journalists said they were prevented from interviewing Katrina victims who had been relocated to government trailers unless a FEMA official was present.[32] Some local law enforcement authorities were also reported to have harassed journalists, particularly those who were reporting on police abuse of criminal suspects. Such harassment included the confiscation of tapes and media equipment, verbal threats, and physical intimidation.[33]

Foreign journalists seeking to cover the United States also face new restrictions in the post-9/11 environment. Foreign correspondents have always been excluded from the government's Visa Waiver Program (under which visitors from 27 countries deemed to be "friendly" can enter the United States without a visa for less than 90 days), and are required to have a special visa to cover news stories in the United States. However, immigration officials routinely ignored these rules until March 2003, when without warning they began to apply them zealously. A number of foreign journalists were stopped for visa violations at U.S. borders, refused entry, and forcibly deported to their home countries, which included Australia, Austria, Denmark, France, and the United Kingdom, among others. Many were

handcuffed, bodily searched, kept in holdover cells or jails over-
night, and prevented from making telephone calls.[34]

In July 2004, a number of press freedom groups criticized
the heightened restrictions, noting that 13 journalists had been
detained and deported in the previous 18-month period.[35]
Partly in response, Democratic Congresswoman Zoe Lofgren
introduced a bill that would allow journalists from the 27
"friendly" countries to enter the United States without a visa
for up to 90 days.[36]

Foreign journalists already in the United States have also faced
new difficulties and scrutiny in the past few years. In July 2004,
the Inter American Press Association asked the State Department to reverse a decision that would require longer-term foreign correspondents to leave the country in order to renew their
visas.[37] In a separate case in March 2003, the accreditation of
two journalists from the Qatar-based satellite television channel
Al-Jazeera was withdrawn for a month by the New York Stock
Exchange (NYSE), amid comments by NYSE officials suggesting that the suspensions may have been linked to the channel's
controversial coverage of the Iraq war.[38]

Overseas Impediments to the Coverage of Sensitive Topics.
American journalists also face new difficulties covering sensitive international stories, particularly those related to the war
on terrorism.

For their coverage of the war in Afghanistan and the initial
invasion of Iraq, many media outlets chose to have their reporters travel with military units in a practice known as embedding.
Victoria Clarke, the assistant secretary of defense for public
affairs at the time of the invasion of Afghanistan, said that "on
the first night of air strikes, 39 journalists from 26 news organizations were aboard U.S. Navy ships involved in the operation."[39] In April 2003, as U.S. and other coalition forces moved
into Baghdad, there were nearly 600 American and foreign correspondents officially embedded with American military units,
including deployed ground units.[40]

Both media and military representatives have observed that embedding during the initial stages of the Iraq war gave journalists unprecedented access to ground combat, which in turn gave the American people a close look at the realities of war. In particular, television coverage of the invasion routinely provided live battlefield video of reporters in protective gear interviewing soldiers in their assigned units; the most striking of these were the occasional interviews interrupted by the onset of combat.

While embedding did provide reporters with new access in some ways, it also limited the story they could tell. Many journalists note that their embedment narrowed their perspective, since they became attached to the military personnel around them and were rarely permitted to leave the unit to cover other news.[41] Many did not even see action that could provide a newsworthy story. In fact, the *New Yorker*'s Jeffrey Goldberg, who declined an embedment, estimated that of the 600 journalists reporting from military units, only 50 to 70 of them saw any interesting combat during their tour.[42]

Many journalists, determined to cover the war without such impediments, chose not to embed. Though this made them more mobile and independent, many claimed that they were often denied equal access to coalition information and were at times even prevented by the military from covering certain stories, like the damage left by the initial invasion in southern Iraqi cities.[43] Nonetheless, most critics agree that coverage of the initial phases of the war was as accurate and free of government control as in any major American conflict abroad. Furthermore, coverage of the war during the period of U.S. occupation has been notable for aggressive reporting on the military setbacks suffered by U.S. forces, political polarization within Iraq, alleged atrocities committed by American troops, scandals involving American contractors, and articles that raise questions about the Bush administration's war policies.

Due to the dangerous nature of reporting from Iraq, journalists have occasionally become casualties of war. In fact, the American military has even been accused of intentionally targeting journalists whose coverage was not favorable.[44] The best-known instances include the 2003 U.S. bombing of Al-Jazeera's Baghdad bureau, which killed one journalist, and the American military assault on the Palestine Hotel—the primary office for most foreign correspondents in Baghdad—which killed two.[45] However, there is no clear evidence that American forces deliberately targeted journalists in these incidents. Foreign journalists have also been detained by forces on both sides of the conflict. In 2003, four foreign correspondents were harassed and imprisoned for eight days by Iraqi officials, and an Al-Jazeera journalist has been held without charge by U.S. forces at Guantanamo Bay since June 2002.

Restrictions on journalists' access to Guantanamo Bay have added to the tension between the media and the Bush administration. More than a thousand journalists have visited the base since it began housing detainees from Iraq and Afghanistan. Despite the insistence of a Pentagon spokesman that Guantanamo Bay is "the most transparent detention facility in the history of warfare,"[46] Associated Press journalist Paisley Dodds has reported that after the war in Iraq began, it became harder to see and interview prison staff and almost impossible to photograph the base or prisoners.[47] Under new media guidelines issued in September 2002, journalists are required to have a media escort with them in areas where detainees are held. These escorts have control over whom journalists may speak with, and have reportedly cut short interviews or prevented interviewees from responding to questions on controversial issues. Journalists have been barred from independently interviewing inmates since the prison opened in January 2002. In June 2006, three U.S. reporters from the *Miami Herald*, the *Charlotte Observer*, and the *Los Angeles Times* were expelled before they could complete an investigation into the alleged suicide of three prisoners, and media access to the base was shut down entirely, though only for a time. Despite the restrictions, the press has published numerous accounts of conditions inside the facility, complaints by detainees, and details of military tribunals held at the site.

Covert Influence Over Media Coverage. Evidence has emerged in recent years that the Bush administration paid to have news stories supporting its point of view placed in the domestic and foreign media, often without accompanying disclosures of its role. Although government funds had been employed to produce such propagandistic media segments under previous administrations, the range of cases detailed below suggests that the Bush administration has made the most extensive use of the practice.

In early 2005, it was revealed that the Bush administration had used federal funds to pay several political commentators who supported some of its domestic policy initiatives. *USA Today* reported in January that the Education Department had paid conservative columnist Armstrong Williams $240,000 to promote the No Child Left Behind Act, an education initiative of the Bush administration. In October 2005, auditors at the Government Accountability Office (GAO) found that "engaging in a purely political activity such as this" was "not a proper use of appropriated funds," and concluded that the administration had intentionally disseminated "covert propaganda."[48] The president asserted that the White House did not know about the payments to Williams.

Soon after the Williams contract was exposed, the *Washington Post* and the *Los Angeles Times* reported that the Health and Human Services Department had paid conservative columnists Maggie Gallagher and Michael McManus $21,500 and $4,000, respectively, to help promote the president's $300 million initiative to encourage marriage.[49] Federal auditors who investigated these contracts discovered other cases in which the government had paid for news stories on television and in newspapers. Most of these stories, two of which were disseminated by the Education Department, did not acknowledge that the government had generated them. As the GAO stated,

> The failure of an agency to identify itself as the source of a prepackaged news story misleads the viewing public by encouraging the audience to believe that the broadcasting news organizations developed the information. The

prepackaged news stories are purposefully designed to be indistinguishable from news segments broadcast to the public.[50]

In the war in Iraq, the struggle to control information has become almost as crucial, albeit not as prominent, as the actual military conflict. In February 2002, the *New York Times* reported that as part of its campaign to win "hearts and minds," the U.S. Defense Department had created an Office of Strategic Influence (OSI) intended to "provide news items" to international media organizations in both friendly and hostile nations. The new office was reportedly given a budget in excess of $100 million for its first year of operation.[51] Barely a week after this story was published, then-Defense Secretary Donald Rumsfeld announced that the government would close down the program. However, in 2005 the *Los Angeles Times* reported that the Pentagon in 2003 had nonetheless continued to place pro-U.S. articles in Iraqi newspapers with the help of a number of private contractors. Among them, the Lincoln Group—a U.S.-based strategic communications firm whose self-described purpose is to help clients "influence their target audience,"[52]— was alone responsible for planting hundreds of stories in Iraqi newspapers.[53] Many papers were paid to publish these articles, and their origins were not disclosed. Referred to by the military as "psychological operations," such efforts to control information and public opinion have persisted along with the war. In July 2005, the Pentagon awarded new contracts worth $300 million to three firms, including the Lincoln Group, to continue placing stories in the Iraqi press.[54]

State Funded Media

Radio and television broadcasting in the United States has historically been private, beginning with the first radio networks— NBC and CBS—in the 1920s, which controlled both the broadcast industry and the technological innovations that fueled it at the time. In this respect, America differs from Europe, where state funding was integral to the formation of broadcast media. In 1927, the British Broadcasting Corporation (BBC) became the first publicly owned broadcasting company in the world, and when the first radio waves were broadcast from the Eiffel Tower in Paris, they were sponsored by the state.

Federal funds were not used to support broadcasting in the United States until the 1962 passage of the Educational Television Facilities Act, and even then they backed only television stations with explicitly educational content.[55] But in 1967, the Public Broadcasting Act provided federal support for the first time to the programming and operational costs of local broadcasting facilities. U.S. public broadcasting was never intended to create a single publicly funded, independently administered network like the BBC. Instead, it was envisioned as a loose association of local outlets supported by government funds. Over the years, however, it has evolved into a more cohesive entity that resembles traditional American broadcast networks in many respects.

From the beginning, government financing of local broadcasters raised concerns about the possibility of political influence over media content. To prevent this, Congress created the private, nonprofit Corporation for Public Broadcasting (CPB) to administer the funds and serve as a barrier between the public broadcasting network and both public and private donors.

U.S. public broadcasting has grown since its inception, but not to the extent of many of its European counterparts. The BBC has become the largest public broadcaster in the world, with a government subsidy of nearly $27 per citizen in 2005, while U.S. government funding for the CPB has rarely exceeded $2 per citizen.[56] The Republican Party, as the traditional advocate of "small government," has been the main source of opposition to increased government financing for public media. In the 1980s, the administration of President Ronald Reagan cut the CPB's budget by $35 million. During the political campaigns of 1994, then-Congressman Newt Gingrich and other Republicans proposed "zeroing out" government funding for public broadcasting as a part of their overall platform, claiming that the CPB was biased against conservatives and asserting that the proliferation of cable television stations rendered government funding unnecessary.[57]

Evidence of political influence at the CPB came to the attention of the American public through the November 2005 resignation of CPB Board Chairman Kenneth Tomlinson. Tomlinson had sought to bring "fairness and balance" to public broadcasting by counteracting what he saw as a liberal bias. However, a CPB internal inquiry found that he had broken federal law by making managerial decisions based on political affiliations. In particular, Tomlinson had advocated the creation of a number of conservative programs and had frequently e-mailed the White House concerning the hiring of former Republican Party co-chairwoman Patricia Harrison as CPB president.

Media Diversity

Broadcast Media. The United States is one of the largest media markets in the world, home to more than 1,500 daily newspapers, 14,000 licensed broadcast radio stations,[58] and 1,900 television stations.[59] The news media are only a subset of the entire media market, but as recently as 2004 there were nearly 45 million television viewers for the morning and evening news programs (combined) at the three main broadcast stations— ABC, CBS, and NBC; this does not include the many cable and satellite television news outlets.[60] Even in the radio industry, audience numbers remain high, particularly for talk shows featuring conservative commentary. The most popular of these, *The Rush Limbaugh Show*, had more than 13.5 million listeners in 2005.[61] Given the size and power of the broadcast industry, it is unsurprising that the diversity of the content consumed as well as the consolidation of outlet ownership have become the topics of contentious debate.

Regulation of the broadcast industry began in 1934 when Congress created the Federal Communications Commission (FCC), an independent government agency responsible for overseeing interstate and international communications, including all forms of television and radio. The Telecommunications Act of 1996 was the first major overhaul of broadcast legislation since the FCC's creation. Passed with little fanfare by a Republican-controlled Congress during the administration of President Bill Clinton, the law was intended to foster competition across all of the telecommunications industries, bringing telephone companies, cable television operators, and terrestrial broadcasters into one another's markets.

However, instead of competition, the result of the law was a wave of mergers between existing companies. In January 2000, internet service provider AOL merged with Time Warner and its Cable News Network (CNN). In September 2003, Vivendi Universal Entertainment merged its entertainment business with General Electric (GE), which, in addition to owning the NBC networks, had significant interests in aircraft manufacturing, medical devices, computers, nuclear reactors, health insurance, home equity, and commercial real estate loans. By 2003, five large companies with diverse media, entertainment, and other corporate holdings controlled just under 75 percent of all prime-time television content: GE, AOL Time Warner, Viacom (which owns CBS), Disney (which owns ABC), and News Corporation (which owns Fox).[62]

The Telecommunications Act also abolished a rule that limited the number of radio or television stations a single company could own. As a direct result, Clear Channel—already the largest single owner of American radio stations in 1996—acquired more stations across the country and within a few years came to own over 1,200 stations in 300 regional markets.[63]

Some argue that the government should impose regulations to limit the influence that any single corporation can have over different media and individual regional markets. Others believe that the media market should be permitted to regulate itself and that government interference works against media diversity. In 1998, Michael Powell—the son of Colin Powell, a former chairman of the Joint Chiefs of Staff who would later serve as secretary of state—was appointed as a commissioner of the FCC. Powell, a member of the deregulation camp, argued that the primary purpose of the FCC was to prevent the government from interfering unduly in the media industry. He was concerned that excessive regulation might suffocate the technological innovation which he believed could enable smaller companies to break into the market.[64] In 2001, Powell was made chairman of the FCC.

The FCC is required by law to conduct a biennial assessment of its rules and determine whether they are still necessary in light of industry changes. As chairman, Powell undertook this assessment and led the FCC to issue a controversial order in June 2003 that modified many existing rules governing media ownership. Most notably, the order would have enabled a company to own a full-service broadcast station, a daily newspaper, and a radio station within the same regional market. The new rules would have also allowed a media company to hold as much as 45 percent (up from 35 percent) of the national television market.[65]

The FCC order received significantly more attention than the 1996 Telecommunications Act. Supporters of deregulation praised it, arguing that despite the recent trend toward consolidation at the highest levels of media ownership, there were more television channels and information sources available to the American public than ever before, enabling a freer press to flourish. According to James Gattuso of the Heritage Foundation, large companies with access to vast resources support variety in news and entertainment, since they are able to finance stations that might not otherwise stay afloat. Gattuso also argues that it is in the best interest of these companies to diversify their programming to appeal to as wide an audience as possible.[66]

However, the FCC's decision also met with considerable opposition from defenders of regulation like the Media Access Project, trade associations like the National Writer's Union, and even a number of socially conservative organizations including the U.S. Conference of Catholic Bishops, the Parents' Television Council, and, at one point, the National Rifle Association. These diverse groups found common ground in the belief that the concentration of media outlets under a few owners would limit the range of voices and lead to programming that was out of touch with local communities.[67] Many organizations, including the International Federation of Journalists, argue that even without the proposed FCC changes, the current trend of multiplying outlets owned by a shrinking number of corporations is already limiting the diversity of opinions that can be accessed by the American public.[68]

Critics of deregulation are particularly concerned that large conglomerates could influence news content under their control to suit their interests in other industries. For example, in 2001 the Environmental Protection Agency (EPA) required GE to pay half a billion dollars to clean up a 40-mile stretch of the Hudson River after it was revealed that the company had dumped more than a million pounds of toxins into the river by the end of the 1970s.[69] While the issue was before the New York City Council, GE engaged in a statewide campaign against the EPA decision that was estimated to have cost tens of millions of dollars, including television, radio, billboard, and internet advertisements.[70] At the same time, Robert Wright—the vice chairman of the GE corporate board and president of NBC—actively advocated against the decision, meeting city council members and defending GE's position.[71] Once the EPA announced its decision, most of the NBC news programs touched only lightly on the issue, and the primary NBC in-depth news magazine program, *Dateline*, has yet to cover it.[72]

In a victory for regulation advocates, a series of legislative decisions and court rulings prevented the new FCC ownership rules from taking effect. A few months after the rules were originally proposed, the Senate passed a resolution voicing its disapproval and calling for them to be withdrawn. Although that demand never became law, the fiscal 2004 Consolidated Appropriations Act instructed the FCC to modify one of the rules and drop the cap on media ownership to 39 percent, from the proposed 45 percent.[73] In 2004, the U.S. 3rd Circuit Court of Appeals in Philadelphia, ruling in *Prometheus Radio Project v. Federal Communications Commission*, suspended all of the 2003 FCC changes and sent most of the ownership rules back for reevaluation.[74] By 2005, the FCC had consulted with the Justice Department and decided against appealing the decision to the Supreme Court. The commission admitted defeat in 2006 and commenced a new review of ownership rules, this time promising more public hearings and attention to the effect its decisions would have on media diversity.

In part as a response to these developments, Michael Powell resigned from the FCC in January 2005. He was succeeded as chairman by Kevin Martin, a Republican commissioner who promised to take a more active interest in public opinion before any further regulations could be passed.

New Media. In the 1990s, when the internet began to emerge as an integral part of the media industry, many at traditional media outlets voiced concerns about whether they could compete. At newspapers in particular, journalists feared that high-quality investigative reporting would suffer along with the traditional print media. A 2006 study by JupiterResearch found that Europeans consistently spend more time online than they do reading newspapers.[75] In the same year, a Pew Research Center study found that "four-in-ten Americans reported reading a newspaper 'yesterday' in the survey, down from 50 percent a decade ago."[76] In the six-month period between March and September 2006, the circulation for six of the 10 most successful papers in the United States declined, with five of them declining by 1.8 percent or more.

It should be stressed that an obituary for the newspaper industry would be premature. Even in 2005—reportedly a bad year for the print media—the top 13 publicly traded newspaper companies reported average profits of 20 percent, while the profit margin of ExxonMobil, the highest ranked Fortune 500 company, was only 11 percent.[77] Many of the largest and most respected national (and local) papers in the United States have adapted well to the advent of the internet, assimilating and capitalizing on the new technology instead of merely competing with it. In fact, online editions of newspapers dominated the 2006 Online News Association awards for quality in journalism.[78]

However, there can be no doubt that the traditional print media confront a serious challenge from the internet. Even with their online success, average profits are declining among most newspaper companies, and the number of print subscriptions continues to decrease annually. This decline is particularly worrisome because subscription fees and advertising revenues for print editions remain the primary sources of profit for most newspapers—the majority still receive no more than 5 or 6 percent of their overall advertising revenue from their websites.[79]

To compensate, many newspapers are closing foreign bureaus and replacing them with local stringers or freelancers. By 2007, all of the largest newspapers, including the *New York Times* and the *Wall Street Journal*, had even closed their bureaus in Canada.[80] This trend costs newspapers precious expertise on international news, threatening the quality of investigative reporting that the American audience has come to expect from the newspaper industry.

One of the most significant challenges faced by the newspaper industry comes from blogs, which provide critical commentary about the media and are also proving to be important sources of information in their own right. Nonetheless, *Washington Post* editor Len Downie has observed that bloggers are sometimes assets to the newspaper industry, because they reference and draw attention to newspaper articles.[81] They are also a boon to media diversity, especially in light of the ownership consolidation affecting traditional media. Blogs offer a platform to anyone interested and dedicated enough to create one. They offer new benefits to readers as well; while the traditional media are consumed more or less passively, blogs allow easy communication and debate between readers and authors.

Political and policy blogs are often highly partisan, and while their proliferation adds to media diversity, it can also contribute to ideological polarization. The Project for Excellence in Journalism found that only 5 percent of blog postings contained "what would be considered journalistic reporting," which involved original research and provided the reader with more substance than commentary.[82] Despite this, or perhaps because of it, the "blogosphere" has already shaped political history in important ways. In 2004, blogs helped presidential candidate Howard Dean rise from obscurity to—for a time—a leading position in the Democratic primary race. Later that year, after the CBS program *60 Minutes* reported that President Bush had evaded the draft for the Vietnam War, conservative bloggers identified the story's sources as fraudulent. Their attacks led CBS to conduct its own investigation, which revealed that a number of the source materials had indeed been fakes. The episode ultimately benefited Bush's reelection campaign.

Blogs have become an influential part of the American media environment and a feature of American life. Because of this, and because many blogs espouse radical or controversial opinions, a number of attempts have been made to regulate the internet. In 1998, Congress passed the Child Online Protection Act (COPA), which made it a crime to publish anything potentially harmful to minors online (particularly pornography and indecent language) without the technological capacity to prevent children from accessing it. However, COPA was quickly blocked by the lower courts, and in 2004 the Supreme Court ruled that the legislation was unconstitutional.[83] According to the Center for Democracy and Technology, lawmakers are now considering legislation that would make internet service providers liable for illegal content. One blogger, Josh Wolf (see above), has already been held in contempt of court and imprisoned for refusing to hand over material published on his website.

Conclusion

The United States has a strong tradition, grounded in precedent and in the First Amendment, of protecting freedom of the press and freedom of expression. But this tradition has faced a variety of threats in recent years. The nation's intensified focus on security concerns since 9/11 is a deepening concern, as is the impact of commercialization and consolidation on media diversity, journalistic independence, and quality of coverage. It remains to be seen whether issues like increased government secrecy, threats to source confidentiality, and government efforts to directly influence media coverage are unique to the current administration, or whether they represent long-term trends. The media's continuing ability to publish stories that discomfit the government—such as revelations about federal surveillance schemes, prisoner abuse in Iraq, or government payments to columnists—is perhaps the best evidence that the American press remains free and robust.

Endnotes

1. David A. Anderson, "Freedom of the Press," *Texas Law Review* 80, no. 3 (2002).
2. Thomas L. Tedford and Dale A. Herbeck, *Freedom of Speech in the United States*, 4th ed. (State College, PA: Strata Publishing, 2001), 24.
3. Ibid., 29.
4. Jodi Icenoggle, *Schenck v. United States and the Freedom of Speech Debate: Debating Supreme Court Decisions* (Berkeley Heights, NJ: Enslow Publishers, 2005), 29.
5. Tedford and Herbeck, *Freedom of Speech*, 59.
6. Ibid., 49–50.
7. Ibid., 64.
8. Ibid., 219.
9. Ibid., 228. In a related ruling, *Miami Herald v. Tornillo* (1974), the Supreme Court struck down a "right of reply" statute, finding that compulsory publication was as much a prior restraint as prohibiting publication altogether.
10. Ibid., 84–88.
11. Jane Kirtley, "Criminal Defamation: An 'Instrument of Destruction'" (background paper, University of Minnesota, Minneapolis, MN, November 18, 2003).
12. Committee to Protect Journalists (CPJ), "Publisher and Editor Convicted of Criminal Defamation," International Freedom of Expression Exchange (IFEX), July 18, 2002, http://www.ifex.org/en/content/view/full/16982.
13. Richard N. Winfield, "An Editorial Controversy Metastasizing: Denmark's Hate Speech Laws," *Communications Lawyer* 24, no. 1 (Spring 2006).
14. Tedford and Herbeck, *Freedom of Speech*, 247–48.
15. Ibid., 244.
16. Ibid., 244.
17. The Reporter's Committee for Freedom of the Press, "Reporter's Privilege," http://www.rcfp.org/privilege/index.html.
18. Ibid.

19. CPJ, "Texas Journalist Released From Jail," IFEX, January 4, 2002, http://www.ifex.org/en/content/view/full/15393.
20. Tedford and Herbeck, *Freedom of Speech*, 246.
21. Lawyers Committee for Human Rights (Human Rights First), *Assessing the New Normal: Liberty and Security for the Post-September 11 United States* (New York: Lawyers Committee for Human Rights, 2003). http://www.lchr.org/pubs/descriptions/Assessing/AssessingtheNewNormal.pdf.
22. Douglas McCollam, "The End of Ambiguity," *Columbia Journalism Review* (July/August 2006): 23.
23. "A Fixation With Secrecy," *New York Times*, August 6, 2006.
24. Laura Parker, Kevin Johnson, and Toni Locy, "Post 9/11, Government Stingy With Information," *USA Today*, May 16, 2002, http://www.usatoday.com/news/nation/2002/05/16/secrecy-usatcov.htm.
25. Gabriel Schoenfeld, "Has the *New York Times* Violated the Espionage Act?" *Commentary* (March 2006).
26. McCollam, "The End of Ambiguity," 21.
27. For a complete list of cases, see the timeline compiled by the First Amendment Center, at http://www.firstamendmentcenter.org/about.aspx?id=16896.
28. Reporters Without Borders (RSF), "Television Reporter Fined for Refusing to Reveal His Sources," IFEX, April 2, 2004, http://www.ifex.org/en/content/view/full/57917; CPJ, "Journalist Convicted of Criminal Contempt," IFEX, November 18, 2004, http://www.ifex.org/en/content/view/full/62652.
29. CPJ, "Judge Jails Freelancer Over Videotape," IFEX, August 2, 2006, http://www.ifex.org/en/content/view/full/76099; CPJ, "CPJ Concerned by Jail Sentences Imposed on Two U.S. Reporters," IFEX, September 22, 2006, http://www.ifex.org/en/content/view/full/77296.
30. "US Reporter Ends Record Jail Term," BBC News, April 3, 2007, http://news.bbc.co.uk/2/hi/americas/6524359.stm.
31. McCollam, "The End of Ambiguity," 25.
32. WorldNetDaily, "Your Government at Work: FEMA Bans Reporters From Katrina Victims: Residents of Trailer Parks Not Permitted to Talk With Media Unless Agent Present,"

July 26, 2006, http://www.worldnetdaily.com/news/article.asp?ARTICLE_ID=51240.

33. For details of several cases, see CPJ, *Attacks on the Press in 2005* (New York: CPJ, 2006), http://www.cpj.org/attacks05/americas05/usa_05.html.

34. International Press Institute (IPI), "IPI Urges United States to Review Visa Policy for Foreign Journalists," IFEX, April 30, 2004, http://www.ifex.org/en/content/view/full/58587.

35. RSF, *Annual Report 2004* (Paris: RSF, 2004), http://www.rsf.org/article.php3?id_article=10003; IPI, *World Press Freedom Review, 2004* (Vienna: IPI, 2005), http://www.freemedia.at/cms/ipi/freedom_detail.html?country=/KW0001/KW0002/KW0031/&year=2004.

36. IFEX, "IFEX Members Urge Visa Rule Change for Journalists," news release, July 28, 2004, http://www.ifex.org/en/content/view/full/60340.

37. Inter American Press Association (IAPA), "IAPA Asks State Department to Reverse Its Decision Stipulating That Foreign Journalists Must Leave the Country to Renew Their Visas," IFEX, July 20, 2004, http://www.ifex.org/en/content/view/full/60183.

38. CPJ, "Al-Jazeera Correspondents Allowed to Return to NYSE," IFEX, May 2, 2003, http://www.ifex.org/en/content/view/full/49493.

39. Victoria Clarke, "Pentagon and the Press—Striking a Balance: Government's Needs Versus Those of the Media," *Columbia Journalism Review* (September/October 2002).

40. Christopher Marquis, "A Nation at War: The Pentagon Spokeswoman; News Media Access Brings Chorus of Criticism and Queries," *New York Times*, April 3, 2003.

41. For example, CPJ noted that a *Los Angeles Times* reporter embedded with 101st Airborne Division was prevented from interviewing enemy Iraqi fighters or survivors of Iraqi civilians killed by coalition forces. CPJ, *Attacks on the Press in 2003* (New York: CPJ, 2004), http://www.cpj.org/attacks03/mideast03/iraq.html.

42. Jack Shafer, "Embeds and Unilaterals," *Slate*, May 1, 2003.

43. Ibid.
44. John Plunkett, "Bush Claim Revives Al-Jazeera Bombing Fears," *Guardian Unlimited*, November 23, 2005, http://www.guardian.co.uk/Iraq/Story/0,2763,1648988,00.html.
45. CPJ, *Attacks on the Press in 2003*.
46. Ben Fox, "Military Blocks Media Access to Guantanamo," *Washington Post*, June 15, 2006.
47. RSF, "RSF Denounces Reporting Restrictions at Guantanamo Military Base," IFEX, October 13, 2003, http://www.ifex.org/en/content/view/full/54218/.
48. Robert Pear, "Buying of News by Bush's Aides Is Ruled Illegal," *New York Times*, October 1, 2005.
49. Howard Kurtz, "Writer Backing Bush Plan Had Gotten Federal Contract," *Washington Post*, January 26, 2005.
50. Ibid.
51. Daniel Schulman, "Mind Games," *Columbia Journalism Review* (May/June 2006).
52. See the home page of the company's website at http://www.lincolngroup.com.
53. Schulman, "Mind Games."
54. Ibid.
55. Public Broadcasting Policy Base, "Educational Television Facilities Act of 1962," Current Newspaper and National Public Broadcasting Archives, http://www.current.org/pbpb/legislation/ETVFacil62.html.
56. Scott Sherman, "Press Watch," *Nation*, August 15, 2005.
57. Public Broadcasting Policy Base, "Curve of Federal Appropriations to CPB, 1969–2001," Current Newspaper and National Public Broadcasting Archives, http://www.current.org/pbpb/statistics/cpbappropscurve.html.
58. Project for Excellence in Journalism, "Number of Licensed Broadcast Radio Stations," in *The State of the News Media 2005*, http://www.stateofthenewsmedia.org/2005/chartland.asp?id=304&ct=line&dir=&sort=&col1_box=1.
59. This figure includes the major networks (ABC, CBS, NBC, FOX, PBS, WB, UPN, and PAX) and the network affiliates, as well as local and public broadcasting stations. Peter Lyman, Hal

R. Varian, Kirsten Swearingen, et al., *How Much Information? 2003*, Regents of the University of California, 2003, http:// www2.sims.berkeley.edu/research/projects/how-much-info-2003/broadcast.htm.

60. Project for Excellence in Journalism, "Morning News Viewership, by Network," in *The State of the News Media 2005*, http:// www.stateofthenewsmedia.org/2005/chartland.asp?id=216&c t=line&dir=&sort=&col1_box=1&col2_box=1&col3_box=1.

61. "Latest Top Host Figures," *Talkers Magazine* (October 2005).

62. Center for Digital Democracy, "Free TV Swallowed by Media Giants: Evidence Contradicts Media Industry Arguments," news release, September 13, 2003, http://www.democraticmedia.org/resources/filings/0915_Free_TV.doc.

63. Gal Beckerman, "Tripping Up Big Media: One of the Strangest Left-Right Coalitions in Recent Memory Has Challenged a Free-Market FCC. What's the Glue That Holds It Together?" *Columbia Journalism Review* (November 2003).

64. Nick Gillespie, Drew Clark, and Jesse Walker, "The Reluctant Planner: FCC Chairman Michael Powell on Indecency, Innovation, Consolidation, and Competition," *Reason* (December 2004), http://www.reason.com/news/show/36417.html.

65. Michael Powell, interview by Terence Smith, *NewsHour with Jim Lehrer*, PBS, June 2, 2003, http://www.pbs. org/newshour/bb/media/jan-june03/powell_6-2.html.

66. James Gattuso, "The Myth of Media Concentration: Why the FCC's Media Ownership Rules Are Unnecessary," Heritage Foundation, May 29, 2003, http://www.heritage.org/ Research/InternetandTechnology/wm284.cfm.

67. Center for Digital Democracy, "FCC Decision Deals a Blow to Diversity and Democracy: New Campaign on Common Carriage for Cable, DSL, and Wireless Broadband Announced," news release, June 2, 2003, http://www.democraticmedia.org/ news/june2.html.

68. International Federation of Journalists, *Who Is in Control? A Primer for the Roundtable Discussion on Global Media—Threats to Free Expression, February 20, 2006* (Brussels: International

Federation of Journalists, 2005), http://www.ifj.org/pdfs/whosincontrol.pdf.

69. Richard Pollak, "Is GE Mightier Than the Hudson?" *Nation*, May 28, 2001, http://www.thenation.com/doc/20010528/pollak/3.

70. Eric Lipton, "NBC President Lobbies City to Block G.E. Dredging Bill," *New York Times*, April 6, 2001, http://select.nytimes.com/search/restricted/article?res=F7091FF63E5A0C758CDDAD0894D9404482.

71. Ibid.

72. Pollak, "Is GE Mightier?"

73. Charles B. Goldfarb, *FCC Media Ownership Rules: Current Status and Issues for Congress* (Washington, DC: Congressional Research Service, August 23, 2004), http://price.house.gov/issues/uploadedfiles/media6.pdf.

74. Ibid.

75. "Study: Europeans Spend More Time Online Than With Print Media," *Editor & Publisher*, October 9, 2006.

76. Pew Research Center for People and the Press, "Online Papers Modestly Boost Readership: Maturing Internet News Audience Broader Than Deep," news release, July 30, 2006, http://people-press.org/reports/display.php3?PageID=1066.

77. Eric Klinenberg, "Breaking the News," *Mother Jones,* March/April 2007),http://www.motherjones.com/news/features/2007/03/breaking_the_news.html.

78. *USA Today*'s website was a finalist for four separate awards, and the *New York Times* online edition received three finalist awards. Robert Niles, "Newspaper Dot-coms Dominate Online Journalism Award Finalists," *Online Journalism Review*, August 29, 2006.

79. Robert Kuttner, "The Race," *Columbia Journalism Review* (March/April 2007), http://www.cjr.org/issues/2007/2/Kuttner.asp.

80. Jeffrey Blythe, "Last US Newspaper Bureau in Canada Closes," *Press Gazette*, April 11, 2007, http://www.pressgazette.co.uk/article/110407/usa_newspapers_journalism.

81. David S. Hirschman, "*Wash Post* Editor Downie: Everyone in Our Newsroom Wants to Be a Blogger," *Editor & Publisher*, October 6, 2006.

82. Project for Excellence in Journalism, "A Day in the Life of the Media: Blogs," in *The State of the News Media 2006*, http://www.stateofthenewsmedia.com/2006/printable_daymedia_blogs.asp.

83. Center for Democracy and Technology, "The Supreme Court Reaffirms First Amendment Protection of Internet Communications," *CDT Policy Post* 10, no. 10 (June 29, 2004).

Religious Liberty: Still a Beacon

Respect for religious liberty in America today is strong, but only as the result of an arduous struggle that predates the founding of the United States and has persisted for nearly four hundred years. In the course of this struggle, major advances in religious liberty have been tempered by periods in which disfavored religious minorities have been persecuted.

The issue of religious liberty traveled to America with her first settlers, who formed a patchwork of colonial governments that addressed the problem in very different ways. When the colonies broke free from British rule and formed a new nation, this variety of approaches had somehow to be reconciled.

The colonies disagreed on three issues of central importance to religious liberty: the establishment of churches, the freedom to worship and engage in other religious speech, and political participation by religious minorities. These controversies helped to shape the four core protections for religious liberty that were ultimately included in the Constitution of the United States: the Establishment Clause, the Free Exercise Clause, the No Religious Test Clause, and the Free Speech Clause.

All of these constitutional protections continue to provoke debate today. Yet in combination—and as interpreted by the judicial and political branches over the years—they have served

153

America well. For evidence, observers need look no further than the status of Protestant Christianity. Protestantism is often closely linked with American culture and government, and it remains the largest single religious group in the United States. Yet despite the vitality of American Protestantism, no single Protestant denomination (nor even a plurality of them) has risen to prominence in American life or enjoyed state support. On the contrary, the United States is noted for its large number of religious organizations, the religiosity of its citizens, and the relative peace in which these diverse peoples and practices coexist.[1]

Four Constitutional Protections

The Establishment Clause. By the time the Constitution was drafted, the colonies' differences over the establishment of religion were particularly bitter. Some colonies, such as Massachusetts, maintained taxpayer-supported churches and feared a powerful anti-establishment guarantee. Other colonies, such as Virginia, had rejected even a mild form of establishment that would have supported a variety of Christian churches, and were opposed to any state church at all in the new federal government. The Constitution's eventual language was therefore the result of a compromise: it prohibited national establishment, but allowed the state and local governments to retain their separate establishments.

Nonetheless, in an era of growing religious diversity, established churches became increasingly unpopular, and the last remaining state establishment, in Massachusetts, ended in 1833. With established churches gone and no national church to worry about, the federal Establishment Clause remained relatively uncontroversial (and was rarely invoked) until 1947.

In that year, the Supreme Court decided *Everson v. Board of Education* (1947), in which the plaintiffs challenged the provision of public school busing to students attending religious schools as a violation of the federal Establishment Clause. Although the court rejected the challenge to that particular program, it affirmed the broader proposition that the federal Establishment Clause applied to the states through the Fourteenth Amendment. Thus, after *Everson*, the provision that once protected state establishments from federal interference was construed to forbid them.

Everson was also important because it first incorporated into Establishment Clause jurisprudence Thomas Jefferson's metaphor of the "wall of separation between church and State" from his 1802 letter to the Danbury Baptists. *Everson* famously declared that the First Amendment "was intended to erect" such a wall, which the court must keep "high and impregnable," "not approv[ing] the slightest breach." Despite its late introduction into First Amendment jurisprudence, this concept has profoundly shaped the law ever since. It ushered in a new era of federal constitutional challenges to governmental conduct, ranging from aid to religious institutions (especially schools), to cultural expression that includes religion, to the accommodation of religion.

The debate over the scope of the Establishment Clause triggered by *Everson* continues to this day.

The Free Exercise Clause. The freedom to worship—or more broadly, the freedom of religious exercise—provoked somewhat less controversy among the drafters of the Constitution. Like the Establishment Clause, the Free Exercise Clause as originally written did not apply to state and local governments and therefore had relatively little impact on the day-to-day religious practices of most citizens. Moreover, from the beginning, most state constitutions protected freedom of worship, often with the proviso that one's religious practices should not disturb the peace and public order.[2]

Still, the scope of the right was the subject of debate in the first Congress. Congress rejected a proposal by James Madison that contained a broad guarantee for "freedom of conscience" for all citizens, as well as a conscientious-objector provision exempting religious objectors from military service.[3] Conscientious objection had arrived in America with the Quakers, who were at the time a disfavored religious minority. Early Quakers (and members of other so-called peace sects) suffered criminal penalties, corporal punishment, and even the threat of death for their refusal to serve in the militia.[4]

Instead, Congress passed more general language in the First Amendment that protected the "free exercise" of religion and remained silent on the issue of conscientious objectors.[5] The problem of religious conscientious objectors again arose during the Civil War, when the federal government at last exempted conscientious objectors from military service, provided that they performed public service in a hospital or elsewhere. Since that time, whenever a military draft has been in place, Congress has provided a similar exemption.[6]

The degree to which "free exercise" exempts religious activities from generally applicable laws remains the subject of sharp debate today. This results partly from the Supreme Court's decision in 1940 to apply the Free Exercise Clause to the states.

The No Religious Test Clause. The framers of the Constitution also adopted a clause to guarantee that "no religious test shall ever be required as a qualification to any office or public trust under the United States." As with the Constitution's other religious protections, however, the "no religious test" clause of Article VI did not originally apply to the states, many of which limited the right to hold political office, to become an officer of the court, or even to vote to favored religious majorities, such as monotheists, Christians, or Protestant Christians. Many colonies also excluded Quakers from political participation on the grounds that they would not take oaths.

While states gradually became more permissive with regard to religious tests over the years, state-level religious requirements for public office were not abolished entirely until 1961, when the Supreme Court in *Torcaso v. Watkins* (1961) invalidated Maryland's requirement that all public officeholders declare belief in the existence of God (see section on religious minorities below).

The Free Speech Clause. Although these three clauses represent the constitutional provisions that explicitly protect religious freedom, they are probably not the most frequently invoked protections. Because so much religious activity entails speech or communication, and because of the Supreme Court's reluctance to apply the Free Exercise Clause vigorously in recent years, the Free Speech Clause of the First Amendment has played an especially prominent role in the constitutional protection of religious freedom.[7] The Supreme Court has rebuffed repeated attempts to exclude religious speech from the protection of the Free Speech Clause, citing the nation's early history of suppressing unpopular religious views.[8]

Core Understandings

What precisely have these protections amounted to, as interpreted by the courts and by Congress? Over the years, several core understandings of the constitutional protection of religion have emerged.

No Religious Coercion. The Supreme Court has interpreted the Free Speech Clause to prohibit American governments from coercion in religious speech. They may not compel citizens to engage in religious speech or compel any speech that would violate religious conscience.[9] Nor may the government exclude speech from a governmental forum simply because it reflects a religious viewpoint.[10] Finally, under the Free Speech Clause, religious organizations enjoy at least the same right as secular "expressive associations" to choose people for leadership and membership in their group based on whether those people share the views the group exists to express.[11]

The Supreme Court has also construed the Establishment Clause to bar the government from coercing citizens to participate in religious services, adopting a very broad conception of what it means to "coerce" participation.[12] The Establishment Clause has also been understood to forbid forced tithing, particularly for the funding of seminaries, which has been a controversial practice of governments with established churches.[13] More broadly, the court has acknowledged the principle that citizens should not be forced through taxation to provide direct financial support to religious instruction or worship with which they may disagree.[14] This represents a narrow exception to the general rule that citizens may *not* sue the government based on objections to its use of their tax money.[15] The court has ruled, however, that the government must not go so far as to exclude religious people or institutions from government benefits simply because of their religious status or beliefs, lest it engage in religious discrimination.[16]

On the other hand, the Establishment Clause does not prevent the government from funding the secular activities of religious people or institutions.[17] Nor does the Establishment Clause forbid the government from providing funds or services that may benefit or support religious instruction or worship incidentally or indirectly.[18] Accordingly, the Supreme Court has repeatedly allowed government-funded educational benefits to be used to advance religious education, so long as the benefits are offered to the religious and nonreligious alike, and the decision to use the benefits for religious purposes is the individual's, not the government's.[19]

No Governmental Religious Indoctrination. This prohibition is based on the principle against compelling taxpayers to support religious instruction, as discussed above, as well as two related principles: that government is theologically incompetent,[20] and that government should not take sides in religious controversies or otherwise insert itself into religious affairs.[21] In practice, these principles have been taken to prohibit school-sponsored religious instruction or worship in public schools,[22] and the direct public funding of religious instruction or worship in religious schools.[23]

Importantly, the prohibition of government indoctrination does *not* forbid the government from providing instruction in public schools *about* the Bible, Christianity, or other religions from a secular and nondevotional perspective.[24] Although the Supreme Court made clear almost 50 years ago—at the same time it struck down government-sponsored devotional studies—that the government may fund and provide education *about* religion, public schools have not offered such instruction widely, and court cases have been few. But in recent years, various groups have offered Bible curricula designed to comply with constitutional requirements for use in public schools, so litigation on whether the curricula succeed in meeting those standards is likely to follow.

No Government Endorsement of Religion. More recently and controversially, the Supreme Court has interpreted the Establishment Clause to forbid the government from "endorsing" religion. This prohibition has emerged over the last 20 years or so, mainly at the initiative of Justice Sandra Day O'Connor and mainly in the context of government-sponsored religious expression on public property, such as Christmas and Hanukkah displays and monuments representing the Ten Commandments.[25] Under the endorsement doctrine, courts will inquire whether a hypothetical "reasonable observer," who is familiar with the full history and context of the religious expression at issue, would deem the government to have endorsed one, some, or all religions. This test has been criticized for relying too heavily on the idiosyncratic judgments of individual justices, and for the corresponding inconsistent results and lack of predictability, which, in turn, provide fertile ground for litigation.

The Supreme Court has specified that the government is not prohibited from expression that *reflects* or *acknowledges* the religiosity of the American people. The Constitution does not require the government to adopt an attitude of "callous indifference" to the faiths of its people, or to feign ignorance of them.[26] The Establishment Clause also does not forbid the government from expressing or engaging in a minimalist "civil religion," which is marked by references to a generic "God" or "Creator," usually as the source and guarantor of the inalienable rights of citizens.[27] Although these general principles are well settled, particular controversies continue to rage over how the principles should be applied, most notably in the recent (and ongoing) constitutional challenge to the presence of the two words "under God" in the Pledge of Allegiance.[28]

No Interference in Church Affairs. Since at least its 1872 decision in *Watson v. Jones*, the Supreme Court has held that civil courts lack the competence or jurisdiction to decide matters of theology, church discipline, ecclesiastical government, or the standards applied to church members.[29] This principle is most often applied to employment-discrimination disputes, in which civil plaintiffs ask the state to gainsay the decisions of religious organizations to hire, fire, promote, or demote ministers and others who formulate or transmit religious doctrine. In this context, the doctrine is commonly called the "ministerial exception" to whatever employment law is applied.[30] More broadly, though, it is called the "church autonomy doctrine," and it protects a wide range of ecclesial decisions from government interference, including decisions regarding the allocation of church property.[31]

This doctrine has recently been invoked—and its limits have been disputed—in cases where ministers have been charged with sexual abuse and their churches have been accused of failing to oversee and manage those ministers and to report allegations of abuse. Importantly, the church autonomy doctrine only *limits* liability or damages for certain tort claims against religious *organizations*, when they are sued on theories of *vicarious* liability for the acts of their ministers. The doctrine does not offer protection against all (or even most) such claims.[32] And, of course, the doctrine does not apply to the abusive ministers themselves, and so does not insulate them from any liability, civil or criminal. Nevertheless, since the sexual abuse scandal in the Roman Catholic Church in 2002, courts have applied these religious freedom principles less consistently, weakening them more broadly.

No Governmental Religious Discrimination. The Religion Clauses forbid governments at all levels from targeting religious people or conduct for special disfavor, whether expressly or covertly. In the jargon of Free Exercise Clause jurisprudence, this is described as the requirement that laws be "neutral" and "generally applicable" with respect to religion. The Establishment Clause provides a similar, if less frequently applied, prohibition against government hostility to religion generally or to specific denominations. More concretely, this means that laws may not discriminate on their face with respect to religion; laws that are facially neutral may not be selectively applied against the religious; the government cannot prohibit conduct because of its religious motivation; and people or groups cannot be denied the protection of the law—or be excluded from participation in government functions or from access to government benefits—based on their religious status or views.[33]

No Substantial Burdens on Religious Exercise. The Free Exercise Clause also prohibits the government from imposing nondiscriminatory, incidental burdens on religious exercise, but this prohibition only applies under certain circumstances. The burden must be "substantial" rather than a mere inconvenience, and must be applied in one of two types of cases. In the first, the system for imposing burdens is highly discretionary or exception ridden, which courts call a "system of individualized assessments." Although the precise meaning of this term is hotly contested, the classic "systems of individualized assessments" are zoning-permit decisions, in which burdens are imposed on religious gatherings based on vague criteria such as whether the gatherings are "consistent with the general plan" or "consistent with neighborhood character." The second type of situation in which "substantial burdens" are forbidden is one where additional fundamental rights—such as freedom of speech, of assembly, or to direct the religious upbringing of children—are implicated.[34] Courts describe these situations as involving "hybrid rights," and once again, the scope of this doctrine is unclear and frequently litigated in the lower courts.

Religious Minorities

Given these many protections, it is not surprising that religion in the United States today is highly diverse, and that members of religious minorities enjoy a degree of freedom and equality with members of mainstream religions that is remarkable by world standards. But these protections evolved over many years, the result of a long and difficult legal and cultural struggle. As late as 1870, for example, Jews and other religious minorities could not vote or hold political office in all states. Accommodations for Orthodox and Hasidic Jews remain controversial to this day.[35] The persecution of Mormons in the nineteenth century entailed not only human but judicial atrocities.[36] The experience of Native Americans has been similar in that respect.[37]

Catholics were singled out for special disfavor in the mid to late nineteenth century, when waves of largely Catholic immigrants prompted political backlash and strong nativist sentiment. The anti-Catholic "Know-Nothing" party briefly gained prominence in the 1850s in Massachusetts. While the party is today little more than a historical footnote, its activities had a lasting impact on the shape of American law more broadly. In that era, Massachusetts amended its state constitution to prohibit government aid to "sectarian" schools and other institutions. The amendment was designed to deny government aid to Catholic schools, while permitting it to continue to flow to the "common schools," which taught the "common religion" of "nonsectarian" Protestantism. Similar amendments that were subsequently passed in other states came to be called "Blaine Amendments," named after the congressman who tried and failed to enact one at the federal level.[38] These amendments remain the law in more than 30 states, and have been invoked in the present day to block school-choice programs that would allow students and their parents to direct public money to "sectarian" schools and, less frequently, to prevent government from contracting with faith-based social service providers to help the needy.

By the late nineteenth century, barriers to political participation by Jews and Catholics were removed (except for required religious oaths, which were invalidated in 1961 as previously noted). In the middle of the twentieth century, the Supreme Court began to construe the Free Exercise and Free Speech Clauses as protecting unpopular religious and political viewpoints. This significantly improved the status of religious minorities. The Jehovah's Witnesses, a relatively new and decidedly unpopular group, won a series of legal victories from the 1930s through the 1960s, establishing strong free speech and free exercise precedent in the process. Most notable is their victory in *West Virginia State Bd. of Educ. v. Barnette* (1943), in which the Supreme Court struck down mandatory recitation of the Pledge of Allegiance in public schools. While this victory did not immediately end the social and political ostracism of Jehovah's Witnesses, it did reinforce the broader ideal of religious freedom that serves that religious minority and so many others.

The Free Exercise Clause has been foundational to the protection of religious minorities. The Supreme Court's decision in *Church of the Lukumi Babalu Aye v. City of Hialeah* (1993) is an excellent, relatively recent example of this principle at work. There, the court struck down a series of local ordinances that did not mention religion or a particular religious sect on their face, but which nonetheless targeted a small and unpopular religious group, Santeria worshippers. The ordinances were written so that they prohibited animal sacrifice in religious rituals, a feature of Santeria worship, while allowing the killing of animals for various other purposes, such as for food, hunting, and pest control.

Religious Freedom Today: Two Conflicts

In recent years, two controversies have emerged that deal with the foundation of the American tradition of religious liberty, and how they are resolved by the Supreme Court will have a profound impact on the character of American government and society for years to come. One relates to the fundamental scope of the Free Exercise Clause: how much religious accommodation may (or must) the government provide, and is it up to the courts, the political branches, or both to decide? The other is the growing conflict between the freedom of religious groups to define their membership and message without government interference, and antidiscrimination statutes that would punish religious groups for making decisions on religious or, increasingly, moral criteria.

The Scope of Protection for Religious Exercise. What happens when a law that does not target religion for special disfavor still imposes a heavy burden on religious exercise? For example, if a county generally prohibits the use of alcohol, could Jews or Catholics be prosecuted for using wine in a seder or mass? If they were prosecuted, could they obtain an exception to the general law in court under the Free Exercise Clause, or would their only recourse be to suffer the penalty this time, and to attempt to revoke or obtain an exception to the rule through the political process? And if they succeeded in obtaining an exception from the legislature or executive, would that represent special favor to religion in violation of the Establishment Clause?

These questions are central to the current debate over religious liberty in the United States today, but they began to emerge in 1963, when the Supreme Court decided *Sherbert v. Verner*. In that case, the court set forth a general test under the Free Exercise Clause such that *anytime* a law imposed a "substantial burden" on religious exercise, courts should apply "strict scrutiny" to that burden. That is, courts should strike down the law as unconstitutional unless the government could prove that the burden represented the means "least restrictive" of religious exercise to serve a "compelling governmental interest." In 1990, in *Employment Division v. Smith*, the court revisited *Sherbert* and narrowed the scope of application of its "substantial burden" test to the two situations discussed above (i.e., where the burdens are imposed through "systems of individualized assessments," or in "hybrid situations" implicating additional fundamental rights).

Outraged by *Smith*'s limitation of *Sherbert*, Congress responded by passing the Religious Freedom Restoration Act of 1993 (RFRA), which was designed to restore application of *Sherbert*'s strict scrutiny to *every* "substantial burden" on religious exercise, not just those involving "individualized assessments" or "hybrid" rights. Several states followed the federal government's lead, passing laws that mirrored RFRA.[39] Some states also interpreted their constitutions so that their free exercise protections maintained the stricter *Sherbert* standard, providing broader protection than the federal First Amendment after *Smith*, and eliminating the need for any state-level RFRA.[40]

Yet the legal battle continued. In 1997, in *City of Boerne v. Flores*, the Supreme Court struck down RFRA as applied to state and local governments, on the theory that it exceeded the federal government's power under the Fourteenth Amendment to enforce civil rights protections. The court faulted RFRA for two main reasons. First, it was too broad in application, covering every area of law rather than targeting certain problem areas. Second, RFRA was unsupported by any legislative record that might indicate a need for heightened protection of religious exercise. (Importantly, the rationale of *Boerne* did not prevent RFRA from being applied to the *federal* government, and in 2006 the Supreme Court applied RFRA with force to block a federal drug prosecution in *Gonzales v. O Centro Espirita Beneficente União do Vegetal.*)

Congress went back to the drawing board with these principles in mind, and the result was the Religious Land Use and Institutionalized Persons Act of 2000 (RLUIPA). The statute was narrower in scope—covering only zoning and prison regulations that burdened religious exercise—and was supported by a substantial legislative record indicating that religious discrimination and excessive burdens on religious exercise were widespread in those areas of law.

RLUIPA elicited a series of constitutional challenges, none of which have succeeded to date. In 2005, in a unanimous decision written by Justice Ruth Bader Ginsburg, the Supreme Court in *Cutter v. Wilkinson* resoundingly rejected an Establishment Clause challenge to the prison provisions of RLUIPA. The theory of the challenge was that laws specially deregulating religion and religion alone represent an impermissible benefit to religion. But as the court explained, if this understanding of the Establishment Clause prevailed, "all manner of religious accommodations would fall." And as Justice William O. Douglas wrote in *Zorach v. Clauson* (1952), not only are such accommodations permissible, but the government in providing them "follows the best of our traditions," because it "respects the religious nature of our people and accommodates the public service to their spiritual needs."

The ability of citizens to secure religious accommodations through the political branches thus remains secure, and continues to serve as an indispensable bulwark of religious freedom in the United States. But this is not a complete solution to the problem. Due to the nature of the political process, only those religious accommodations that earn the support of a majority will be enacted by the political branches. So in practice, the substantial withdrawal of the judiciary from the business of religious accommodation operates to the disadvantage of religious minorities, i.e., those who are both more likely to have idiosyncratic needs and less likely to have the political muscle necessary to secure a legislative or executive accommodation.

Moreover, the minorities that suffer for lack of judicial intervention are not only national minorities, but local ones. Of course, religious groups that are minorities both nationally and locally are worst off under *Smith*. But religious groups that are well-represented nationally routinely find themselves unable to secure political exceptions to religiously burdensome state or local laws because they are politically weak in those particular places. In this way, *Smith* hurts religious minorities all of the time and larger groups some of the time.

The Supreme Court's decision in *Smith* remains among its most controversial, and ongoing litigation under RLUIPA and RFRA may well provide the court with an occasion to reconsider that decision and, along with it, the scope of protection afforded under the Free Exercise Clause.

Church Autonomy or Antidiscrimination? As described above, the Constitution prohibits government from engaging in religious discrimination, and statutes may reinforce that protection by providing an additional measure of accommodation and deregulation. But statutes perform another important religious-freedom function in American law. Federal, state, and local governments have established a broad network of statutory prohibitions against religious discrimination by *private* actors in a wide range of economic activities—most notably employment, but also housing, public accommodations, education, and many others. These laws were passed principally to combat racial discrimination, but they almost always prohibit discrimination based on religion as well. Foremost among these statutes is Title VII of the Civil Rights Act of 1964, the federal protection against discrimination in employment.

These laws provide an important protection for the religious liberty of *individuals*, in that they prevent people from having to choose between observing their faith and making a living, finding housing, or having access to various goods and services in the marketplace. But the laws pose a risk to religious *organizations* by interfering with their ability to choose their members and leaders based on religion. So, for example, a synagogue must be able to consider religion in its decision to hire or fire its rabbi. In order to respect this important right, Title VII (like most of its state-level analogs) exempts religious organizations from the otherwise applicable prohibition on religious discrimination.[41]

Recently, this tension between antidiscrimination statutes and the right of religious organizations to choose members and leaders based on religion has come to the fore in two controversial areas: the faith-based initiative and gay rights.

First, when the government purchases social services from a religious organization, some have argued that the organization waives its right to hire based on religion, on the theory that government should not fund "discrimination." Others argue that the "discrimination" government would fund in this context is not pernicious, but constitutionally protected activity that is indispensable for any religious organization (or, indeed, any expressive association) to maintain its message and mission over time.

Second, religious groups that teach that homosexual conduct is immoral—and correspondingly hire and fire employees based on their agreement with that teaching—will likely find themselves at odds with the growing number of laws prohibiting discrimination based on sexual orientation. Additionally, in jurisdictions where same-sex marriage is legal, religious groups whose convictions prevent them from treating legally married same-sex couples exactly like legally married different-sex couples will face an additional layer of conflict.

In both contexts, the disputes are only beginning to percolate through the courts, and it remains unclear how they will ultimately be resolved.

Comparisons to Other Democracies

The great number and vitality of American religious organizations and the religiosity of the American people are all unusual among industrialized Western nations. America is highly religious even compared to Western European nations, such as the United Kingdom and Norway, that have maintained state churches for generations; these churches, either despite or because of their governmental support, have only weakened over time.[42]

But it is not simply the absence of an established church that appears to have served religious Americans so well. The American system has eschewed the extreme church-state separation of some of its European counterparts, in part because its simultaneous commitments to free speech and free exercise require toleration of even unpopular religious speech in the public square. The *laïcité* laws in France, for example, prohibit even private religious expression on government property, such as the wearing of religious garb (*hijab*, turbans, and prominent crosses) by students in public schools.

In short, the twin policies of non-establishment and the special deregulation of religion have helped not only religious Americans and their institutions to flourish, but American government and society more broadly as well.

Endnotes

1. See, e.g., Edward A. Tiryakian, "American Religious Exceptionalism: A Reconsideration," *Annals of the American Academy of Political and Social Science* 527 (May 1993): 40, 43–45 (describing this "exceptionalism" and collecting sources).

2. See, e.g., Md. Const. Art. XXXIII (1776); Va. Const. § 16 (1776); N.J. Const. Art. XIX (1776); N.Y. Const. Art. XXVIII (1777).

3. John Witte, *Religion and the American Constitutional Experiment*, 2nd ed. (Boulder: Westview Press, 2005), 80–89.

4. At the time, the United States had no standing army, so all able-bodied men were expected to serve in their local militia. Militias could be called up in a time of war to create a national army. See Kevin Seamus Hasson, *The Right to Be Wrong* (San Francisco: Encounter Books, 2005), 49–52 (discussing history of conscientious objection in the colonies).

5. The degree to which conduct (as opposed to pure belief) is protected has varied over time. See, e.g., *Reynolds v. United States*, 98 U.S. 145, 166 (1878) ("Laws are made for the government of actions, and while they cannot interfere with mere religious belief and opinions, they may with practices.")

6. In the 1960s, the Supreme Court enlarged conscientious objection (CO) status to cover nonreligious objectors who demonstrated a deeply held moral view that all war is wrong. The court refused to extend CO status to those who opposed only a particular war, or opposed the war on political or pragmatic grounds.

7. *Murdock v. Pennsylvania*, 319 U.S. 105, 108–09 (1943) (listing "hand distribution of religious tracts," "worship in the churches and preaching from the pulpits" as religious activities enjoying Free Speech and Free Exercise protections).

8. *Capitol Square Rev. Bd. v. Pinette*, 515 U.S. 753, 760 (1995) (declining to exclude religious speech from free speech protections, noting that "in Anglo-American history, at least, government suppression of speech has so commonly been directed *precisely* at religious speech that a free-speech clause without religion would be Hamlet without the prince").

9. See, e.g., *West Virginia State Bd. of Educ. v. Barnette*, 319 U.S. 624 (1943) (striking down mandatory Pledge of Allegiance).
10. *Good News Club v. Milford Central Sch.*, 533 U.S. 98 (2001) (applying Free Speech Clause to strike down public school's exclusion of Christian group from school facilities based on religious viewpoint); *Rosenberger v. Rector and Visitors of Univ. of Va.*, 515 U.S. 819 (1995) (applying Free Speech Clause to strike down state university's exclusion of Christian group from participation in student activity fees based on religious viewpoint); *Lamb's Chapel v. Center Moriches Union Free Sch. Dist.*, 508 U.S. 384 (1993) (applying Free Speech Clause to strike down public school's exclusion of Christian group from school facilities based on religious viewpoint); *Widmar v. Vincent*, 454 U.S. 263 (1981) (applying Free Speech Clause to strike down state university's exclusion of Christian group from school facilities based on religious viewpoint).
11. *Boy Scouts v. Dale*, 530 U.S. 640 (2001) (applying Free Speech Clause to protect the right of the Boy Scouts to exclude from leadership those who disagree with the Scouts' views on sexual morality).
12. See, e.g., *Lee v. Weisman*, 505 U.S. 577 (1992) (striking down nondenominational prayer at public high school graduation as "coercive," where participation in ceremony was voluntary and where students were not required to listen to or recite prayer, but only to be silent).
13. See *Locke v. Davey*, 540 U.S. 712, 722 (2004) ("Since the founding of our country, there have been popular uprisings against procuring taxpayer funds to support church leaders, which was one of the hallmarks of an 'established' religion.")
14. See *Doremus v. Board of Education*, 342 U.S. 429 (1952); *Flast v. Cohen*, 392 U.S. 83 (1968); *Valley Forge Christian College v. Americans United for the Separation of Church and State*, 454 U.S. 464 (1982).
15. See, e.g., *DaimlerChrysler Corp. v. Cuno*, 126 S. Ct. 1854, 1865 (2006) (reaffirming general rule against taxpayer standing). The scope of the *Flast* exception to the general rule against taxpayer standing is, at the time of this writing, pending before

the Supreme Court: *Hein v. Freedom from Religion Foundation*, No. 06-157, *cert. granted*, 127 S. Ct. 722 (December 1, 2006).

16. *McDaniel v. Paty*, 435 U.S. 618 (1978) (applying Free Exercise Clause to strike down state constitution's exclusion of ministers from participation as delegates in state constitutional convention); *Rosenberger v. Rector and Visitors of the Univ. of Va.*, 515 U.S. 819 (1995) (applying Free Speech Clause to strike down state university's exclusion of Christian group from participation in student activity fees based on religious viewpoint).

17. See *Tilton v. Richardson*, 403 U.S. 672 (1971) (rejecting claim that Establishment Clause prohibits government funding of buildings used for teaching secular subjects at a religious university).

18. See *Zelman v. Simmons-Harris*, 536 U.S. 639 (2002) (distinguishing direct and indirect government funding of activities by religious institutions, and allowing indirect aid to fund even religious instruction consistent with Establishment Clause); *Everson v. Board of Education*, 330 U.S. 1, 17–18 (1947) ("Similarly, parents might be reluctant to permit their children to attend schools which the state had cut off from such general government services as ordinary police and fire protection, connections for sewage disposal, public highways and sidewalks. Of course, cutting off church schools from these services, so separate and so indisputably marked off from the religious function, would make it far more difficult for the schools to operate. But such is obviously not the purpose of the First Amendment.")

19. See *Witters v. Washington Dept. of Services for the Blind*, 474 U.S. 481 (1986) (allowing vocational assistance for the blind); *Zobrest v. Catalina Foothills Sch. Dist.*, 509 U.S. 1 (1993) (allowing sign-language interpreter); *Zelman v. Simmons-Harris*, 536 U.S. 639 (2002) (allowing tuition vouchers).

20. See, e.g., *Watson v. Jones*, 80 U.S. 679, 728 (1871) ("The law knows no heresy, and is committed to the support of no dogma, the establishment of no sect."); *West Virginia State Bd. of Education v. Barnette*, 319 U.S. 624, 642 (1943) ("If there is any fixed star in our constitutional constellation, it is that no official, high or petty, can prescribe what shall be orthodox in politics,

nationalism, religion, or other matters of opinion or force citizens to confess by word or act their faith therein.")

21. See, e.g., *Thomas v. Review Board*, 450 U.S. 707, 717 (1981) ("Courts are not arbiters of scriptural interpretation.") See also *Kedroff v. St. Nicholas Cathedral*, 344 U.S. 94 (1952). (First Amendment assures "a spirit of freedom for religious organizations, an independence from secular control or manipulation, in short, power to decide for themselves, free from state interference, matters of church government as well as those of faith and doctrine.")

22. See, e.g., *Edwards v. Aguillard*, 482 U.S. 578 (1987) (striking down law requiring "balanced treatment" of evolution and creationism in public schools); *Epperson v. Arkansas*, 393 U.S. 97 (1968) (striking down law prohibiting teaching of evolution in public schools and universities); *School Dist. of Abington v. Schempp*, 374 U.S. 203 (1963) (striking down daily Bible reading and recitation of Lord's Prayer in public schools); *Engel v. Vitale*, 370 U.S. 421 (1962) (striking down teacher-led recitation of "Regents' prayer" in public school).

23. See, e.g., *Committee for Public Education v. Nyquist*, 413 U.S. 756 (1973) (applying Establishment Clause to strike down various forms of direct state aid to parochial schools).

24. See *Abington Twp. School Dist. v. Schempp*, 374 U.S. 203, 225 (1963) ("It might well be said that one's education is not complete without a study of comparative religion or the history of religion and its relationship to the advancement of civilization. It certainly may be said that the Bible is worthy of study for its literary and historic qualities. Nothing we have said here indicates that such study of the Bible or of religion, when presented objectively as part of a secular program of education, may not be effected consistently with the First Amendment."); *Stone v. Graham*, 449 U.S. 39, 42 (1980) (noting that "the Bible may constitutionally be used in an appropriate study of history, civilization, ethics, comparative religion, or the like").

25. See, e.g., *Van Orden v. Perry*, 544 U.S. 677 (2005) (upholding Ten Commandments display); *McCreary County v. ACLU of Ky.*, 545 U.S. 844 (2005) (striking down Ten Command-

ments display); *Allegheny County v. ACLU of Pittsburgh*, 492 U.S. 573 (1989) (upholding holiday display consisting of crèche and menorah, but striking down crèche-only display); *Lynch v. Donnelly*, 465 U.S. 668 (1984) (upholding display consisting of crèche and secular elements).

26. *Lynch v. Donnelly*, 465 U.S. 668, 673 (1984) (quoting *Zorach v. Clauson*, 343 U.S. 306, 314 [1952]).

27. See *Marsh v. Chambers*, 463 U.S. 783 (1983) (rejecting Establishment Clause challenge to legislative prayer because it represents permissible "civil religion"). See also Declaration of Independence, preamble (the people are "endowed by their Creator with certain unalienable rights," which governments are instituted to secure).

28. See *Elk Grove Unified Sch. Dist. v. Newdow*, 542 U.S. 1 (2004) (rejecting for lack of standing Establishment Clause challenge to "under God" in Pledge of Allegiance); *Newdow v. Congress of the United States*, 383 F. Supp. 2d 1229 (E.D. Cal. 2005) (accepting Establishment Clause challenge to "under God" in Pledge of Allegiance), *on appeal sub nom.*, *Newdow v. Carey*, Nos. 05-17257, 05-17344, 06-15093 (9th Cir.).

29. *Watson v. Jones*, 13 Wall. 679, 733 (1872).

30. Two recent appellate court decisions applying the ministerial exception, *Petruska v. Gannon University*, 462 F.3d 294 (3d Cir. 2006), and *Tomic v. Catholic Diocese of Peoria*, 442 F.3d 1036 (7th Cir. 2006) (Posner, J.), provide excellent explanations of the exception and the legal principles underlying it.

31. *Kedroff v. St. Nicholas Cathedral*, 344 U.S. 94 (1952) ("church autonomy doctrine" "a spirit of freedom for religious organizations, an independence from secular control or manipulation, in short, power to decide for themselves, free from state interference, matters of church government as well as those of faith and doctrine"). See also *Jones v. Wolf*, 443 U.S. 595, 608 (1979) (court proceedings "involv[ing] considerations of religious doctrine *and polity*" unacceptable).

32. See, e.g., Mark E. Chopko, "Stating Claims Against Religious Institutions," *Boston College Law Review* 44 (2003): 1089.

33. See, e.g., *McDaniel v. Paty*, 435 U.S. 618 (1978) (striking down prohibition on clergy participation in state constitutional convention); *Torcaso v. Watkins*, 367 U.S. 488 (1961) (striking down requirement of religious oath to hold public office).

34. See *Employment Div. v. Smith*, 494 U.S. 872, 881, 884–85 (1990).

35. See *Kiryas Joel v. Grumet*, 512 U.S. 687 (1994) (applying Establishment Clause to strike down public school district designed to accommodate Orthodox Jewish religious requirements); *Tenafly Eruv Ass'n, Inc. v. Borough of Tenafly*, 309 F.3d 144 (3d Cir. 2002) (applying Free Exercise Clause to strike down local government denial of permission to erect *eruv*, or ceremonial barrier to facilitate Orthodox Jewish observance of the Sabbath); *Grosz v. City of Miami Beach*, 82 F.3d 1005 (11th Cir. 1996) (rejecting Free Exercise Clause challenge to denial of permission to gather for Orthodox Jewish worship).

36. See, e.g., *Late Corporation of the Church of Jesus Christ of Latter-Day Saints v. United States*, 136 U.S. 1 (1890) (upholding federal statute dissolving charter of Mormon church and seizing its property).

37. See, e.g., *Lyng v. Northwest Indian Cemetery Protective Ass'n*, 485 U.S. 439 (1988) (upholding federal administrative decision to build paved road through land sacred to Native Americans).

38. The Blaine Amendments are named after Representative James G. Blaine, who as Speaker of the House of Representatives attempted to pass a constitutional amendment banning public aid to sectarian institutions. The amendment failed at the national level, but similar amendments passed in many states.

39. Those 13 states are Alabama, see Ala. Const. amend. 622; Arizona, see Ariz. Rev. Stat. Ann. §§ 41-1493 et seq. (West 2003); Connecticut, see Conn. Gen. Stat. Ann. § 52-571b (West 2003); Florida, see Fla. Stat. Ann. §§ 761.01-761.04 (West 2003); Idaho, see Idaho Code §§ 73-401 et seq. (Supp. 2002); Illinois, see 775 Ill. Comp. Stat. Ann. §§ 35/1-35/99 (West 2002); Missouri, see V.A.M.S. §§ 1.302 & 1.307 (West 2004); New Mexico, see N.M. Stat. Ann. §§ 28-22-1 to 28-22-5 (Michie 2002); Oklahoma, see Okla. Stat. Ann. tit. 51, § 251 (West

2003); Pennsylvania, 71 Pa. Cons. Stat. Ann. 2401 et seq.; Rhode Island, see R.I. Gen. Laws §§ 42-80.1-1 to 42-80.1-4 (2001); South Carolina, see S.C. Stat. Ann. § 1-32-10 (Law. Co-op. 1999); and Texas, see Tex. Civ. Prac. & Rem. Code Ann. §§ 110.001 et seq. (West 2003).

40. See, e.g., *Humphrey v. Lane*, 728 N.E.2d 1039 (Ohio 2000); *In re Browning*, 476 S.E.2d 465 (N.C. 1996); *State v. Miller*, 549 N.W.2d 235 (Wis. 1996); *Attorney Gen. v. Desilets*, 636 N.E.2d 233 (Mass. 1994); *Swanner v. Anchorage Equal Rights Comm'n*, 874 P.2d 274 (Alaska 1994); *Rourke v. N.Y. State Dep't of Corr. Servs.*, 603 N.Y.S.2d 647 (N.Y. Sup. Ct. 1993), aff'd, 615 N.Y.S.2d 470 (N.Y. App. Div. 1994); *Rupert v. City of Portland*, 605 A.2d 63 (Me. 1992); *St. John's Lutheran Church v. State Comp. Ins. Fund*, 830 P.2d 1271 (Mont. 1992); *First Covenant Church of Seattle v. City of Seattle*, 840 P.2d 174 (Wash. 1992); *State v. Evans*, 796 P.2d 178 (Kan. 1990); *State v. Hershberger*, 462 N.W.2d 393 (Minn. 1990).

41. This exemption was challenged under the Establishment Clause, on the theory that it provided a benefit to religious employers without simultaneously benefiting secular ones. The Supreme Court rejected that theory in *Corporation of the Presiding Bishop v. Amos*, 483 U.S. 327 (1987).

42. See, e.g., Frank Bruni, "Faith Fades Where It Once Burned Strong," *New York Times*, October 13, 2003 (discussing decline of religious affiliation, particularly among established churches, in Western Europe).

Academic Freedom: Withstanding Pressures From Left and Right

cademic freedom as we know it today originated in Germany. It dates to the founding of the world's first research university, the University of Berlin, in 1810. Previous universities had regarded truth as something already known and needing only to be transmitted to younger generations. The University of Berlin, however, was dedicated to the idea that truth must be sought, studied, and revised, free from political and religious authority.

In 1850 *Lehrfreiheit*, or the right of university faculty to teach on any subject, was enshrined in the Prussian constitution.[1] And in 1876, the German model was transplanted to the United States with the founding of Johns Hopkins University.

Hopkins was the first American institution of higher learning to be organized around scholarly research, the pursuit of new knowledge, and the training of future scholars and researchers through graduate studies.[2] Previous American colleges and universities, beginning with Harvard College in 1636, had been based on the British model. They were founded and managed primarily by Protestant denominations (Congregational, Episcopal, and Presbyterian) with the expectation that they would transmit established knowledge to students preparing for vocations such as teaching, the clergy, and law.

However, after the founding of Hopkins, the research-university model proliferated in the United States, taking root and supplanting its predecessors. Established institutions began to sever ties with religious authorities. In the 1890s previously undergraduate institutions such as Harvard and the University of California organized associated graduate schools. Wealthy businessmen and state governments began to replace the churches as underwriters of higher education. Stanford University and the University of Chicago were founded as full-fledged research universities. Between 1890 and 1910, the number of college and university teachers in the United States increased by 90 percent,[3] and student enrollment rose from 50,000 to 350,000.[4]

But professors were not simply more numerous following the establishment of the research university. They also performed a different function. Once viewed primarily as teachers and mentors of the country's elite young men and women, they were now considered independent scholars and were expected to create or discover new knowledge. As a result, professors began to group themselves into specialized "disciplines" within their own universities and colleges and to form academic associations with scholars from other institutions. In 1884 the American Historical Association was established, followed soon after by the American Economic Association (1885), the American Physical Foundation (1899), the American Political Science Association (1903), and the American Sociological Association (1905).[5]

These associations enabled academics to collaborate in their scholarly endeavors and devise mutual rules for study, research, and publication. As the status of professors came to depend more and more on their published research, many associations created academic journals in which their disciplines' preeminent works were published. Once considered mere employees of universities and colleges, by the early 1900s professors saw themselves as "professional scholars who were answerable to the professional judgment of their peers."[6]

Rights

Academic freedom in America today is centered on the rights of three interested parties: professors, students, and the institutions themselves. The modern understanding of these rights can be traced to the founding of the American Association of University Professors (AAUP).

The Rights of Professors. The AAUP was founded in 1915 by philosophers Arthur O. Lovejoy and John Dewey. The founding was a somewhat belated reaction to the controversial 1900 firing of Stanford economist Edward Ross for advocating ideas on monetary policy and trade with which Mrs. Leland Stanford— the university's then owner—disagreed.[7] The AAUP's 1915 General Report of the Committee on Academic Freedom and Academic Tenure was the first official American statement on the professoriate's right to academic freedom. At its core were the ideas of professorial self-regulation and independence from traditional employer-employee relations:

> For once appointed, the scholar has professional functions to perform in which the appointing authorities have neither the competency nor moral right to intervene. The responsibility of the University teacher is primarily to the public itself and to the judgment of his own profession.[8]

The statement also identified three main components of professorial academic freedom: freedom of inquiry and research, freedom to teach in the university or college, and freedom of extramural utterance and action.

In 1940 the AAUP joined with the Association of American Colleges to issue a Statement of Principles on Academic Freedom and Tenure. The 1940 statement mirrors the 1915 statement but provides greater detail on the freedom to which "teachers are entitled":

a. Teachers are entitled to full freedom in research and... publication, subject to the adequate performance of other academic duties....

b. Teachers are entitled to freedom in the classroom in discussing their subject, but they should be careful not to introduce...controversial matter which has no relation to their subject....

c. [While speaking as citizens, teachers] should be free from institutional censorship or discipline, but their special position...imposes special obligations.... Hence they should at all times be accurate, should exercise appropriate restraint, should show respect for the opinions of others, and should... indicate that they are not speaking for the institution.[9]

The statement also establishes the association's position on tenure, which it describes as a way of attaining "freedom and economic security" and which it calls "indispensable to the success of an institution in fulfilling its obligations to its students and to society."

Although the 1940 statement permitted "church-related institutions" to "[depart] from the principles of academic freedom," interpretive comments added in 1970 revoked this permission. The 1970 comments also noted that "a faculty member's expression of opinion as a citizen cannot constitute grounds for dismissal unless it clearly demonstrates...unfitness for his or her position."[10]

Although the statement has no legal power, it is today considered to define academic freedom in the United States. All major colleges and universities have adopted it or a variant of it, and implementation is monitored by the AAUP. Guided by this statement—and influenced by the nation's legal, political, and social traditions of individualism—academic freedom in the United States is understood to mean the freedom of the individual professor vis-à-vis institutional, governmental, and religious authorities.

The Rights of Students. The AAUP acknowledged in its 1915 statement that "academic freedom has traditionally had two applications—to the freedom of the teacher and to that of the student." However, the association's original understanding of students' freedom mainly concerned voluntary chapel attendance and an elective system of courses. It did not include rights vis-à-vis a professor.[11]

A broader understanding of students' rights was not articulated until 1967, when efforts by student groups, civil liberties organizations, and professional groups culminated in the drafting of the Joint Statement on Rights and Freedoms of Students by representatives of the AAUP, the U.S. National Student Association, the Association of American Colleges, the National Association of Student Personnel Administrators, and the National Association of Women Deans and Counselors.[12] The joint statement specifies that "within the limits of its facilities, each college and university should be open to all students who are qualified according to its admission standards." Preferences of private religious institutions for students of a specific religious background should therefore be clearly indicated, the statement says. In the classroom, students are entitled to three primary protections: of freedom of expression, against improper evaluation, and against the improper disclosure of their "views, beliefs, and political associations." The joint statement also declares a student's right to freedom of association (to belong to student organizations), freedom of expression ("to support causes by orderly means [and] to invite and to hear any person of their own choosing"), participation in student government, and free student publications.

The Rights of Institutions. Unlike academic freedom for professors and students, institutional academic freedom in America has never been explicated in a formal document. However, the independence of colleges and universities from outside influences is the hallmark of academic freedom in Britain, the model on which the first American colleges were based.

In imitation of this model, therefore, colleges and universities in the United States are free to hire and fire faculty, admit students, and determine curricula, all as needed to pursue their institutional mission. This mission is now understood to be the unhampered search for truth for the benefit of society, although it is also understood that some religious institutions may have other purposes.

It should be noted that *institutional* academic freedom can conflict with *individual* academic freedom.

To speak of the academic freedom of a college or university is to beg the question: freedom from what? Over the centuries and worldwide, political, social, and religious forces have all been known to threaten this freedom. In the United States, however, the only force truly capable of threatening the independence of a college or university is judicial.

Academic Freedom and the Judiciary

While documents such as the AAUP's 1940 statement and the 1967 joint statement are widely heeded, they do not have the force of law. As a result, the courts have been crucial to the development and current state of academic freedom in the United States.

Much of this judicial history is based on the First Amendment. Although some legal scholars argue that the First Amendment does not protect academic freedom,[13] most federal courts have held that it does.[14]

The courts' early applications of the First Amendment to academic freedom were prompted by the anti-Communist "loyalty" investigations associated with Senator Joseph McCarthy of Wisconsin in the 1950s. It should be noted that scholars disagree about both the severity of the McCarthy threat and the appropriateness of the judiciary's response to it. Ellen Schrecker of Yeshiva University believes that the threat was significant and that "academic freedom was no protection." She cites "an academic blacklist" and dismissals of Communist or formerly Communist professors from institutions such as the University of Washington and Rutgers University for their refusal to take loyalty oaths or "name names."[15] On the other hand, John P. Roche of the Fletcher School of Law and Diplomacy contends that the "antics of McCarthy, the House Un-American Activities Committee, and various state roadshows" did not threaten academic freedom substantially. Roche notes that McCarthy was not responsible for any of the 140 people "jailed under the Smith Act for conspiring to teach and advocate the violent overthrow of the government, or for contempt of Congress."[16]

Nonetheless, American courts did intervene. The first major Supreme Court case was *Sweezy v. New Hampshire* in 1957. Paul Sweezy was a Marxist journalist who lectured at the University of New Hampshire and refused to answer questions from the state attorney general about the content of his lectures. A plurality opinion drafted by Chief Justice Earl Warren judged the government's investigation to be "unquestionably an invasion of petitioner's liberties in the areas of academic freedom and political expression." Warren wrote that academic freedoms are "areas in which the government should be extremely reticent to tread.... Teachers and students must always remain free to inquire, to study and to evaluate, to gain new maturity and understanding; otherwise our civilization will stagnate and die."

In a concurring opinion, Justice Felix Frankfurter cited "the dependence of a free society on free universities."[17] Citing a South African statement on the topic, Frankfurter endorsed "'four essential freedoms' of a university—to determine for itself on academic grounds who may teach, what may be taught, how it shall be taught, and who may be admitted to study."[18]

Another major McCarthy-era Supreme Court case concerned anti-Communist loyalty oaths for professors. Relying on *Sweezy*, the majority in 1967's *Keyishian v. Board of Regents* [of the State University of New York (SUNY)] found the oaths unconstitutional.[19] In explaining his decision, Justice William J. Brennan located the academic freedom of professors squarely within the First Amendment:

Our Nation is deeply committed to safeguarding academic freedom, which is of transcendent value to all of us and not merely to the teachers concerned. That freedom is therefore a special concern of the First Amendment, which does not tolerate laws that cast a pall of orthodoxy over the classroom.

The federal judiciary therefore protected academic freedom against the investigations, loyalty oaths, and compelled testimonies of the McCarthy era. It could be argued, though, that the judiciary only really began to recognize the academic freedom of the university in the landmark 1978 affirmative action case, *Regents of the University of California v. Bakke*.[20] Here Justice Lewis F. Powell Jr., who provided the fifth vote for the Supreme Court's majority, identified institutional academic freedom (a university's right to determine "who may be admitted to study") as a First Amendment right in maintaining that it was constitutional for a university to make race a factor in student admissions.

Three years later, in *Widmar v. Vincent*, the court again cited institutional academic freedom, this time as it permitted an evangelical Christian student group to meet on a public university campus. Educational decisions, wrote Justice John Paul Stevens, "should be made by academicians, not by federal judges."[21]

It has been noted that the academic freedom of an individual professor can conflict with the freedom of the college or university where he or she works. In the 1985 case *Piarowski v. Illinois Community College District*, the U.S. 7th Circuit Court of Appeals in Chicago permitted a college to remove a professor's controversial artwork from its main building. Judge Richard Posner wrote:

Though many decisions describe "academic freedom" as an aspect of freedom of speech that is protected against governmental abridgement by the First Amendment, the term is equivocal. It is used to denote both the freedom of the academy to pursue its ends without interference from the government...and the freedom of the individual teacher...to pursue his ends without interference from the academy; and these two freedoms are in conflict.

Unsurprisingly, when this conflict arises different courts rule differently. In *Edwards v. California University of Pennsylvania* (1998), the U.S. 3rd Circuit Court of Appeals in Philadelphia ruled that under the First Amendment the institution, and not the individual professor, has the freedom to decide on curriculum. A similar decision concerning grades was reached by a different 3rd Circuit panel in *Brown v. Armenti* (1991). In *Urofsky v. Gilmore* (2000), the U.S. 4th Circuit Court of Appeals in Richmond agreed, finding that the academic freedoms attributed to professors in the 1940 AAUP statement are not protected by the First Amendment, whether they are widely accepted professional norms or not.[22] Instead, the majority judged that "to the extent that the Constitution recognizes any right of 'academic freedom' above and beyond the First Amendment..., the right inheres in the University, not in individual professors."[23]

However, in the 1989 case *Parate v. Isibor*, the U.S. 6th Circuit Court of Appeals in Cincinnati ruled that a university administration could not order a professor to change a grade because of the professor's First Amendment right to academic freedom. Former AAUP general counsel David Rabban has asserted that "five other federal circuit courts...have recognized that the First Amendment safeguards the academic speech of professors."[24]

For some time the Supreme Court declined to deal explicitly with the First Amendment rights of students. But in 1995, in *Rosenberger v. Rector & Visitors of the University of Virginia*, the court's majority, led by Justice Anthony M. Kennedy, ruled that the university's refusal to allocate activity fees to a Christian student organization for the publication of its magazine was viewpoint discrimination and violated the students' First Amendment rights:

For the University, by regulation, to cast disapproval on particular viewpoints of its students risks the suppression of free speech and creative inquiry in one of the vital centers for the Nation's intellectual life, its college and university campuses.[25]

Of course, the academic freedom of students could just as easily conflict with the freedoms of professors and institutions as those freedoms do with each other. Indeed, much of the current debate about academic freedom in the United States is based on the conflicting claims of teachers and students. And when these claims go head to head, teachers tend to prevail. In the words of AAUP counsel Donna R. Euben, "the legal academic freedom rights of faculty and students are not equally weighted. Faculty academic freedom…[is] a collective right…informed by professional expertise and peer review." Consequently, "students do not have the legal right to demand that classes be viewpoint neutral or 'balanced.'"[26]

Two recent federal cases support Euben. In *Board of Regents v. Southworth* (2000), student Scott Southworth sued the University of Wisconsin for violating his First Amendment rights by requiring payment of activity fees that funded various student groups, some of which offended him. Ruling against Southworth, Supreme Court Justice David H. Souter wrote that "[university] students are inevitably required to support the expression of personally offensive viewpoints in a way that cannot be thought constitutionally objectionable." The 2003 ruling in a case before the U.S. 9th Circuit Court of Appeals in San Francisco, *Brown v. Li*, echoed: "A teacher may require a student to write a paper from a particular viewpoint, even if it is a viewpoint with which the student disagrees, so long as the requirement serves a legitimate pedagogical purpose."

Academic Freedom Since September 11

Since the terrorist attacks of September 11, 2001, new debates about academic freedom have arisen. Some have argued that both government and nongovernmental groups have attempted to suppress academic freedom in the wake of 9/11. Others contend that while "academic freedom has indeed suffered as a result of government measures," the consequences have "been less severe than many of us would have feared."[27] The latter conclusion is that of the AAUP's Special Committee on Academic Freedom and National Security in Times of Crisis, set up several months after 9/11 to protect professors' (and, to a lesser extent, students') academic freedom from anticipated violations.

The passage of the USA PATRIOT Act in 2001 sparked fears throughout the academy that freedom and access to information would be restricted. However, the impact of some of the act's provisions—such as the federal government's new authority to demand library records (and thus information on scholarly research)—is still unclear, either because of security considerations or a genuine lack of information on the part of researchers. A University of Illinois Library Research Center survey of 1,505 public libraries across the country found that of the 906 respondents, 215 libraries had explicitly cooperated with law enforcement requests for information about patrons' reading and internet habits, and 225 specified that they had not cooperated. In addition, most libraries had not altered their policies on book or internet use.[28]

The impact of post-9/11 restrictions on foreign students has been far clearer. The implementation of the Student and Exchange Visitor Information System by the Department of Homeland Security has discouraged foreign students—particularly those from sensitive areas like the Middle East and South Asia—from pursuing higher or graduate education in the United States. Foreign students already in the country have been subjected to more onerous registration, student visa, and identification requirements, and have occasionally been detained on dubious grounds. In December 2002, for example, several foreign students in Colorado who reported to immigration officials in compliance with new requirements were briefly arrested and jailed for not having enrolled in the required number of credit hours. In addition, the law has enhanced restrictions on who may participate in sensitive government research. This has reduced opportunities for noncitizens and for collaboration with foreign researchers as well.[29]

The USA PATRIOT Act has also raised bureaucratic and security barriers to domestic research in sensitive fields. A number of controversial investigations have resulted. In 2002, Dr. Thomas Butler of Texas Tech University was investigated and criminally prosecuted for violating the act's reporting provisions for the use and transport of specific biological agents. Though Butler was eventually cleared of 14 out of 15 PATRIOT Act–related charges (he was found guilty of failing to obtain a required transport permit), the government's investigation led to 54 charges of tax evasion, fraud, and theft that were unrelated to the act. When anthrax attacks followed 9/11 in 2001, the Justice Department declared Louisiana State University's Dr. Steven J. Hatfill a "person of interest." Though Hatfill was never charged with a crime, he was fired "because of the accusation and intervention of the Justice Department."[30]

The most publicized prosecution of a university professor in the PATRIOT Act era, however, is that of University of South Florida (USF) computer science professor Sami Al-Arian. Even before 9/11, Al-Arian had been controversial for his support of the Palestinian Islamic Jihad (PIJ) terrorist organization. After the attacks, though, he was accused of making statements in support of the perpetrators on national television. In December 2001 USF filed suit, seeking to clarify whether it had the authority to terminate his tenured appointment.

A federal judge dismissed the suit, declaring it a campus matter. Al-Arian was placed on indefinite suspension with pay. Several advocacy organizations, including the AAUP and the American Civil Liberties Union (ACLU), then criticized USF for failing to follow the proper charge and termination procedures, while others declared Al-Arian the victim of a political witch-hunt.

In February 2003, Al-Arian was indicted on nine counts, including providing material support to a terrorist organization, conspiracy to maim or murder, perjury, and immigration violations. The charges were based on evidence gathered using surveillance methods approved under the PATRIOT Act. A week later, USF officially terminated his appointment. In April 2006, Al-

Arian—after being found not guilty on eight of the nine counts against him in 2005—pleaded guilty to one count of conspiring to provide support to PIJ. He agreed to be deported.

An attempt to terminate tenured professor Ward Churchill of the University of Colorado at Boulder proved almost as contentious. Soon after 9/11, Churchill, whose field is ethnic studies, published an essay arguing that U.S. policies had provoked the attacks and that those who died in the collapsed towers of New York City's World Trade Center, whom he called "little Eichmanns," deserved their fate. The essay escaped broad notice until 2005, when the media picked it up and a controversy erupted. While university alumni and some government officials called for Churchill's termination, others defended his right to free speech.

The Standing Committee on Research Misconduct at Churchill's university declared that his essay was protected by the university's academic freedom code, but authorized an investigation into charges that he had plagiarized and falsified some of his work and lied about his Native American roots. The committee ultimately found Churchill guilty of serious "research misconduct" and recommended to the Board of Regents that he be dismissed.

In a similar case, Columbia University anthropology professor Nicholas De Genova was criticized for his behavior at an antiwar "teach-in" where he wished military defeat and "a million Mogadishus" on American troops poised to invade Iraq in 2003. According to then provost Jonathan Cole, irate alumni and 62 members of Congress urged Columbia to dismiss De Genova.[31] In the end, university president Lee Bollinger condemned De Genova for his remarks, but defended his right to free expression and withheld disciplinary action.

In the wake of 9/11, not just individual professors but the field of Middle Eastern Studies itself came under enhanced scrutiny. Charging that Middle Eastern Studies was rife with "analytical failures, the mixing of politics with scholarship, intolerance of alternative views, apologetics, and the abuse of power over students," academics and activists Martin Kramer and Daniel Pipes established Campus Watch in November 2002 to "improve" the discipline.[32]

At first the organization's website maintained dossiers on individual scholars, departments, and academic institutions, and invited students to contribute. Campus Watch also called for changes in the government's Title VI funding of area studies programs, to ensure that such funds were not used to promote anti-Americanism or ideas potentially threatening to U.S. security.

Academics, nonacademics, and professional organizations responded with a wave of criticism and charges of a "new McCarthyism." Critics accused Campus Watch and its supporters of perpetrating a "witch hunt" against critics of Israeli and U.S. policies by way of "a virtually limitless campaign of harassment and intimidation."[33] In September 2002, the organization removed its dossiers on individual professors.

A related dispute emerged at Columbia University in 2002. A group of Jewish students, supported by the Boston-based David Project, claimed that certain professors of Middle Eastern politics and history—particularly Dr. Joseph Massad—were aggressively promoting an ideological anti-Israel agenda and expressing anti-Semitism in the classroom. The group produced a short film documenting their charges, and a media and political storm ensued. Supporters of Massad accused the David Project of attempting to silence academic critics of Israel and the United States under the guise of combating anti-Semitism.

Bollinger led an investigation into the allegations on both sides. Eventually Massad was criticized but exonerated of any charges.

"Political Correctness"

Perhaps the leading controversy over academic freedom in America today concerns the charge that colleges and universities are dominated by a left-wing political and cultural orthodoxy known derisively as "political correctness." According to this view, dissenting (i.e., conservative) voices are rarely heard on campus, limiting both the quality of students' educations and their academic freedom. Meanwhile, academics with conservative viewpoints are denied opportunities for professional advancement.

There is some empirical support for these claims. Recent studies have found that most academics identify themselves as politically "liberal" and as supporters of the Democratic Party. A 2003 study by Daniel Klein (Santa Clara University) and his student Andrew Western found that self-described "liberals" outnumber "conservatives" 7-to-1 among members of anthropology, economics, history, philosophy, political science, and sociology associations. A 2005 Klein and Western study of 22 departments in two universities found that Democrats outnumber Republicans 8-to-1 at Stanford University and 10-to-1 at the University of California–Berkeley.

A 2005 study by Stanley Rothman (Smith College), S. Robert Lichter (Center of Media and Public Affairs), and Neil Nevitte (University of Toronto)—the most comprehensive and rigorous study to date—surveyed 1,643 faculty members from 183 universities and colleges in the United States and Canada. Rothman and his colleagues found that: (1) the academy overwhelmingly identifies itself as "liberal" rather than "conservative" (72 percent to 15 percent) and Democratic rather than Republican (50 percent to 11 percent); (2) these identifications are not limited to particular disciplines or institutions; (3) the academy has shifted substantially leftward since the 1960s and especially since the 1980s; and (4) the results of the study are "consistent with the hypothesis that political conservatism confers a disadvantage in the competition for professional advancement." The study also found that women and religious Christians suffer from disadvantages in professional advancement that have no basis in merit.[34]

Many critics have questioned these studies' methods. A detailed review of such methodological disputes is beyond the scope of this chapter, but the most significant objections are that: (1) the way faculty members describe themselves ideologically does not necessarily reveal their opinions about specific issues, and does not indicate the moderation or extremism of their views; (2) outside the more "political" disciplines such as political science or sociology, the ideological and political affiliations of faculty and potential faculty are often unknown to students and other faculty; and (3) the prevalence of self-identified "liberals" and Democrats in academia reflects professional self-selection more than disciplinary or institutional biases.[35]

Some conservatives counter that the ideological homogeneity of the academy, and more importantly its suppression of dissenting perspectives, are nonetheless problems. Students for Academic Freedom (SAF), founded by conservative commentator and former leftist radical David Horowitz, has led this campaign. SAF promotes a document it calls the Academic Bill of Rights (ABR), which asserts that "the central purposes of a university are the pursuit of truth...and [the] discovery of new knowledge" and "the teaching and general development of students to help them become creative individuals and productive citizens of a pluralistic democracy." It declares that "no party or intellectual faction has a monopoly on wisdom" and defines academic freedom as "protecting [the] intellectual independence of professors, researchers, and students from legislators and university authorities." The ABR also identifies eight "principles" intended to ensure academic freedom for both teachers and students.

While most of these principles are generally accepted, the ABR's agenda is not. The document demands that faculty decisions foster "a plurality of methodologies and perspectives," that lectures and curricula provide students with "dissenting sources and viewpoints," and that academic institutions and professional societies maintain "neutrality" with respect to disagreements on questions inside and outside the discipline. Also controversial is the ABR's declaration that the freedom to teach and learn depend upon "the creation of appropriate conditions and opportunities" on campus, in classrooms, and in lecture halls.

SAF is attempting to win passage of the ABR or some variant of it in state and federal legislatures. While 21 state legislatures and the U.S. House of Representatives have considered such legislation, so far none has been passed. The legislation's failure can be attributed in part to lobbying by opponents, foremost among them the AAUP.

The AAUP's objections to the ABR have been summarized by its Committee A on Academic Freedom and Tenure. While the committee agrees that the faculty selection process should not impose orthodoxies on professors or researchers, it contends that the ABR is "an improper and dangerous method" for preventing this. It disagrees that faculty should be hired "with a view toward fostering a plurality of methodologies and perspectives," arguing that this approach would undermine professorial self-regulation and "invite diversity to be measured by political standards that diverge from the academic criteria." The AAUP panel also argues that the ABR transfers "the pedagogical authority required to make evaluative judgments" from faculty to administrators and courts, and thus "undermines the very academic freedom it claims to support."

Another major debate concerns the "speech codes" that have been adopted at hundreds of colleges and universities since the 1980s. These codes generally do one or more of the following: they protect students from harassment (general, sexual, discriminatory, and "protected group") and "intolerant," "insensitive," or "hate" speech; they encourage or in some cases require "diversity" and "multiculturalism"; and they encourage or require loyalty oaths and honor codes.[36] Proponents of speech codes say they are intended to create a nonthreatening and thus more open and diverse campus environment. Opponents say they result in both harmful self-censorship and unconstitutional official censorship of student speech.

Like other academic freedom issues involving the First Amendment, the debate over speech codes has raged most fiercely in the context of public colleges and universities. However, opponents of speech codes argue that private institutions, particularly those that represent themselves as places of free and open inquiry, also violate students' rights by enforcing these policies.

Speech codes have not fared well in court. In 1989, a federal court struck down a speech code at the University of Michigan (*Doe v. University of Michigan*), ruling that "statutes punishing speech or conduct solely on the grounds that they are unseemly or offensive are unconstitutionally overbroad."[37] In 1991, the University of Wisconsin implemented a speech code prohibiting "racist or discriminatory" comments that are directed at individuals. A student newspaper and several individual students challenged the code in court (*UWM Post v. Board of Regents of University of Wisconsin*). A federal court found that because the policy was targeted not at violence but at the "demeaning" of students and the creation of a "hostile" environment, it could not be constitutionally defended as prohibiting "fighting words."

Students themselves have also restricted academic freedom and free expression by suppressing dissenting viewpoints on college and university campuses. On campuses such as the University of California–Berkeley, Columbia University, Washington State University, Williams University, and the University of Connecticut, student activists have shouted down or otherwise silenced controversial speakers at university venues. In addition, students at Berkeley and San Francisco State University have forcibly occupied buildings where classes were in session and destroyed literature with which they disagreed. According to the Foundation for Individual Rights in Education (FIRE), this behavior constitutes a major contemporary academic freedom issue.

Evolution and Intelligent Design

The teaching of evolution, with its many implications for religious doctrine, has been a source of controversy in the United States since the Scopes trial of 1925 (*State of Tennessee v. John Thomas Scopes*), in which a high school teacher was convicted of violating a Tennessee statute that made it illegal "to teach any theory that denies the story of the Divine Creation of man as taught in the Bible, and to teach instead that man has descended from a lower order of animals." The conviction was later overturned by the state Supreme Court.[38] Teaching evolution remains contentious today, as its opponents increasingly demand that a theory called "intelligent design" (ID) be taught along with it.

The debate over ID and evolution is waged mostly in the context of public primary and secondary education, rather than colleges and universities. In the past the central issue in this debate has been understood to be the separation of church and state. Today, however, proponents of ID argue that it touches on academic freedom as well.

Opponents of ID, who include the great majority of scientists, argue that it "remains a quintessentially religious doctrine." They claim that it is at bottom no different from the doctrine of biblical creationism, since both hold "that biological entities in the physical world have not evolved naturally from lower-order to higher-order beings, and...that a supernatural intelligence intervened in the natural world to dictate the nature and ordering of all biological species."[39] These opponents therefore believe that the teaching of ID violates the constitutionally mandated separation of church and state.

However, proponents of ID define it as a "theory...[that] holds that certain features of the universe and of living things are best explained by an intelligent cause, not an undirected process such as natural selection." These supporters argue that the theory is not based on the Bible and is agnostic regarding the source of nature's "apparent design."[40] While it is incompatible with "neo-Darwinism" or "purposeless" natural selection, they say, it is not incompatible with the theory of evolution. As a result, they argue that ID is scientifically valid and should be taught in public schools, and that the refusal to teach it violates students' academic freedom.

Advocates of ID have worked through political channels to introduce it into American classrooms. In October 2004, the school board in Dover, Pennsylvania, mandated that intelligent design be taught in high school biology classes. After a group of families sued in federal court on church-state separation grounds, Judge John E. Jones III declared ID to be "a religious view, a mere re-labeling of creationism, and not a scientific theory."[41] In November 2005, the Kansas Board of Education approved new science education standards that required students to learn about scientific criticisms of modern evolutionary theory, including

ID. In elections in August 2006, however, the "pro-ID" faction that had approved the new standards lost control of the board. Whether or not it affects academic freedom, the battle for the American classroom that has been waged for nearly a century by evolutionists and their foes will not be resolved anytime soon.

Endnotes

1. Robert B. Standler, "Academic Freedom in the USA" (1999), http://www.rbs2.com/afree.htm.
2. James Pierson, "The Left University," *The Weekly Standard*, October 3, 2005: 22.
3. Scott McLemee, "Academic Freedom, Then and Now," *Inside Higher Ed*, February 17, 2005, http://www.insidehighered.com/views/2005/02/17/mclemee6.
4. Pierson, 23.
5. Ibid., 23.
6. Robert Post, "Academic Freedom: Its History and Evolution Within the UC System" (lecture, Academic Freedom Forum, June 11, 2003), www.universityofcalifornia.edu/senate/committees/ucaf/afforum/post.pdf.
7. The American Association of University Professors (AAUP), "History of the AAUP," http://www.aaup.org/aboutaaup/hist.HTM.
8. AAUP, "1915 General Report of the Committee on Academic Freedom and Academic Tenure."
9. AAUP, "1940 Statement of Principles on Academic Freedom and Tenure."
10. Ibid.
11. Walter P. Metzger, *Academic Freedom in the Age of the University* (New York: Columbia University Press, 1961).
12. Philip P. Wiener, ed., "Academic Freedom," *Dictionary of the History of Ideas* (The Electronic Text Center at the University of Virginia), http://etext.virginia.edu/cgi-local/DHI/dhi.cgi?id=dv1-02.
13. For example, see J. Peter Byrne, "Academic Freedom," 99 *Yale Law Journal* 251 (1989).
14. Donna R. Euben, "Political and Religious Belief Discrimination on Campus: Faculty and Student Academic Freedom and the First Amendment" (paper, National Association of College and University Attorneys, March 2005).

15. Ellen Schrecker, "Political Tests for Professors: Academic Freedom During the McCarthy Years" (address, symposium: The University Loyalty Oath: a 50th Anniversary Retrospective, October 7, 1999).
16. John P. Roche, "The New Left Vigilantes: Academic Freedom," *National Review*, December 8, 1989.
17. *Sweezy v. New Hampshire*, 354 U.S. 234 (1957).
18. David M. Rabban, "Academic freedom, Individual or Institutional?" *Academe*, November 1, 2001.
19. Rabban, 1.
20. Rabban, 2.
21. Rabban, 2.
22. Rabban, 4.
23. *Urofsky v. Gilmore*, 216 F.3d 401 (4th Cir. 2000).
24. Rabban, 5.
25. *Rosenberger v. Rector & Visitors of the UVA*, 515 U.S. 819, 835-36 (1995).
26. Euben, 5.
27. Robert O'Neil, "Academic Freedom and National Security in a Time of Crisis," *Academe*, May 1, 2003.
28. The Library Research Center, "Public Libraries and Civil Liberties" (The Graduate School of Library and Information Science, University of Illinois at Urbana-Champaign), http://lrc.lis.uiuc.edu/web/PLCL.html.
29. O'Neil, 4.
30. Jonathan Cole, "Academic Freedom Under Fire," *Daedalus*, Spring 2005.
31. Ibid., 3.
32. Campus Watch, "About Campus Watch," http://www.campuswatch.org/about.php.
33. Kristine McNeil, "The War on Academic Freedom," *The Nation*, October 11, 2002.
34. Stanley Rothman, S. Robert Lichter, and Neil Nevitte, "Politics and Professional Advancement Among College Faculty," *The Forum*, Volume 3 (1), 2005.
35. Barry Ames, David C. Barker, Chris W. Bonneau, and Christopher J. Carman, "Hide the Republicans, the Christians, and the

Women: A Response to 'Politics and Professional Advancement Among College Faculty,'" *The Forum*, Volume 3 (2), 2005. Ethan B. Cohen-Cole and Steven N. Durlauf, "Evaluating Claims of Bias in Academia: A Comment on Klein and Western's 'How Many Democrats per Republican at UC Berkeley and Stanford?'" (University of Wisconsin–Madison, April 23, 3005).

36. Foundation for Individual Rights in Education (FIRE), "About Speech Codes," *The Spotlight*, http://www.thefire.org/index.php/article/5822.html.

37. David L. Hudson Jr., "Hate Speech and Campus Speech Codes: Overview," First Amendment Center, http://www.firstamendmentcenter.org/speech/pubcollege/topic.aspx?topic=campus_speech_codes.

38. Matthew J. Brauer, Barbara Forrest, and Steven J. Gey, "Is it Science Yet?: Intelligent Design, Creationism, and the Constitution," *Washington University Law Quarterly*, Volume 83 (1), 2005: 3.

39. Brauer et al., 6.

40. The Discovery Institute Center for Science and Culture, "Top Questions: What Is the Theory of Intelligent Design?" http://www.discovery.org/csc/topQuestions.php.

41. National Public Radio online, "Teaching Evolution: A State-by-State Debate," December 20, 2005, http://www.npr.org/templates/story/story.php?storyId=4630737.

Equality of Opportunity
in an Age of Globalization

Almost since the founding of the republic, equality of opportunity has been recognized as a value that is fundamental to the American idea. From the beginning, Americans believed that their society was in a basic sense different from Europe, where a man's destiny was largely determined by his social class. In the United States, by contrast, a man's success depended on his ability, ingenuity, and character. The phrase "the American Dream" expresses the ideal that everyone, no matter how humble his or her station, has the potential to attain a degree of middle-class prosperity.

The United States has often observed its commitment to equality of opportunity in the breach. Under slavery and segregation, blacks were denied practically every avenue to prosperity, save for those involved in businesses that catered specifically to the black community. Other nonwhite groups faced similar, if less systematically applied, discrimination. Until relatively recently, women were discouraged from entering the professions and excluded from positions of authority. More generally, in America, as in every other society, the wealthy and increasingly the well educated enjoy advantages that they are able to pass on to their heirs.

Yet despite its failure to live up to its ideals consistently, for many in the world the United States remains the land of opportunity. America is today, as it was a century ago, a land where both freedom and the chance to succeed beckon to those in other nations who suffer poverty, repression, or both. Where previously wave after wave of European immigrants sought a better life, today immigrants from Latin America, Asia, the Middle East, and Africa do the same. Darker-skinned people were for years denied entry to the United States. The fact that the current immigration flow is overwhelmingly drawn from non-European populations represents a dramatic change in American policy. The proven ability of these new immigrants to hold down jobs, raise families, learn English, and assimilate into American society is an impressive achievement by global standards and a reaffirmation of the idea of America as the land of opportunity.

Furthermore, the era that followed World War II brought the promise of equal opportunity much closer to reality for groups that had historically been excluded from the American Dream. The civil rights revolution ended legal discrimination against native-born blacks, nonwhite immigrants, and women. The explosive growth of higher education enabled the children of working-class families to pursue college degrees for the first time. New laws and policies enhanced the role of merit in decisions on hiring, firing, promotions, and university admissions.

For evidence of America's enhanced commitment to equality of opportunity, one need go no further than the local hospital or courthouse. In both, jobs that were once monopolized by white men are now held by a diverse group of blacks, Latinos, Asians, immigrants (in the case of hospitals), and of course women. Indeed, women are almost as likely to enroll in medical or law school today as are men.

Not only did the United States make significant progress toward equality of opportunity during the civil rights era, it also significantly equalized outcomes, especially among the races. High rates of growth and industrial expansion during the 1950s and 1960s facilitated the entry into the working class of millions of black workers, who found jobs making automobiles, processing steel, or building machine tools.

Since the early 1970s, however, the American economy has experienced something of a transformation. The old industry-based model has been supplanted by a model based on education and technological expertise, along with services. The result has been a growth in opportunity for those with the relevant credentials and abilities, and stagnation or decline for those who lack such skills.

As is always the case during periods of economic change, there have been winners and losers. But the bulk of the evidence suggests that in the current transition the winners are restricted to a small proportion at the top while everyone else is experiencing economic stagnation or decline. Over the past decade, economic gain has been limited to those in the top 10 percent while conditions for the vast majority have been flat or declined. Some statistics even suggest that, looked at from the perspective of educational attainment, only those with advanced degrees are moving ahead while those with a college degree or high school education are treading water or losing ground. Some critics further contend that the losers include many workers who have been consigned to the substantial and growing low-wage economy. Others go further, arguing that in recent years equality of opportunity has diminished both as an ideal and as an on-the-ground reality in the United States. Although this criticism comes principally from the left, some conservatives have also acknowledged that the United States has become a more unequal society as a result of such trends as globalization and technological advancement. Alan Greenspan, the former chairman of the Federal Reserve Bank, has gone so far as to assert that the capitalist system is threatened by growing inequality.

The question of whether American workers "need a raise," in the words of John J. Sweeney, president of the American Federation of Labor–Congress of Industrial Organizations (AFL-CIO), has entered the political debate. During his initial presidential bid in 1992, Bill Clinton campaigned on the theme that most Americans were not sharing in the riches generated by the economic policies of former president Ronald Reagan; Clinton promised a better deal for Americans who "work hard and play by the rules." Similar ideas were touted by Democratic candidates during the congressional campaign of 2006.

In making the case that American workers suffer from growing inequality, the critics cite statistics that place the average earnings for a corporate chief executive officer (CEO) at 475 times that of the average worker, compared with a differential of 40–1 during the 1960s. The disparity is especially glaring when compared with CEO compensation in Japan, where the differential is 11–1, or in Britain, where the differential is 22–1. Others point to the decades-long stagnation in U.S. wages and, some say, the creation of a two-tiered economy in which many jobs are held by illegal immigrants.

Compared with other developed democracies, the United States indeed has a mixed record. There is more absolute poverty in the United States than in the countries of Western Europe. At the same time, the United States has a higher proportion of immigrants from poor countries than does Europe, and has by most accounts done a better job of integrating the new immigrants into the country's social and economic fabric. The United States has a lower minimum wage than do most European countries and differs from Europe in its willingness to tolerate a substantial class of low-wage workers. But the United States has a lower rate of unemployment than do most countries in Europe, some of which have suffered jobless rates of 10 percent or more for many years.

This study examines the condition of freedom in America. Certainly equality of opportunity is essential to freedom, both as a value and as a factor that affects the functioning of a free country. As has been seen in Russia and in some Latin American countries, people lose faith in democracy under conditions of massive poverty, huge gaps between rich and poor, rampant corruption, and economic volatility.

At the same time, in an economically stable liberal democracy, the degree of freedom does not neatly correlate with the gains and losses in the stock market, the unemployment rate, the rate of inflation, interest rates, or other broad indicators of economic performance. Is it a violation of Americans' rights and freedoms that Wal-Mart pays many of its workers less than $10 an hour without medical insurance? Some would argue that the Wal-Mart phenomenon, whereby large, powerful corporations maintain their competitive advantage through the exploitation of low-wage workers, does represent an abuse of power and a violation of rights. Others would maintain that Wal-Mart's labor policies are a function of market forces and are less a violation of rights—since they do not reflect national economic policy—than France's rigid labor code, which contributes to a high unemployment rate and erects barriers to the career prospects of hundreds of thousands of young people.

However, other economic issues bear more directly on the freedoms enjoyed by individual Americans. One such issue is the right of workers to enjoy trade-union representation. In the United States, the great movement of the working class into middle-class status coincided with the period of trade unionism's greatest success. Conversely, the period of wage stagnation and the spread of low-wage jobs that began in the 1970s took place during a period of decline in union membership and influence that is unprecedented in the modern era among developed democracies. Some of organized labor's decline is clearly due to broad economic trends such as globalization, intensified trade, the integration of China into the global market, and technological change. High-visibility corruption has also damaged trade unionism's image. But the decrease in union membership in the private sector can also be attributed to an increasingly hostile political and legal environment, combined with the American business community's traditional antiunion animus.

A second issue is discrimination. This subject is dealt with at some length in the chapters on race relations and immigration. This chapter will assess how government policies and the actions of private institutions have affected the status of women in education and in the economic arena.

Unions Under Duress

More than in any other developed democracy, the history of organized labor in America has been marked by violence, unrest, and intense efforts by management to thwart union objectives. That unions in the United States have encountered such stubborn resistance may seem odd given that, unlike those in Europe, American unions have historically accepted capitalism and eschewed the goal of refashioning the economic system along socialist lines. Samuel Gompers, the first president of the American Federation of Labor, scorned political radicals and refused to tie labor to a political party. For years, his successors maintained a tradition of political bipartisanship, although recently labor has opted for a more organic relationship with the Democratic Party.

Unions' often violent struggles to organize the steel and automobile industries during the 1930s established them as a major force in economic life. After World War II, labor's rolls rose steadily as the American industrial sector grew, until by the mid-1950s some 35 percent of the labor force was unionized, with labor's strength overwhelmingly centered in the private sector. Yet even at the pinnacle of its strength, labor confronted opposition within the business community and among elements of the political leadership that union movements in Western Europe did not have to face. From the standpoint of labor's future ability to organize workers on a truly nationwide basis, the most important consequence was the series of so-called right-to-work laws that were adopted after the 1947 passage of the Taft-Hartley Act, which was meant to curb what its supporters claimed was excessive union power. Among other provisions, Taft-Hartley gave states the authority to pass right-to-work laws. Under these statutes, unions are forbidden to make union membership or payment of union dues a condition of employment, either before or after a worker is hired. Right-to-work laws were quickly enacted by nearly all of the Southern states; today, 22 states have some form of right-to-work provision in their labor codes.[1]

The principal effect of right-to-work laws has been to restrict labor's growth in the South and the Sun Belt region. During the 1950s and 1960s, unions enjoyed saturation strength in key industries in the Northeast, Midwest, and some Western states, but they remained weak in the South. The impact of Taft-Hartley was less significant during the 1950s due to the South's economic backwardness. However, the law's influence became more problematic as industries began to migrate to the region, in part due to the South's antiunion environment and comparatively low labor costs.

By the mid-1970s, union membership had declined to 25 percent of the workforce. The reasons were complex, and included the gradual shift of the American economy from one based on industrial production to one based on services and knowledge. Even more important were advances in technology that rendered some jobs—and in a few cases entire occupations—obsolete. Trade was also a factor; whereas America had been the world's export giant, it now began to import large quantities of goods from Japan and other economies that paid their workers less than in the United States.[2]

In addition to these broad economic trends, unions were confronted with mounting resistance from employers. To a substantial degree, unions suffered from the transformation of the American economy from one based in internal markets to one based on globalized competition. Unions have historically fared poorly under conditions of a competitive economy, where labor costs figure prominently in a corporation's ability to achieve profitability. Management used a variety of tactics to forestall unionization, including the intimidation of union activists. Often, corporations were willing to violate labor law if it would result in the defeat of a unionization campaign. One specific problem was the stalling tactics management resorted to when confronted with a representation vote that was likely to favor the union. Another problem was the inability of union activists to obtain timely justice for acts of reprisal by management; it took on average two years for a worker to win reinstatement after a finding of illegal dismissal for union activity. Furthermore, when found guilty by the courts or the National Labor Relations Board (NLRB), companies were compelled to do nothing more than provide back pay, a slap-on-the-wrist penalty that failed to discourage management from summarily firing union supporters.

To rectify the situation, labor in the late 1970s pressed for the adoption of a bill that was meant to correct what union leaders felt was an imbalance in labor-management relations. The bill would have expanded the NLRB in order to expedite hearings on cases of alleged violations, permitted two board members instead of the full board to adjudicate routine cases, and established strict time limits for a recognition vote once a union had gathered enough authorization cards from the workers. Although the bill won majority support in both the House and Senate, a filibuster backed by Republicans and Southern Democrats succeeded in killing the bill in the Senate by two votes.[3]

Labor's membership decline accelerated during the administration of Ronald Reagan in the 1980s. Much of the decline was due to "deindustrialization," whereby steel mills, automobile factories, and other industrial facilities were shut down or significantly reduced in size, devastating once-thriving communities and creating what came to be referred to as the Rust Belt. To this relentless force of an evolving market economy was added a generally unfriendly political environment. Whereas previous Republican administrations had maintained cordial relations with organized labor, the Reagan administration adopted policies that were often antithetical to labor's interests. Especially important were its appointments to the NLRB. The Reagan administration's appointees tended to support management's positions on labor-relations issues and were determined to move the board in a pro-employer direction. Once these appointees were in place, the board began issuing decisions that reversed earlier judgments supporting the rights of unions and unionized workers. In case after case, the NLRB gave management more latitude to abrogate union contracts, dismiss workers, and discipline union activists.

The political changes spurred corporations to take a tougher line in negotiations with existing unions and to resist further unionization even more forcefully. This resulted in an increase in the number of union activists fired during organizing campaigns, an increased use of fear tactics to discourage unionization efforts, and an increased resort to stalling tactics to thwart agreement on contracts. Another new wrinkle in labor-management relations was the replacement of striking workers by nonunion workers on a permanent basis. Striker replacement, though legal, had seldom been seen in the postwar era. Its reappearance had the effect of nullifying the strike as a significant weapon in labor relations.

The willingness of corporations to fire striking workers, including some corporations with histories of friendly relations with unions, had a powerful effect on organizing and collective bargaining. Even though only a relatively small number of companies took this extreme step, the threat that other businesses might follow suit discouraged workers from striking. The impact of the corporate world's antiunion tactics can be observed in Bureau of Labor Statistics figures, which indicated that among companies with over 1,000 workers, the average annual number of strikes during the 1980s was 80 (only 45 in 1990). By contrast, in the previous three decades, the lowest number of strikes in one year was 181, in 1963; the highest, 437, came in 1953.[4]

The loss of the strike as an instrument in labor-management relations, changes in the political atmosphere, employers' resistance to unions, a shift in attitude at the NLRB—all of these factors contributed to a steady weakening of labor's ability to represent workers effectively in the private sector. In 2006, only 12 percent of American workers were represented by unions, a remarkably low figure for a developed democracy. An even more telling statistic is the unionization figure for the private sector: 7.4 percent (by contrast, 36.2 percent of public employees were unionized). Furthermore, the trajectory has continued downward even as unions have adopted a number of new organizing strategies and campaigns and have greatly increased the resources devoted to organizing workers in areas where union-ization rates have historically been low.[5]

American union representation is well below that of practically every other developed democracy. In Canada, the proportion of union representation is close to 30 percent; for Germany, it is 22 percent; for the European Union as a whole, it is a little over 26 percent. But it should be noted that in almost every developed country, union membership has decreased over roughly the same period as America's trade-union decline, sometimes by greater margins than in the United States. Between 1970 and 2003, union membership as a percentage of the workforce dropped by 11.1 percentage points in the United States. The decline in Australia over a similar period was 27.3; for Japan, 15.4; for Germany, 9.5; for France, 11.4; for Great Britain, 15.5; and for the European Union as a whole, 11.5 percentage points, about the same as America's.[6]

Yet even within the context of a global decline in union strength, the American situation is unique. Although the governments of some developed countries—Great Britain and Australia, for example—have adopted policies to curb union strength, none of the established democracies has gone as far as the United States in tolerating employer practices that discourage union membership.

Advocates of workers' rights have multiple complaints about the current state of labor policies, labor law, and the institutions that adjudicate labor issues. Among the more significant issues are the following:

•While the National Labor Relations Act enshrines the rights of workers to form unions and engage in collective bargaining as a basic principle, those rights are frequently denied because of weak enforcement by the Department of Labor, the courts, and the NLRB.

•Union supporters at many companies are subject to discrimination, harassment, and dismissal. While dismissal for union advocacy is illegal under U.S. law, many companies ignore the law due to the weak penalties for violations of worker rights, which are usually limited to reinstatement and back pay.

•There is a lack of balance in a union's ability to present its case to workers. At many corporations, antiunion arguments are presented to workers from the day they are hired, including at captive-audience meetings and in frequent one-on-one discussions with supervisors about the problems of union representation.

•Employers warn of plant closure should unionization occur. According to labor law, it is illegal for management to threaten to close a facility if the employees opt for union representation. Increasingly, management representatives have been "predicting" that closure was possible or likely under union conditions, a practice which, union advocates contend, has had a powerful impact on workers' willingness to organize.

•There are lengthy delays in the judicial system and at the NLRB. Union advocates complain that cases of unfair labor practices are often stuck in litigation for years, denying justice to workers who have been unfairly penalized and discouraging workers from pursuing union representation.

•Management often bargains in bad faith. Unions frequently encounter situations where collective bargaining for a contract takes place, but management goes through the motions without any intention of reaching a contract.

•The number of workers eligible for union representation has declined. Under U.S. law, supervisors are exempted from normal labor-law coverage. In recent years, the courts and the NLRB have issued decisions that have continually expanded the roster of workers lumped under the supervisory category, thus rendering them ineligible for union protection and other benefits.[7]

Like much else today, the debate over union decline has become increasingly polarized. Employers and their political allies contend that union decline has little to do with government policy and much to do with shifts in the economy, technological advances, changes in the workforce that favor part-time workers and the self-employed, union corruption, and worker contentment with job conditions. Attitudinal surveys have generally found that Americans favor most of the benefits and protections that come with union representation while at the same time harboring mixed or negative feelings about unions themselves.

Another problem facing unions stems from an increase in the role of government in the economy. Many workplace issues that might be dealt with by unions are increasingly the responsibility of the federal government, including job safety, discrimination, and sexual harassment. A further problem for labor is that in an era of global competition, the ability of unions to offer substantially higher rates of pay at levels that would protect members from inflation has dwindled, especially in the private sector.

It is unclear whether the legal environment will change. Over the past four decades, attempts to bolster the ability of unions to organize workers and negotiate contracts have regularly failed. The most recent attempt to reform labor law is the proposed Employee Free Choice Act, now pending in Congress. Under the bill, once a union gets a majority of workers at a given facility to sign a card expressing the desire for a union, that union is automatically certified as the bargaining representative of all the workers at the facility. The bill has many critics, including some who generally support union objectives, due to its bias against elections as the principal vehicle for union recognition. If adopted, the bill would represent a major change in labor-management relations, since unions have traditionally gained bargaining-representative status only through secret-ballot votes by the workers involved. The measure has been endorsed by the Democratic Party leadership and might be able to gain a majority in Congress. It would, however, face a certain veto by President George W. Bush, and its prospects for adoption under a future Democratic president are questionable at best.[8]

Revolution in Women's Status

The role and status of women in the United States have undergone a major transformation in the past four decades. Testifying to their progress is the fact that three women—Secretary of State Condoleezza Rice, senator and presidential candidate Hillary Rodham Clinton, and Speaker of the House Nancy Pelosi—rank among the most influential public figures in the United States. Women, in fact, hold influential positions throughout the political field: in the administration, in the party leaderships, and in the constellation of trade associations, lobbying firms, think tanks, and nongovernmental organizations that play a crucial role in American government. In Congress, the number of women has grown steadily over the past three decades. After the 2006 midterm elections, there were 61 women in the House of Representatives and 13 in the Senate, both record numbers.

The legal foundation for the equality of women was enshrined in the 1964 Civil Rights Act, a measure that applied to both women and minority groups. Especially important was Title VII, which barred discrimination in the workplace and set in motion a movement of women into jobs from which they had traditionally been excluded or in which they had been significantly underrepresented. Another important measure was the Equal Pay Act of 1963, which made it illegal to pay men and women at different rates for jobs requiring equal skill, effort, and responsibility.

Although initially there was considerable resistance to the "women's liberation" agenda, a good deal of that agenda has been achieved. In particular, numerous occupations that were overwhelmingly or even totally the province of men now include a strong contingent of women. For example, there are currently more than 215,000 women in the military, compared with 1.2 million men as of 2003. Sixteen percent of 1991 Persian Gulf War veterans were women, compared with 5 percent in World War II, and women are substantially represented in the officer ranks.[9] In sports, 2.9 million girls participated in high school athletics in the 2002–03 school year, compared with 800,000 girls 30 years earlier.[10] Women are more likely than men to have graduated from college (88 percent versus 85 percent), and more likely to have a college degree in the crucial age bracket between 25 and 29 (31 percent versus 26 percent).[11]

In the professions, too, the numbers show a remarkable transformation. In 1970, only 7.6 percent of physicians were women. By 2004 that figure had risen to over 26 percent.[12] Moreover, statistics for enrollment in medical colleges suggest that the percentage of women in medicine is destined to grow substantially. For the 1969–70 school year, just 9 percent of medical school enrollees were women; for the academic year 2002–03, women's enrollment was over 46 percent, and for the year 2004–05, it was 48.6 percent, near parity with men.[13] Similar trajectories obtain for law school enrollment. Women made up 11.1 percent of law school students in the academic year 1972–73. For the academic year 2005–06, that figure had risen to 47.5 percent, again near parity.[14] The increase in business school enrollment has also been dramatic. In the class of 1965 at Harvard Business School, a mere 2 percent of enrollees were female; in 2007, that figure was 38 percent.[15]

Despite the huge increase in women in high-paying professions, women still lag behind men in average income. The most recent figures suggest that for 2004, the median earnings for women were 80 percent of those for men. This ratio varied significantly between demographic groups: for blacks it was 89 percent; for Latinos, 87 percent; for whites, 80 percent; and for Asians, 76 percent. Yet in 1979, women earned just 63 percent of what men earned. Significantly, for the youngest age cohort,

16 to 24 years old, women earned 94 percent of the median male earnings. By contrast, for those aged 35 and older, women earned 75 percent of their male counterparts' pay.

The reasons for the gap between men's and women's wages are the subject of considerable debate. Many researchers hold that women are more likely to drop out of the workforce for lengthy periods in order to care for children.[16] According to the Labor Department, the number of women who have chosen to stay at home has risen recently, and the increase has been especially sharp among highly educated mothers who might otherwise be earning high salaries. This could account for a recent stagnation in the earnings gap for college graduates. Others, however, point to the "feminization of poverty," a phenomenon driven by the increase in female-headed households. In 2000, about 11 percent of American families lived in poverty, but 28 percent of female-headed families did so. Most of these women were divorced or never married. Many have little education or job skills, and thus qualify only for poorly paid positions in the service sector.

In the 1980s, some women's rights organizations sought to rectify what they claimed were continued inequities in the workplace through a policy known as comparable worth. According to civil rights law, American workers regardless of race or sex were to be given equal pay for equal work, whether they were receptionists, cab drivers, or electricians. But according to some feminist theorists, the doctrine of equal pay for equal work was insufficient. They asserted that jobs traditionally held by women were devalued precisely because they were women's occupations. To rectify this state of affairs, they promoted a new doctrine. Instead of equal pay for equal work, the law should require equal pay for jobs of comparable worth.

Comparable worth or, as it was sometimes called, pay equity, sought to rearrange wage scales not simply for workers doing jobs that were relatively similar, such as a subway motorman and a long-haul trucker, but also for jobs that were highly dissimilar—a truck driver and a registered nurse, for example. Pay equity called for sweeping job evaluations to determine whether certain positions were undervalued because they were predominantly filled by women, and whether some jobs were overvalued because they were predominantly held by men. Comparable-worth plans encountered considerable resistance in the court system, and their impact has thus far been largely restricted to the public sector.

Women's rights advocates have been more successful in persuading the government and the courts to take steps against sexual harassment in the workplace and in education. A series of court decisions have held both individuals and corporations responsible for acts of sexual harassment, patterns of harassment, or a work environment that is deemed hostile to women. Title VII of the 1964 Civil Rights Act, which bans discrimination on the basis of sex in the workplace, is the key federal law cited in harassment cases. Another important statute is the Civil Rights Act of 1991, which added provisions to Title VII that expanded the rights of women to sue and collect punitive damages in harassment cases. In 1980, the Equal Employment Opportunity Commission (EEOC) had issued regulations defining sexual harassment and stating that it was a form of discrimination outlawed by the Civil Rights Act.

The federal judiciary has been equally important in curtailing sexual harassment. In case after case, the courts, including the Supreme Court, have defined sexual harassment; set standards for employer liability; established whether speech, as opposed to conduct, can create a hostile environment; allowed psychological effects to be included in the assessment of damages; set standards for assessing same-sex harassment; and set standards for giving harassment suits class-action status. Approximately 15,000 sexual harassment cases are brought before the EEOC each year.

Access to Education

The American economy has evolved into one in which good jobs require knowledge and specialized skills, elevating the role of education as an instrument of social mobility. In the past, many new immigrants and working-class households were able to attain middle-class status through well-paid union jobs in industry and construction, or in certain skilled trades. The dwindling of the blue-collar option has put particular pressure on segments of the population that may have relied on it for generations, whether out of tradition or due to past bias that excluded them from higher education.

Critics like William Julius Wilson have pointed to the decline of the blue-collar sector as the principal reason for the failure of African Americans to make more substantial strides toward economic equality. Others have pointed to the danger of an emerging two-tiered economy, in which the well educated and their children attain interesting careers and prosperity, while those without higher education and very often their children are relegated to a low-wage, dead-end fate.

The principal flaw in this argument is that it ignores the multilayered university system that has evolved in the United States and offers diverse opportunities to obtain a higher education. There are literally thousands of colleges in America, including two-year community colleges, state colleges and universities, religion-based private institutions, and prestigious Ivy League schools.

However, four-year colleges offer advantages over two-year colleges, and most students do not attend four-year institutions. Of the roughly four million young people who were of age to enter college in 2002, only 35 percent actually entered a four-year college. Furthermore, minorities were much less likely than whites to enroll in college when they reached the normal age of high school graduation. The relevant figures were 37 percent for whites, 26 percent for blacks, and 15 percent for Latinos.

It is widely believed that a lack of money is a major impediment to access to higher education for the poor, and especially for low-income minority students. Certainly it is true that college is expensive. In 2003, the average tuition, room, and board in public colleges cost $10,700 a year; the average was over $25,000 for private colleges. However, financial aid is readily available for deserving students. In the same year, 76 percent of students in four-year colleges and 89 percent in private colleges received some assistance. Most of this aid—59 percent in public universities and 82 percent in private institutions—took the form of outright grants.

The bigger obstacle to college enrollment is not money, but preparation. Richard D. Kahlenberg, a scholar of American education at the Century Foundation, asserts that "there's almost no gap between college ready high school graduates and the number of students starting college. Virtually everyone who is academically qualified to go to college actually goes to college." However, not everyone is qualified. Studies have shown that some two-thirds of college-age Americans either do not graduate from high school or do graduate but lack the basic academic prerequisites for college admission.[17] Because the primary cause of the racial gap in college enrollment is that students are graduating from high school without being academically prepared for college, the problem is not likely to be solved until reforms are made in primary and secondary education.

Conclusion

Globalization has widened the gulf between those with skills and education and the traditional working class, not only in America but around the world. The gap between the rich and poor has expanded, sometimes by substantial amounts, in Russia, China, and India, as well as throughout Latin America. The same process has occurred even in Europe.

Economic globalization has also contributed to the decline of the traditional institution of working-class solidarity and power, the trade union. While the erosion of labor's ability to organize and represent workers has proceeded further in the United States than in many other countries, trade-union decline has occurred worldwide, including in countries where the political and legal environment is friendlier than in America.

What has distinguished the United States from most other societies is that inequality, as measured in the narrowest terms of income and wealth, barely figures in the American political debate. To be sure, Americans have responded politically to fears over economic insecurity during times of mass layoffs by major corporations, and have expressed a desire for a more robust level of social welfare benefits. But the reports of huge salaries for CEOs or the excessive lifestyles of entertainers and professional athletes, not to mention the mundane statistics that demonstrate the increased level of inequality, have had surprisingly little resonance among ordinary Americans. This, however, may be changing. Opinion surveys show a major increase in the proportion of Americans who are concerned about rising inequality and who believe that they are among society's "have-nots." According to a poll conducted by the Pew Research Center, in 2007 fully 48 percent of Americans believe the country is divided into "haves" and "have-nots," compared to 26 percent in 1988. During that same period the percentage of Americans who identified themselves as part of the have-nots doubled from 17 to 34 percent.

At the same time, the United States in many important ways remains committed to equal opportunity in employment and education. The pillars of the country's antidiscrimination regime are detailed here and in other chapters in this study. The progress that women have made, especially in education and the economy, stands as powerful evidence of the seriousness of the American commitment. It also reminds us of the importance of the openness of American society to new ideas, demands, and causes. Without freedom of association, freedom of expression, and the freedom to advocate for a political agenda, gains for women would not have been possible. Likewise, the integration of immigrant groups, especially those of non-European origin, testifies to the ability of American society to judge people by their character and achievements rather than by religion or skin color. The high-profile representation of Asians and Latinos in the upper echelons of the Bush administration reflects a broader reality within the corporate world, in small business, and in the nonprofit sector. In no other society would one find as many women, minorities, or children of immigrants in high positions of power and authority as in the United States.

And while the United States has taken little direct action to ameliorate the negative effects of economic change, it must be credited with having established a system of higher education that offers an efficient route to success for both elites and ordinary citizens in an era in which knowledge often determines destiny. The United States boasts a system of colleges and universities that offers education to students with a broad range of abilities, interests, and income levels.

At the same time, the decline of organized labor represents a decline in workers' right to associate and a serious blemish on American democracy. Labor's critics argue that workers today are simply not interested in unions and are content with their conditions of employment. The fact that trade-union membership in the private sector in Canada is four times that of the United States casts doubt on this contention. More to the point, it is impossible to know whether American workers would opt for union representation in substantial numbers as long as the playing field is tilted against organized labor.

Endnotes

1. National Right to Work Foundation website, http://www.nrtw. org/.
2. Helen Dewar, "Labor Plight in '78; Ambitious Program Is Proving Elusive," *Washington Post*, September 4, 1978.
3. Philip Shabecoff, "Business Interests Unite to Fight Over Labor Laws," *New York Times*, June 24, 1977.
4. Peter T. Kilborn, "Ban on Replacing Strikers Faces Veto Threat," *New York Times*, March 7, 1991.
5. Steven Greenhouse, "Sharp Decline in Union Members in '06," *New York Times*, January 26, 2007.
6. Jelle Visser, "Union Membership Statistics in 24 Countries," *Monthly Labor Review*, January 2006.
7. Human Rights Watch, "Unfair Advantage: Workers' Freedom of Association in the United States Under International Human Rights Standards," August 2000, 17–32.
8. Bryan O'Keefe and Whitney Blake, "Rebound of Labor?" *New York Sun*, February 9, 2007.
9. U.S. Census Bureau, "Women's History Month," news release, March 2006.
10. Ibid.
11. Ibid.
12. American Medical Association, *Physician Characteristics and Distribution in the U.S.* (American Medical Association Press, 2006).
13. Ibid.
14. American Bar Association, "First Year and Total J.D. Enrollment by Gender, 1947–2005," http://www.abanet.org/legaled/statistics/charts/stats%20-%206.pdf.
15. Harvard Business School, "Statistics: MBA Program," http://www.hbs.edu/about/mba.html.
16. U.S. Bureau of Labor Statistics, "Highlights of Women's Earnings in 2004," http://www.bls.gov/cps/cpswom2004.pdf.
17. Greg Forster, "The Embarrassing Good News About College Access," *Chronicle of Higher Education*, March 10, 2006.

Political Process: Needs Repair

Aided by a vigorous press, an energetic civil society, and the determination of whichever party comprises the "loyal opposition" at each level of the system, today's American is free to choose who holds political power and has at least as much influence on the workings of government as citizens in any other democracy. The process through which citizens compete for political office, and more generally for influence over government actions and the substance of public policy, is relatively transparent and accessible to those who choose to take part.

Yet, as the world famously learned in November and December 2000, the United States has a remarkably decentralized and diverse set of electoral arrangements in which a closely decided contest can lead to political firestorms and diminished public confidence in the integrity of the process. Controversy continues about how the country can compile an accurate registry of eligible voters, ascertain that these persons each vote only once in elections when they desire to participate, and be confident in the announced results. Several major efforts have been undertaken to find solutions consistent with the American federal system. A bipartisan commission led by former President Jimmy Carter and former Secretary of State James Baker produced one of the more compelling proposals as part of a comprehensive set of recommendations in September 2005.[1] Yet efforts to improve electoral administration are often stymied by partisans who insist that the main issue is either voter fraud or voter disenfranchisement. Dismayingly, because the most consistent demographic correlation in voting habits is that African Americans tend disproportionately to vote for Democrats, partisan scuffling for advantage in this regard often veers into racial stereotyping and race-baiting that complicates resolution.

Other aspects of the national political process are problematic or controversial. In late 2007, the rules of the game are still being established for the presidential contest that is already well under way, as conflict simmers within the political parties and among the states about the calendar of primary election dates.[2] As in much of American society, the proper boundaries between private and public responsibility are difficult to discern and often disputed. (Are the primaries an internal matter for privately organized political parties? Or does the public interest in the large sums of money spent on elections at every level of government, and the interest in fair elections that extends well beyond party members, mean that these are matters of public policy?) The role of money in politics—who gets to spend how much on which aspects of the electoral and governing processes—is hotly debated. The power of incumbency is much studied and analyzed: while some argue that the institutionalization of constituency service by legislators confers an unfair electoral advantage on those already in office, others see the same dynamic as proof that a democratic system makes officials responsive to citizen demands.

The predominance of two political parties that have successfully established barriers to entry for independent candidates and third parties, draw most electoral boundaries for the protection of incumbents on both sides, and control the electoral machinery itself, is also noteworthy. Opinion surveys suggest popular disquiet with the existing system, though voters also tend not to support alternatives when they appear. Moreover, major third-party bids for the presidency, even when relatively well-funded and successful in attracting voters, have generally been highly personalized epiphenomena rather than the products of lasting political organizations. In the current presidential election season, a new effort called Unity08 has brought together prominent campaigners from both the Republican and Democratic establishments who seek to launch a bipartisan ticket, avoiding both the formation of a permanent third party and a focus on any single personality. Using secure internet voting, the project's backers intend to craft a centrist alternative to what they see as polarizing and unconstructive partisanship.[3]

More than two centuries after the adoption of the Constitution, the American political system is, in many critical aspects and depending on one's perspective, either still a work in progress or in need of serious repair. Some points of contention date back several decades (low voter turnout) or even to the adoption of the Constitution (the Electoral College), while others have crystallized in the modern era (campaign finance regulation). No American would say the United States is a perfect democracy, or even that it administers elections as well it should. All three branches of government, every one of the 50 states, and more than 3,100 counties each play a distinct role in defining and implementing the political process in our federal system. This means not only that ours is a broadly inclusive, locally based democracy, but that many, many people and entities have collaborated in the construction of an electoral framework that has lately dismayed America's admirers, and brought glee to critics of the United States.

Nevertheless, and notwithstanding the flaws discussed below, the American political system basically works. New actors constantly enter the arena, while incumbents and majority parties are turned from office at each election. Public opinion matters, and those citizens who choose to mobilize can affect outcomes very directly. The country is almost continually engaged in debate about how to improve the system.

In the 2006 midterm elections, owing to the corrupt practices of a handful of officeholders and rising opposition to the president's policies in Iraq, the dominant Republican Party lost its majorities in both chambers of Congress. It remains to be seen, of course, whether the Congress now controlled by Democrats will address either the corruption issue or the war in

Iraq in ways that satisfy the recently energized voters. But the election results demonstrated anew that, despite concerns about the impact of gerrymandering, the presumed fund-raising and other advantages of incumbency, and efforts at vote suppression in key areas, the American people can change who governs them when they choose to do so.

Incumbency Advantage

Gerrymandering. The practice of gerrymandering, perhaps the most visible means by which incumbents seek to engineer their reelection, is an American political tradition rooted in the system of single-member legislative districts. It dates back at least to 1812, when Governor Elbridge Gerry of Massachusetts, at the behest of Jeffersonian Democrats, approved a district that had been tortured for political purposes into the shape of a salamander. He was promptly excoriated in the press by opponents of the plan, who preserved the governor's name for posterity by coining the term "gerrymander." Two centuries later, the growing power of computing enables mapmakers to draw lines with great precision based not only on election statistics, but on data about voters' history of political contributions, race, education, income level, and other factors that may correlate with voting behavior. Because gerrymandering is designed to increase the number of "wasted votes" among the electorate, as the majority interest packs its opponents' voters into designated districts, the relative representation of particular groups, whether ideological, ethnic, or economic, can diverge from their actual share of the voting population.

Gerrymandering has become a central feature of the American political system, as state legislators fulfill their constitutional obligation to accommodate changes in the population by adjusting state and federal legislative districts after each decennial census. In the process, both major parties utilize their positions in the state legislatures and gubernatorial mansions to carve out personal and partisan advantage. Even in states where bipartisan commissions have been established to draw districts, they sometimes break down amid partisan standoffs, prompting the courts to step in and replace district maps that would have egregiously violated equal protection clauses of the Constitution and federal legislation.

The self-interested nature of this process, as it occurs in 49 states, is *prima facie* corrupt. That alternatives are possible is made clear by the practice in the state of Iowa, where redistricting is entrusted to the nonpartisan Legislative Services Bureau with specific instructions not to consider the location of incumbents or party interest. Indeed, in 2002, two of Iowa's incumbent House members—Jim Leach (R) and Leonard Boswell (D)—had to move their place of residence in order to run in newly configured districts.[4] Those looking for proof that gerrymandering achieves its aims typically point to the longevity in office of its practitioners and beneficiaries. Since the 1950s, elections to the U.S. House of Representatives in particular have been marked by an increasingly conspicuous lack of competitiveness. In 2002, only four incumbents in the 435-seat House lost to nonincumbent challengers (though others retired, and four were defeated by rival incumbents in newly reconfigured districts)—the fewest ever in the country's history. In 2004, only five of the 404 incumbents seeking reelection were defeated at the polls, a reelection rate of 99 percent.[5]

Nevertheless, American scholars are divided on the impact of redistricting and gerrymandering on incumbency, with some asserting that there is, in fact, little hard evidence that it works as well as popularly believed.[6] A major reason for the lack of consensus is the difficultly of separating the effect of redistricting from other incumbency advantages, discussed below, as well as from social and political trends at the national, regional, and local levels. Complicating the issue further—and apparently leading many scholars to support the null hypothesis when, in fact, a small but real effect may exist—is the observation that the effects of redistricting can vary widely depending on the type of gerrymander employed.

An incumbent-protecting gerrymander creates safer seats for current members on both sides of the aisle, so it decreases the number of competitive, marginal districts contested by incumbents in the election cycle immediately following redistricting. In partisan gerrymandering, however, the party in power will often attempt to concentrate opposition supporters into as few districts as possible (and sometimes dilute its own advantage in secure areas) in order to increase its overall majority. Depending on how far this process is taken, it can have the effect of increasing the number of marginal seats. Moreover, redistricting plans are frequently hybrids combining some aspects of each kind of gerrymander. Many argue that, in the aggregate, the decrease in electoral competition created by incumbency-protection gerrymandering is balanced by the increase in competition resulting from partisan gerrymandering.[7]

Calculating Incumbency Advantage. Before addressing the other tools available to incumbents, it is worthwhile to note the difficulty of producing a precise calculation of their overall electoral edge. As noted above, recent House reelection figures are fairly impressive. Over the last five election cycles, incumbents have been returned to office an average of 97 percent of the time. Even in the Democrats' sweeping victory of 2006, House members running for reelection managed to win 94.5 percent of their races. Similarly, an examination of the proportion of congressional elections over the last 50 years that have been decided by less than 20 percentage points provides a panoramic view of the rising level of stagnation in congressional elections. From 1960 to 1968, House incumbents won by at least a 20-point margin, 64 percent of the time.[8] Then, during the 1970s, they won by that margin 73 percent of the time. From 1980 to 1988 the trend continued, with incumbents winning handily in 79 percent of all districts in which they ran for reelection. Between 1990 and 1998, the tide temporarily reversed, as only 71 percent of incumbents won reelection by more than 20 percent.[9] But the elections since the turn of the millennium have been the most stagnant of any decade since Reconstruction. Over the last four election cycles, 83 percent of House incumbents won by more than 20 points. Again, in the tumultuous 2006 elections, 79 percent of those seeking reelection were returned via landslide margins of 20 points or more.

Nonetheless, incumbency reelection rates are an incomplete measure of incumbency advantage. They assume that incumbents and challengers are essentially equal, as if selected at random, when they are not. Incumbents have already won an election and are thus, *ipso facto*, better-than-average campaigners. Furthermore, challengers who choose—or are chosen—to run in districts that are deemed safe for the incumbent party or lawmaker are typically not as competitive as the average candidate. And incumbents who perceive that they are unlikely to be reelected, due to personal problems or broader political trends, often retire strategically. Thus a discussion focused mainly on reelection rates tends to overstate the incumbent's entrenchment.

Among the first scholars to address this problem and present a more nuanced estimate of incumbency advantage was Robert Erikson, who in 1971 measured its magnitude as the difference between a candidate's success in an initial electoral win and that of subsequent victories. His measure also controls for redistricting, partisan electoral tides, and the effect of running against an incumbent—for members who did not enter Congress through an open seat. Erikson found that, on average, incumbency in the 1960s was worth about two percentage points on election day.[10] Recent studies, using essentially the same methodology, have shown that incumbency advantage has grown drastically since 1960 and place its current value at between 8 and 11 percentage points.[11]

Professionalization and Earmarking. Some analysts attribute the longevity of lawmakers in office to the growing professionalization of the nation's legislatures during the 20th century.[12] On the one hand, professionalization increases legislative effectiveness, leads to higher productivity, expands membership diversity, and brings in savvier, more adept representatives.[13] On the other hand, over the last 60 years, career-minded legislators have developed tools and provided themselves with resources that both raise the barrier for entry and serve them well in reelection bids.

A popular perception of congressional dynamics juxtaposes the major political parties in fierce battle with one another, locked in a zero-sum game with the majority attempting to push their partisan agenda through, while the minority works diligently to stymie such efforts. Scholars of congressional organization, though, offer a very different picture: a more decentralized legislature with relatively weak parties, where members seek seats on committees that have jurisdiction over the portion of the budget they believe is most important to the localities they represent.[14] Members then engage in a positive-sum game: they use their committee positions to appropriate funds for projects that benefit a particular interest or visibly bring federal resources into their district or state, and then trade votes in order to secure funding for their pet projects.[15]

By catering in this manner to diverse—and sometimes deserving—special interests, members create powerful allies and potential campaign contributors, which provide them with financial and organizational advantages in subsequent elections. Given the electoral benefits of this distributive brand of politics, it is little surprise that pork-barrel projects, in the form of "earmarks" attached to appropriations bills, are both quite common and on the rise. According to the Congressional Research Service, in 1994 members of Congress allocated $27 billion on 4,202 pet projects; in 2005, they set aside $52.1 billion for 16,050 such projects.[16]

The 2006 election season was roiled by unfolding news about the outsized influence that lobbyist Jack Abramoff seemed to have on the work of Congress and the practice of earmarking. (Abramoff, Representative Robert Ney of Ohio, and at least 10 others have since been convicted of criminal charges in this context.[17]) In an effort to increase the transparency of these spending decisions and decrease the influence of hired lobbyists on Washington lawmakers, the Congress elected that year passed an ethics reform bill entitled the Honest Leadership and Open Government Act of 2007. The new law prohibits members of

Congress and their staffs from accepting gifts, free meals, and travel, and extends the time a former member must wait before becoming a lobbyist. In addition, the bill requires the disclosure of, among other things, the legislative author of all earmarks for federal projects in appropriations bills, and an accounting of any earmarks contained in bills and conference reports before they are voted on. Critics of the legislation point out that while it does restrict the use of earmarks, it also creates a number of loopholes, for instance by increasing—from one or two to 40—the number of senators it takes to prevent provisions not passed by the House or the Senate from being inserted into legislation. That would make it easier, not harder, to enact special interest measures without public scrutiny.[18]

While earmarks have been popularly described as a means for lawmakers to divert taxpayer dollars into wasteful pork-barrel projects of limited public utility, some elected officials have spoken up in favor of the practice. Democratic Representative Rahm Emanuel of Illinois, for instance, noted that while "some members of Congress, on both sides of the aisle, eschew earmarks... most members believe it is their prerogative and their duty to channel federal resources to important public purposes."[19]

Nearly every president in the past century has sought to obtain the authority of a line-item veto as a tool for controlling supposedly wasteful spending added to bills by lawmakers. Most governors have similar authority over state spending. In a curious triangulation, Democratic President Bill Clinton collaborated with congressional Republicans to enact the Line Item Veto Act of 1996, and Clinton used the new power 82 times before it was declared unconstitutional in a 6-to-3 ruling by the Supreme Court in 1998.[20]

Constituency Service and District Ties. Constituency service is another means by which members of Congress can improve their image within their districts and create an electoral advantage over challengers. Although helping constituents to obtain veterans' benefits, Social Security checks, and civil service pensions, or to navigate some other facet of the federal bureaucracy, is a legitimate and important function performed by representatives, it is also a significant electoral advantage, as it allows members to stand apart from their party, and from Congress as a whole, at election time.[21] In contrast to Canada or the United Kingdom, where party organizations play a stronger role in politics, a large and growing proportion of U.S. representatives' electoral support is attributed to their personal qualities and local activities, making it less susceptible to changing partisan tides and negative views of Congress.[22] Not surprisingly, opinion polls consistently find that voters rate their own representatives much higher than they rate Congress.[23] To more effectively reap the electoral benefits of casework, members maintain increasingly well-staffed offices in their districts. Some may wonder whether there are more efficient, systematic fixes to the bureaucratic problems these offices seek to address for constituents, but the current system in which elected officials serve as brokers for federal benefits clearly is seen to be worth continuing.

In addition, federal legislators have allocated to themselves resources that enable them to maintain visibility in their districts throughout the year. From 1962 to 1997, for instance, members gradually raised the number of annual trips they could take to their districts at public expense elevenfold, from 3 to 33.[24] Of course, it must be noted on behalf of these perquisites that frequent visits also increase legislators' ability to understand their constituents' concerns and advocate better for them in Washington.

Included among each representative's personal communications expenditure is the franking privilege, which allows members of Congress to use the U.S. Postal Service for all "official business," at no charge to them personally or to their campaign organizations. Although the privilege has been around in one form or another since 1789, in 1968 the standards for what constitutes official business were relaxed considerably, and representatives began blanketing their districts with literature that was likely to assist them in their reelection efforts. Yet members' use of the mail is on the wane in today's Congress, as the use of more advanced technologies increases sharply. Incumbents, for example, now cultivate huge taxpayer-funded databases with detailed information about their constituents' interests and interactions with the federal bureaucracy, which they can use to send out issue-specific e-mails to well-targeted groups of voters within their districts.[25]

Term Limits. Concern about the permanent hold that some politicians, especially legislators, seem to have on their jobs has given rise to a civic movement in favor of legal limits on the number of terms they may serve. Some jurisdictions have always required the regular rotation of officeholders, and 36 of the 50 states have limits on the ability of governors to be reelected, usually restricting them to one or two terms. At the presidential level, a two-term tradition launched by George Washington, who declined to stand for a third term, was broken only by Franklin D. Roosevelt, who was elected four times. The presidential two-term limit became mandatory under a 1951 constitutional amendment. In the 1980s and early 1990s, a private organization called U.S. Term Limits Inc. persuaded a large number of candidates for state and federal office to pledge that they would only serve three terms in a lower house or two terms in a senate, and the Republican Party's "Contract With America," the platform for their successful takeover of Congress in the 1994 elections, included term-limit provisions. In 23 states, measures were enacted to limit federal legislators' terms in office, though in 1995 the Supreme Court ruled that states could not impose limits on the terms of federal lawmakers.[26] That same year, the Republican leadership in the House brought a constitutional amendment on the subject to the full chamber. It secured a majority, but not the two-thirds required to pass.

In 2007, political action was under way in California, Pennsylvania, and Missouri to trim or eliminate existing term limits on state legislators. However, U.S. Term Limits Inc. remains active in supporting initiatives, filing related lawsuits, and publicizing the issue. Opponents of term limits argue that they are an unnecessary and unreasonable restriction on the rights of voters and candidates alike, insisting that voters should be able to decide for themselves whether to back an incumbent or one of the alternatives on the ballot.

Enhanced Fairness in Redistricting and Reapportionment

One Man, One Vote. Notwithstanding the real and imagined advantages that decision makers seek to extract in the course of redrawing district boundaries, the American system has seen a clear improvement in many dimensions of fairness over several decades, often due to the intervention of the courts. Since the Supreme Court handed down *Baker v. Carr* in 1962, the level of both partisan bias and malapportionment within the electoral framework has decreased markedly, at both the state and national level. Prior to 1964, when, in *Reynolds v. Sims,* the Supreme Court applied its "one man, one vote" principle nationwide,[27] legislative districts in many states were seriously malapportioned, and a strong bias favoring rural over urban areas prevailed. In the 1962 Alabama state legislature, for example, a majority of state senators represented just 25 percent of all Alabamans, and the rural county of Bullock (population 13,500) had two House seats while Mobile (population 314,000) had just one.[28] Similarly, based on the 1960 census, the most populous district in Vermont's General Assembly had 33,000 residents, while the least populated district contained only 238.[29] Other egregious examples include Connecticut, where the population ratio between the most and least populated districts was 424 to 1; California, where the ratio in the state Senate was 428 to 1; and Utah, with a 196 to 1 ratio in the state House. In the U.S. House of Representatives, the level of malapportionment was much less extreme, but ratios of 2 to 1 were not uncommon.

The redistricting revolution that followed *Baker v. Carr* and other decisions in the early 1960s shifted the balance of power from rural to urban and suburban voters, and greatly reduced malapportionment at both the state and federal level.[30] Subsequent court decisions outlined more specific standards and have worked to further reduce malapportionment. By the conclusion of the 2002 round of redistricting, the deviation between the most and least populous U.S. House district of any state was less than two-thirds of one percent. In short, Supreme Court decisions and the redistricting efforts of the 1960s, 1970s, and 1980s have nearly eradicated malapportionment and, as a result, greatly increased representative equality in the United States. A recent study by leading political scientists concludes that population equalization altered the flow of state funds, diverting approximately $7 billion annually from formerly overrepresented to formerly underrepresented counties.[31] The authors concluded that "as long as people have equal representation, they will get a fair share of public expenditures."[32]

Declining Partisan Bias. By examining the effect of change in the proportion of the vote received by each party on change in their respective shares of House seats, scholars have estimated a pro-Republican bias, in non-Southern states, of about six percentage points as of 1962 (meaning that with 50 percent of the vote for the two main parties, the Republican Party could expect about 56 percent of the seats). After the wave of redistricting in 1966, this bias all but disappeared.[33] Southern states, it should be noted, are almost universally omitted from redistricting studies of this period since, at the time, the Democratic Party utterly dominated the vote in the South, general elections there were rarely competitive, and turnout was much lower than in the North. However, once the Republican Party established a presence in the South, evidence of a Democratic partisan bias became clear. Since then, pro-Republican gerrymanders have largely corrected this advantage, though at the state level some have significantly overcompensated. Moreover, the net effect of partisan gerrymandering since 1966 is generally believed to be small and, on the whole, has been found to reduce rather than exaggerate overall partisan biases in the American political system.[34]

Analyses of the individual redistricting cycles are consistent in finding minimal or no partisan effects, but due to varying methodologies, they often differ as to which party benefited when they do find effects. In examining the 1970 redistricting efforts, one study argues that the status quo was maintained, producing no noticeable partisan advantage, while another found a small pro-Republican bias.[35] Similarly, in 1980, one study identifies a pro-Democratic bias, and a second shows a small pro-Republican advantage.[36] The 1990 cycle is thought to have either benefited only incumbents or evinced a latent pro-Republican advantage.[37] Finally, the available literature on the 2000 redistricting cycle shows no real partisan consequence. While the 2003 out-of-cycle redistricting efforts in Texas and Georgia had substantial pro-Republican effects, they both seem to have worked to offset large preexisting pro-Democratic bias in those states. When the Supreme Court reviewed the constitutionality of the Texas redistricting plan famously orchestrated by former Representative Tom DeLay, in *League of United Latin American Citizens et al. v. Perry et al.*, it confirmed that gerrymandering for partisan purposes is not unconstitutional. With some minor adjustments to correct for violations of the race requirements established in the Voting Rights Act of 1964, the Texas plan was left intact.

Clearly, partisan redistricting has the potential to create a significant and sustainable bias within the political system and overrepresent the interest of one party at the expense of the other. However, since 1966 the most effective partisan gerrymanders have typically moved the state in question from a severe bias favoring one party to a slight bias favoring the other, and collectively, the redistricting efforts of the last 40 years seem to have worked to reduce the overall level of partisan bias within the political system.[38]

Counting Prisoners and Citizens Overseas. The census data that Congress uses to reapportion seats and that most state legislatures use to redraw district lines is often quite controversial, since nominally technical or administrative determinations have obvious and immediate political impact. The census includes children, noncitizens, institutionalized people, and other groups that are not permitted to vote. It also counts federal employees and military personnel who are overseas, adding them to the totals for their home states and districts, but excludes nongovernmental workers living abroad.

One of the more contentious outcomes of the 2000 census was the allocation of the 435th House seat to North Carolina, which edged out Utah by just 857 residents. In an unsuccessful suit brought in federal court, Utah argued that Mormon missionaries serving overseas should be treated no differently than federal employees working abroad.[39] In fact, if Mormons on missions overseas were counted, Utah, with 11,176, would have been awarded the extra seat, since North Carolina had only 107.[40] Alternatively, if all residents living overseas were excluded for purposes of reapportionment, Utah, with just 3,545 residents working abroad as federal employees, still would have been awarded the seat, given that North Carolina had 18,360 residents in that category.

While in this instance the effect on the overall equality and level of representation in the United States is quite small, the extra seat would have increased Utah's modest influence in the House by 25 percent and its impact on presidential elections by about 18 percent. Furthermore, to the extent that the interests of the 4.1 million non–federally employed American citizens currently residing abroad are different from those who *are* counted in the census, not counting them distorts the substantive representativeness of American democracy to some degree.[41]

A related concern is the Census Bureau practice of counting prison inmates where they are incarcerated rather than in the inmate's previous place of residence. A disproportionate number of state prisons are located in sparsely populated areas, while the two million inmates they house are predominately from densely populated cities in other electoral districts. Because inmates are not permitted to vote (in all but two states), the ballots cast by citizens of rural districts with large prison populations are effectively given more weight than those of voters in other districts. Fifteen percent of Montana's 85th state House district, for instance, are incarcerated. One county in Louisiana, a second in Florida, and a third in Texas get more than 30 percent of their population totals from prisons.[42]

In New York, 91 percent of the state's prisons are located upstate, but 66 percent of the inmates are from New York City.[43] The seven New York State Senate districts with the largest prison populations are rural upstate districts represented by conservative senators, who vote quite differently than those from the city. This pro-rural bias is further exacerbated by the fact that New York City is systematically underrepresented in the Senate, with each of the 29 districts in its five boroughs containing between 1.69 percent and 4.83 percent more individuals than average. If the state's prison population were excluded, each of the seven rural upstate districts noted above would have between 5.8 and 6.8 percent fewer people than the average district, and all seven of the districts in the Democratic-dominated borough of Queens would have 4.1 percent more people than average. That would raise the deviation between the most and least populous districts beyond the 10 percent limit set by the Supreme Court. It should be noted that in the New York State Assembly, the lower house of the legislature, the situation is somewhat reversed. New York City is overrepresented by just under 1 percent; if the prison population is omitted, this bias drops to ½ of 1 percent.

The Electoral College

Another institution that affects the representative character of American government is the presidential Electoral College, adopted in 1789 as part of the grand federal bargain that is the U.S. Constitution. The number of electors in each state is equivalent to the number of representatives a state has in both the Senate and the House of Representatives. As a result, the states with smaller populations receive added weight, and the 10 largest states have 35 fewer electors than they would if the nation's 538 electoral votes were distributed purely on the basis of population; California alone has 10 fewer electoral votes than it might. In addition, to maximize their influence over the selection of the president, states have an interest in maintaining a winner-take-all system, allocating all their electoral votes to a single candidate; 48 states currently do so. This creates a structural bias that also heightens the influence of "swing states," where party preferences are about evenly divided, and whose Electoral College votes would essentially cancel one another out if they were allocated proportionately to each candidate.

Four times in U.S. presidential election history (1824, 1876, 1888, and 2000), the winner of the popular vote has failed to win the White House. There have only been 54 presidential elections to date. Therefore, almost 8 percent of the time, the Electoral College system has led to the election of a candidate other than the one who received the most votes nationwide—a modest, but by no means insignificant, proportion. However, candidate and voter behavior under a system without the Electoral College would likely be different in ways that are not entirely predictable. For instance, the perceived closeness of the presidential contest in a particular state currently has a significant impact on voter turnout in that state.[44] It is unclear how turnout would be affected if every vote in the country were counted equally.

Even when the structural biases of the Electoral College are not sufficiently significant to change the outcome of the election, they may still have considerable impact on substantive representation. Election-minded first-term presidents, for instance, are much more likely to be responsive to the interests of voters in swing states than those in noncompetitive states. The Electoral College endures, however, because it is generally understood to be a part of the federal inheritance, in which states are seen as historically sovereign entities rather than mere administrative divisions. Proponents, moreover, often argue that the Electoral College obliges candidates to marshal popular support in multiple parts of the country, preventing the victory of those who rely on the exploitation of regional interests or prejudices. The system also discourages third-party candidates, which, all else being equal, results in more stable, centrist policies than alternative frameworks.

Voting Administration and Equal Access

A major issue of concern is equality of access to and influence over the political process. Despite universal suffrage and the great strides made in protecting individual voting rights, not all citizens in today's America have an equal voice with which to influence government decision-making. The problem starts with access to the ballot. In recent election cycles, observers reported what are, at best, inconsistent practices regarding the purging of voter rolls and voter registration. The updating of voter lists and the vetting of incoming registration cards are necessary to maintain the integrity and manageability of the electoral process. But the improper purging of voter rolls, inequitable distribution of voting machinery, unreasonable rejection of provisional ballots, and unlawful voter intimidation tactics effectively suppress voter turnout at critical times and places—and do so disproportionately along ethnic, partisan, and socioeconomic lines.

For nearly 100 years after the constitutional enfranchisement of all African Americans and the extension of equal protection under the law to all citizens, the voting power of ethnic minorities throughout the country, and particularly in the South, was suppressed by aggressive intimidation tactics, the widespread use of violence, unconstitutional voting rules, and the lack of effective means of recourse. The passage of the Voting Rights Act in 1965 provided the federal government additional tools with which to enforce the rights guaranteed under the 14th and 15th amendments, and specifically outlawed many voter-suppression practices. The statute required large-scale Justice Department monitoring of elections in states with a poor history of ensuring voting rights, and paved the way for legal challenges against those who continued disenfranchisement efforts.

From 1964 to 1974, in the seven Southern states covered by Section 5 of the Voting Rights Act, registration of black voters increased from 29 to over 56 percent, and the disparity between white and black registration decreased from 44.1 to 11.2 percent.[45] Over the last 30 years the situation has continued to improve. In Louisiana and Mississippi, the registration rate among blacks today exceeds that of whites. Problems persist nonetheless. In modern presidential elections, about 2 percent of all ballots are spoiled (at the low end of the range in well-established democracies),[46] and hundreds of thousands of additional voters are not permitted to cast their vote on election day due to problems in the registration process.[47] Thousands more are deliberately targeted in efforts to suppress their vote. The effect on election outcomes is often minute, but the voters in question are disproportionately minority and urban, meaning their collective political voice is muffled and their access to the political process is reduced relative to white, nonurban voters. Because African Americans tend overwhelmingly to vote Democratic when they do vote—and because problems in obtaining government-issued photo identification, rates of arrest and imprisonment, and poverty tend to affect African Americans disproportionately—the purely partisan interests of Republicans in affecting election outcomes assume an unfortunate racial character.

"Majority-minority" districts spawned by the Voting Rights Acts of 1965 and 1982 have added to the presence of minorities in legislatures, as boundaries have been drawn to concentrate minority voters. The 1992 elections, the first based on lines drawn after the 1982 law was enacted, led to a jump in the number of minorities in the House of Representatives, from 38 to 58.[48] While this has clearly been beneficial to minorities (and the Democratic Party) at one level of analysis, subsequent studies have raised the question of whether broader minority interests have truly been enhanced, since the districts created have left adjoining districts bereft of the reliable Democratic voters that minority candidates often represent.[49]

Even after the legislative reforms of the past 50 years, some ethnic minorities, particularly African Americans, continue to face voter intimidation and disenfranchisement efforts, although the methods are often less crude than in the past.

In New Jersey in 1981, the Republican National Committee (RNC) set up "ballot security" task forces, exclusively in precincts with a majority of ethnic minority voters, to purge voter rolls of citizens whose mail was returned as undeliverable. It then deployed hired armed guards at polling places on election day. In response, a U.S. District Court issued a ban on efforts to target specific groups for disenfranchisement or intimidation, even if the means are otherwise legitimate.[50]

Despite the ban, an internal party document indicated that the RNC launched a similar effort in 1986 in order to "keep the black vote down" in Louisiana, Georgia, Missouri, Pennsylvania, Michigan, and Indiana;[51] the RNC worked to have 31,000 mostly black voters purged from registration rolls in Louisiana alone.[52] Likewise, in 1988 armed guards were placed at polling places in heavily Hispanic precincts in Orange County, California; in 1990, 125,000 postcards were mailed primarily to black North Carolinians, intentionally misinforming them about residency requirements;[53] and intimidating mailers, fliers, and signs threatening jail time and deportation for those who did not follow registration requirements were frequently deployed in minority neighborhoods in New York City, Texas, and the Carolinas during the 1990s.[54]

Following the 2000 presidential election in Florida, there were similar allegations of intimidation and improper purging of eligible voters from registration rolls in heavily African American precincts. That election also brought to light the unequal allocation of voting machinery, and its disparate impact on black voters. Throughout the state, 4 percent of all punch-card ballots were excluded, compared with 1.4 percent of optical-scan ballots.[55] Punch-card machines are located disproportionately in African American areas, in Florida and elsewhere.

In response to concerns that the allocation of voting machines and the practice of purging voter registration lists effectively dilute the vote of ethnic minorities, Congress passed the Help America Vote Act (HAVA) in October 2002. The legislation allows voters who have been removed from voter registration lists to cast provisional ballots that may be counted at a later time if they were in fact improperly purged. It also mandates minimum standards for election machinery. Overall, HAVA seems to have significantly reduced the total number of spoiled ballots nationwide. Charles Stewart III, an expert on voting behavior and equipment at the Massachusetts Institute of Technology, estimates that HAVA saved about one million votes across the country in 2004.[56]

Nevertheless, voters faced familiar problems at the polls that year. A court order to make public a purge list of 47,000 "potential felons" in Florida revealed that thousands of those listed were actually eligible to vote. It appeared that the list, which consisted overwhelmingly of African Americans, had been deliberately cleared of Hispanics, who tend to vote Republican in Florida.[57] The list was scrapped nine days after it was made public. The most extensive reports of vote suppression in 2004 were in Ohio. At the center of most of the electoral controversies was Ohio Secretary of State Ken Blackwell, whose position as cochairman of the Committee to Reelect George W. Bush in the state led many to allege a conflict of interest. Blackwell was ultimately named in 16 election-related lawsuits.

In the months leading up to the 2004 presidential election, there was an unprecedented surge in the registration of new voters in Ohio, which was thought to favor the Democratic Party. In a county-by-county analysis, the *New York Times* found that new registrations between January and September were 250 percent higher than in 2000 in areas that typically vote Democratic, but only 25 percent higher in Republican neighborhoods.[58] During this time, Blackwell took several steps to invalidate new voter registrations, purge names from the existing rolls, and establish more scrupulous standards for the state to follow when considering the validity of provisional ballots. Certainly, some such measures are necessary to eliminate erroneous voter registration applications and remove former residents from the current roll, but many in this case were clearly intended to achieve partisan electoral advantage.

For example, citing an arcane Ohio law, Blackwell for three weeks in September instructed county election boards to reject any registration applications submitted on paper thinner than 80-pound stock (most commonly used for postcards). This excluded standard 20-pound copier paper, used by most Ohioans who printed out their applications from the secretary of state's website.[59] In a separate effort to purge registration rolls of likely Democrats, the Ohio Republican Party unlawfully targeted hundreds of thousands of predominantly minority voters by sending registered mail to their given addresses. If the letters were not signed and returned, or were returned as undeliverable, those registrations were challenged.[60]

Most of the complaints from Ohio concerned the misallocation of voting machines, resulting in four- to ten-hour lines outside dozens of polling places in Cleveland, Columbus, and Cincinnati. Many voters were deterred by the long wait and did not cast ballots. Part of the problem was an overall shortage of voting machines in some parts of the state. Franklin County, for instance, received only 2,866 machines, despite the fact that the Election Board's own analysis indicated that it needed 5,000.[61] There was also a bias in the allocation of machines within counties that worked against precincts with predominately minority and lower-income populations. House Judiciary Committee staff members received reports that, adjacent to two heavily African American precincts in Columbus with five- and seven-hour waits, there was a suburban district with just 184 voters per machine and less than a 15-minute wait.[62] In the whole of Franklin County, where Columbus is located, there were 262 registered voters per machine in precincts with low proportions of African Americans and 324 registered voters per machine in precincts with a high proportion of African Americans, a difference of 23.7 percent; if calculated using the Election Board's measure of "active voters," the disparity is still 13.6 percent.[63]

With control of both houses of Congress at stake in the 2006 midterm elections, several states passed legislation that significantly hindered voter registration drives. In Ohio, the state legislature passed new laws requiring individual registration workers to personally submit completed forms to an election office rather than allowing the organization for which they work to submit them in bulk.[64] The new laws hold the workers *criminally* liable for any irregularities in the forms. In response to similar laws passed in Florida, the League of Women Voters halted their voter registration efforts in that state for the first time in 67 years.[65] However, a federal judge blocked enforcement of the Florida law, which imposed fines of between $250 and $5,000 for the "mishandling" of voter registration cards.

In March 2006, Georgia enacted a law requiring voters to show a passport, driver's license, or other official form of identification before casting a ballot. In contrast to past elections, for which any of 17 different types of documents could be used as proof of identity and residency, the new state law would require Georgians lacking government-issued IDs to purchase a $20 state ID card before voting. A federal judge struck down the law, likening the requirement to a Jim Crow–era poll tax.[66] A subsequent version of the law eliminated the $20 fee; the Supreme Court is currently considering the validity of a similar measure in Indiana.

According to press reports in April 2007, a leaked bipartisan study commissioned by the Election Assistance Commission, a government panel created under HAVA, concluded in 2006 that "there is widespread but not unanimous agreement that there is little polling place fraud." Republicans generally insist that voter fraud is widespread and justifies the voter identification laws that have been passed in at least two dozen states. Democrats, on the other hand, say the threat is overstated and have opposed voter identification laws on the grounds that they tend to disenfranchise the poor, members of minority groups, and the elderly, who are less likely to have photo IDs and are more likely to be Democrats.[67]

Campaign Finance

It is a widely held view that money in the American political system is pervasive and problematic, from the consuming race for campaign contributions to the special political access enjoyed by lobbyists and donors, and that contributions and spending associated with politics need to be regulated closely. Yet an equally compelling argument can be made that the amount of money raised and spent in American politics is by itself a red herring. The more important concern is whether political contributions, or services provided to candidates and officeholders, oblige the recipients to depart from the proper performance of their duties.

New policymaking in this area is rare. Indeed, when the Bipartisan Campaign Reform Act, also known as McCain-Feingold (or Shays-Meehan), was enacted in November 2002, it was the first major reform of campaign finance law in 28 years. There is widespread unease about the central role that fund-raising plays in the life of elected officials, and concern about the fairness of citizen access to officeholders for those without the means to contribute. But finding a regulatory framework consistent with the Constitution's First Amendment guarantees of free speech has proven difficult. The columnist George F. Will, in keeping with America's libertarian tradition, regularly decries the "attacks on free speech" he sees in campaign finance regulation.[68] The Supreme Court, which is currently considered conservative, has acknowledged the validity of viewing campaign donations as a form of free speech, but in a 2006 decision overturning a Vermont law that had imposed a $400 limit on contributions to candidates for statewide office, the court upheld the established principle of permitting contribution limits in the name of thwarting corruption, or the appearance thereof.

McCain-Feingold bans soft money contributions to national political parties, but permits up to $10,000 in soft money contributions to state and local parties. "Soft money" refers to contributions to parties and other political organizations that are not directed to any specific candidate or campaign, meaning it is not subject to older restrictions. The 2002 law also stops so-called issue advertisements, which advocate positions on specific topics, from targeting specific candidates. The ads have been seen as an indirect way of aiding certain campaigns without running afoul of contribution and spending limits. Whether that provision accomplished its main purpose, to curtail the activities of tax-exempt advocacy groups (dubbed 527s after the provision in the tax code that covers them), is disputed.[69] Another portion of McCain-Feingold raised the individual contribution limit from $1,000 to $2,000 per election for House and Senate candidates (the figure increased in the 2008 cycle to $2,300 for each candidate in each federal election for individual donors). A "Millionaire's Amendment" to the law increases the contribution limits for candidates facing wealthy opponents, whose personal spending on their own campaigns remains unrestricted.[70] Many advocates assert that the solution to problems associated with fund-raising is mandatory public financing of federal campaigns, especially since the viability of the current system of voluntary partial public funding of presidential elections appears to have all but collapsed. The top tier of candidates from both parties in 2004 chose to forgo the public financing that was available to them in order to free themselves from the spending limits it entailed, and the same pattern is emerging in the 2008 race. Public financing has become the redoubt of troubled campaigns that are unable to raise funds to compete head-to-head with the front-runners.[71] As the cost of airtime on television and radio is often the largest expense associated with campaigning, some have proposed that the airwaves be harnessed to provide equal access to candidates as a public service.[72]

Voting Rights for the District of Columbia

The 585,000 residents of the District of Columbia do not enjoy the same political rights as other U.S. citizens. There are also a number of small U.S. island territories that have limited access to the federal political process, including American Samoa, Guam, Puerto Rico, and the U.S. Virgin Islands. Puerto Rico is the largest, though its citizens have consistently voted to retain the island's current intermediary status as a commonwealth rather than seek full statehood or independence. As U.S. territories that are not states, these five jurisdictions fall into a constitutional lacuna that leaves their residents with many of the obligations of citizenship but without a say in the election of full voting members of Congress. Their elected delegates have long been permitted to participate in the deliberations of the House and to vote in House committees. In 1993 and again in 2007, Democratic majorities in the House adopted a procedural rule that permits the five delegates to vote with the full House, but their votes count only if they have no effect on a measure's ultimate outcome. None of the five territories are represented in the Senate.

The District is noteworthy in this group because it is the seat of the national government and because, unlike Puerto Rico, its citizens do not control their own destiny. Unfortunately, the intertwined issues of race and partisanship that arise in other aspects of the American political process are evident in this issue as well. Since the population of the District is mostly African American and overwhelmingly Democratic in its political preferences, consideration of how to provide equitable political representation to these citizens is often hampered by partisan wrangling.[73] Fortuitously, the grievance felt by predominantly Republican Utah, which narrowly missed receiving the 435th seat in the House of Representatives following the 2000 census, as discussed earlier, provided the basis for a compromise in 2007 that would have extended full voting rights to a representative from the District. The proposal would have enlarged the House of Representatives to 437 and given one seat each to the District and Utah. However, the measure was blocked in the Senate by the threat of a filibuster and appears to have died for the time being.[74]

In 1961, the 23rd Amendment to the U.S. Constitution was ratified, granting the District electors in the Electoral College. District residents have thus participated in presidential elections since 1964. In 1978, Congress passed another constitutional amendment that would have given the District its own voting members of Congress, making it virtually a state. However, the amendment was given a seven-year time limit for ratification by the states, and only 16 states gave their approval in that time, far short of the three-quarters (currently 38) required.

District sympathizers have tried to craft solutions that would pass constitutional muster and also avoid inflaming partisan or other passions. Congressman Ralph Regula, a Republican from

Ohio, believes that the time is long past to fix the "appalling breach in our democracy" that deprives District residents of voting representation in the House and Senate. His solution is to shrink the District down to a tiny enclave of federal buildings and return the office and residential areas to Maryland, of which the territory was originally a part. This notion is often referred to as retrocession. "Retrocession would allow D.C. to use Maryland state facilities and all other state-funded institutions," Regula has said. "The District could also finally be run like any other major city in the U.S."[75]

Conclusion

There are enduring problems of inequity in the U.S. political system that lead to diminished access for certain groups of voters, frequently the poor and people of color, to full participation in the political process. Efforts to correct these injustices are ongoing, though the federal nature of the American system sometimes disperses decision-making and responsibility and makes resolution more difficult.

Longevity in office and apparently uncompetitive elections are an affront to a significant minority, abetted by gerrymandering, the capture of public resources, and other advantages of incumbency. Yet, as has been discussed, the nature of the problem is frequently misstated, and the potential virtues of long incumbency in the legislature are often overlooked. For instance, a secure district enables a lawmaker to challenge the president, or leaders of his own party, on important issues, and lengthy service allows legislators to develop areas of expertise that enhance the quality of their oversight of the executive branch.

Debate about regulatory limits on contributions to and spending by candidates will surely continue. The corruption of public officials, in which they take action—whether spending public money, enacting laws or regulations, or wielding some other form of influence—in return for personal payments or campaign donations, occurs regularly and in both parties, but does not describe the behavior of the vast majority of elected officials in

America. Indeed, many incur financial hardship or forgo other opportunities in order to serve in public office.

Today's American is able to choose the country's leaders in increasingly fair processes. U.S. citizens have demonstrated again and again that they can oust incumbent officials at all levels whose performance is not satisfactory. Despite its flaws, the system fundamentally works, providing a substantial measure of democratic accountability and regular rotation in government.

Endnotes

1. See the commission's final report and other related documents at http://www.american.edu/ia/cfer/. The recommendations are consistent with the American federal system and also draw on the best practices in electoral administration that have emerged internationally in recent years.
2. As this chapter went to press, the Democratic Party of the state of Florida was engaged in a standoff with the national party over rules about the dates of presidential primaries.
3. Jim VandeHei, "From the Internet to the White House; Political Veterans Work to Organize Bipartisan 2008 Ticket With Online Balloting," *Washington Post*, May 31, 2006.
4. Kelly Buck, "Iowa's Redistricting Process: An Example of the Right Way to Draw Legislative Districts," Centrists.org, July 22, 2004, http://www.centrists.org/pages/2004/07/7_buck_trust.html.
5. Jim VandeHei and Charles Babington, "Technology Sharpens the Incumbents' Edge," *Washington Post*, June 7, 2006.
6. For a review of the academic literature on redistricting and its effects, see Gary Cox and Jonathan Katz, *Elbridge Gerry's Salamander: The Electoral Consequences of the Reapportionment Revolution* (Cambridge: Cambridge University Press, 2002).
7. Alan Abramowitz, Brad Alexander, and Matthew Gunning, "Incumbency, Redistricting, and the Decline of Competition in U.S. House Elections," *Journal of Politics* 68, no. 1 (February 2006); Lawrence Dodd and Bruce Oppenheimer, *Congress Reconsidered*, 8th ed. (Washington, DC: CQ Press, 2004).
8. Norman Ornstein, Thomas Mann, and Michael Malbin, *Vital Statistics on Congress* (Washington, DC: CQ Press, 1992).
9. Compiled by author.
10. Robert Erikson, "The Advantage of Incumbency in Congressional Elections," *Polity* 3, no. 3 (Spring 1971): 395–405.
11. Cox and Katz, *Elbridge Gerry's Salamander*, 132; Gary King and Andrew Gelman, "Enhancing Democracy Through Legislative Redistricting," *American Political Science Review* 88, no. 3 (September 1994): 541–559.

12. For the seminal work on the professionalization of the U.S. House and the argument that professionalization establishes barriers to entry and reduces turnover, see Nelson Polsby, "The Institutionalization of the House of Representatives," *American Political Science Review* 62, no. 1 (March 1968).

13. Peverill Squire, "Membership Turnover and the Efficient Processing of Legislation," *Legislative Studies Quarterly* 23, no. 1 (February 1998); Gerard Padro Miquel and James Snyder, "Legislative Effectiveness and Legislative Careers," *Legislative Studies Quarterly* 31, no. 3 (August 2006): 347–81. Squire finds that efficiency is related to the level of professionalization. Similarly, Miquel and Snyder provide strong statistical support for the claim that careerism leads to increased effectiveness and that effectiveness has a positive impact on incumbent electoral success.

14. Committees formed by each party's lawmakers in the House and Senate make recommendations for committee assignments based on member requests. These recommendations must be approved by the party's full membership in the chamber, and then by the chamber as a whole. In *The Giant Jigsaw Puzzle: Democratic Committee Assignment in the Modern House* (Chicago: University of Chicago Press, 1978), Kenneth Shepsle examines all committee requests from Democratic members of Congress between 1958 and 1974. He finds strong statistical evidence that freshman members self-select onto committees that most benefit local interests and are usually given that assignment (his model predicts successful committee self-selection between 74 and 87 percent of the time). For more on the distributive theory of legislative organization see Shepsle, "Institutional Arrangements and Equilibrium in Multidimensional Voting Models," *American Journal of Political Science* 23, no. 1 (February 1979); and David Baron and John Ferejohn, "Bargaining in Legislatures," *American Political Science Review* 83, no. 4 (December 1989).

15. Barry Weingast and William Marshall, "The Industrial Organization of Congress," *Journal of Political Economy* 96, no. 1 (1988).

16. Amounts tabulated by author from Congressional Research Service, "Earmarks in Appropriation Acts: FY1994, FY1996,

FY1998, FY2000, FY2002, FY2004, FY2005," memorandum, January 26, 2006.

17. Susan Schmidt, James V. Grimaldi, and R. Jeffrey Smith, "Investigating Abramoff—Special Report," *Washington Post*, http://www.washingtonpost.com/wp-dyn/content/link-set/2005/06/22/LI2005062200936.html.

18. Robert D. Novak, "The Senate's Ethics Sleight of Hand," *Washington Post*, September 10, 2007.

19. Rahm Emmanuel, "Don't Get Rid of Earmarks," *New York Times*, August 24, 2007.

20. "Supreme Court Deletes Line-Item Veto; Clinton Disappointed; Opponents of Veto Call It a Victory for the Constitution," CNN AllPolitics, June 25, 1998, http://www.cnn.com/ALLPOLI-TICS/1998/06/25/scotus.lineitem/.

21. Morris Fiorina, "The Case of the Vanishing Marginals: The Bureaucracy Did It," *American Political Science Review* 71, no. 1 (March 1977): 177–181.

22. Bruce Cain, John Ferejohn, and Morris Fiorina, *The Personal Vote: Constituency Service and Electoral Independence* (Cambridge: Harvard University Press, 1990).

23. Glenn Parker and Roger Davidson, "Why Do Americans Love Their Congressmen So Much More Than Their Congress?" *Legislative Studies Quarterly* 4, no. 1 (February 1979): 53–61.

24. Ibid., 32.

25. Jim VandeHei and Charles Babington, "Technology Sharpens the Incumbents' Edge," *Washington Post*, June 7, 2006.

26. *U.S. Term Limits, Inc. v. Thornton*, 514 U.S. 779 (1995).

27. *Wesberry v. Sanders*, 376 U.S. 1 (1964).

28. *Reynolds v. Sims*, 377 U.S. 533 (1964).

29. U.S. State Department, "*Reynolds v. Sims* (1964)," in *Basic Readings in U.S. Democracy*, http://usinfo.state.gov/usa/infousa/facts/democrac/68.htm.

30. The other rulings included *Reynolds v. Sims*, 377 U.S. 533 (1964) and *Wesberry v. Sanders* 376 U.S. 1 (1964).

31. Stephen Ansolabehere, Alan Gerber, and James M. Snyder Jr., "Equal Votes, Equal Money: Court-Ordered Re-Districting and the Distribution of Public Expenditures in the American States"

(unpublished paper), http://web.mit.edu/polisci/research/ ansolabehere/equal_votes_final.pdf), 19–20.
32. Ibid., 22.
33. Robert Erikson, "Malapportionment, Gerrymandering, and Party Fortunes in Congressional Elections," *American Political Science Review* 66, no. 4 (December 1972); Gary Jacobson, *The Electoral Origins of Divided Government: Competition in U.S. House Elections, 1946–1988* (Boulder: Westview Press, 1990); David Brady and Bernard Grofman, "Sectional Differences in Partisan Bias and Electoral Responsiveness in U.S. House Elections, 1850–1980," *British Journal of Political Science* 21, no. 2 (April 1991); and Cox and Katz, *Elbridge Gerry's Salamander.*
34. King and Gelman, "Enhancing Democracy."
35. Amihai Glazer, Bernard Grofman, and Marc Robbins, "Partisan and Incumbency Effects of 1970s Congressional Redistricting," *American Journal of Political Science* 31, no. 3 (August 1987); Richard G. Niemi and Laura R. Winsky, "The Persistence of Partisan Redistricting Effects in the 1970s and 1980s," *Journal of Politics* 54, no. 2 (May 1992).
36. Alan Abromowitz, "Partisan Redistricting and the 1982 Congressional Elections," *Journal of Politics* 45, no. 3 (August 1983); Janet Campagna and Bernard Grofman, "Party Control and Partisan Bias in 1980's Congressional Redistricting," *Journal of Politics* 52, no. 4 (November 1990).
37. Niemi and Abromowitz, "Partisan Redistricting and the 1992 Congressional Elections," *Journal of Politics* 56, no. 3 (August 1994); John W. Swain, Stephen A. Borrelli, and Brian C. Reed, "Partisan Consequences of the Post-1990 Redistricting for the U.S. House of Representatives," *Political Research Quarterly* 51, no. 4 (December 1998).
38. King and Gelman, "Enhancing Democracy," 541–559.
39. Utah's appeal to the Supreme Court was *Utah v. Evans,* 01-283.
40. Linda Greenhouse, "Justices Deal Utah a Setback in Its Bid to Gain a House Seat," *New York Times,* November 27, 2001.

41. According to 1999 estimates by the U.S. State Department, 4.1 million (non–federally employed) Americans were living abroad at that time.

42. Eric Lotke and Peter Wagner, "Prisoners of the Census: Electoral and Financial Consequences of Counting Prisoners Where They Go, Not Where They Come From," *Pace Law Review* 24, no. 2 (2004).

43. Department of Correctional Services, State of New York, *The Hub System: Profile of Inmates Under Custody on January 1, 2000* (2000), 8.

44. Patrick Kenny and Tom Rice, "Voter Turnout in Presidential Primaries: A Cross-Sectional Examination," *Political Behavior* 7, no. 1 (1985); W. Mark Crain and Thomas H. Deaton, "A Note on Political Participation as Consumption Behavior," *Public Choice* 32, no. 1 (December 1977); Russell F. Settle and Burton A. Abrams, "The Determinants of Voter Participation: A More General Model," *Public Choice* 27, no. 1 (September 1976). In a comparative study, G. Bingham Powell Jr. finds that lack of competitiveness accounts for 10 percent of the difference in turnout between U.S. presidential elections and those in 20 other developed democracies. Powell, "American Voter Turnout in Comparative Perspective," *American Political Science Review* 80, no. 1 (March 1986).

45. U.S. Commission on Civil Rights, *The Voting Rights Act: 10 Years After* (Washington, DC: U.S. Commission on Civil Rights, January 1975).

46. Martin Merzer, ed., *The Miami Herald Report: Democracy Held Hostage* (New York: St. Martin's Press, 2001), 51.

47. A Cal Tech/MIT report estimates that of the four to six million lost votes in American presidential elections, approximately three million result from problems in the states' voter registration process. This chapter suggests that only "hundreds of thousands" are disenfranchised because, according to the same scholars, the aggressive use of provisional ballots following the passage of HAVA in 2002 has most probably reduced this problem substantially. Michael Alvarez, Stephen Ansolabehere, Erik Antons-

son, and Jehoshua Bruck, "Voting: What Is, What Could Be" (2001).

48. John Meacham, "Voting Wrongs—Racial Reapportionment," *Washington Monthly*, March 1993.

49. For instance, see Grant Hayden, "Majority-Minority Voting Districts and Their Role in Politics: Their Advantages, Their Drawbacks, and the Current Law," FindLaw, October 7, 2004, http://writ.news.findlaw.com/commentary/20041007_hayden.html#bio.

50. Editorial, "Illegalities in New Jersey?" *New York Times*, November 14, 1993.

51. Editorial, "Bad New Days for Voting Rights," *New York Times*, April 18, 2004.

52. Jo Becker, "GOP Challenging Voter Registrations," *Washington Post*, October 29, 2004.

53. B. Drummond Ayres Jr., "The 1990 Campaign; Judge Assails GOP Mailing in Carolina," *New York Times*, November 6, 1990.

54. People for the American Way, "The Long Shadow of Jim Crow: Voter Suppression in America (2004)," http://www.pfaw.org/pfaw/general/default.aspx?oid=16383.

55. Josh Barbanel and Ford Fessenden, "Contesting the Vote: The Tools; Racial Pattern in Demographics of Error-Prone Ballots," *New York Times*, November 29, 2000.

56. Michael Powell and Peter Slevin, "Several Factors Contributed to 'Lost' Voters in Ohio," *Washington Post*, December 15, 2004, http://www.washingtonpost.com/wp-dyn/articles/A64737-2004Dec14.html.

57. Matthew Waite, "Florida Scraps Felon Vote List," *St. Petersburg Times*, July 11, 2004, http://www.sptimes.com/2004/07/11/State/Florida_scraps_felon_.shtml.

58. Ford Fessenden, "A Big Increase of New Voters in Swing States," *New York Times*, September 26, 2004.

59. Editorial, "Block the Vote, Ohio Remix," *New York Times*, June 7, 2006.

60. Bill Sloat, "Judge Orders Halt to County Hearings Challenging Voters," *Plain Dealer*, October 30, 2004.

61. Powell and Slevin, "Several Factors."
62. House Judiciary Committee Democratic Staff, "Preserving Democracy: What Went Wrong in Ohio," January 5, 2005, available at http://election04.ssrc.org/research/preserving_democracy.pdf.
63. Powell and Slevin, "Several Factors."
64. Ian Urbina, "New Registration Rules Stir Voter Debate in Ohio," *New York Times*, August 6, 2006
65. Editorial, "Block the Vote, Ohio Remix."
66. Darryl Fears, "Voter ID Law Is Overturned," *Washington Post*, October 28, 2005, http://www.washingtonpost.com/wp-dyn/content/article/2005/10/27/AR2005102702171.html.
67. Ian Urbina, "Panel Said to Alter Finding on Voter Fraud," *New York Times*, April 11, 2007.
68. See, *inter alia,* George F. Will, "Free Speech Under Siege," *Newsweek*, December 5, 2005; Will, "Corrupt Campaign Finance 'Reform,'" *Washington Post*, June 29, 2006.
69. Richard Hasen and Robert Bauer, "Has Campaign Finance Reform Failed?" *Legal Affairs*, October 14, 2004, http://www.legalaffairs.org/webexclusive/debateclub_527s1004.msp.
70. Project Vote Smart, "Government 101: Campaign Finance," http://www.vote-smart.org/resource_govt101_07.php.
71. David D. Kirkpatrick, "Edwards to Accept Public Financing After All," *New York Times*, September 28, 2007.
72. Paul Taylor, "Campaign Reform: A Way Forward," *Washington Monthly*, March 1999; Taylor, "Free Airtime for Political Candidates," *Yes! Magazine*, Winter 2003, http://www.yesmagazine.org/article.asp?ID=573.
73. See U.S. Census Bureau estimates for 2006 at http://quickfacts.census.gov/qfd/states/11000.html.
74. Mary Beth Sheridan, "Senators Block D.C. Vote Bill, Delivering Possibly Fatal Blow," *Washington Post*, September 19, 2007.
75. See the website of the DC Voting Rights Movement at http://www.dcvote.org/trellis/denial/dcvotingrightshistoricaltimeline.cfm.

Corruption: Money and Politics

The road to the 2006 congressional elections was fraught with revelations of waste, fraud, inappropriate conduct, and other misuses of government office by elected officials. Shortly after the 2004 elections, allegations began to surface that the House majority leader, Tom DeLay, had accepted lavish trips, gifts, and political donations from lobbyist Jack Abramoff. In early April 2005, as the Abramoff investigation gained traction, the media reexamined reports of a 1998 trip that DeLay, his family, and several members of his staff had taken to the island of Saipan in the Northern Marianas. The stay had been arranged and financed by Abramoff, who accepted $1.36 million from Saipan officials to lobby against a bill aimed at cracking down on the sex trade and sweatshops in the U.S. territory. DeLay reportedly promised Abramoff's clients that he would not let the bill reach the House floor.[1]

DeLay was also among several power brokers treated to an extravagant Scottish golf excursion in 2000, a trip that was paid for in part by the internet gambling company and Abramoff client eLottery. Shortly after the trip, the Texas congressman used a parliamentary procedure to help kill the proposed Internet Gambling Prohibition Act, which had majority support in the House but was fervently opposed by eLottery. DeLay's name was sullied further in May 2005, when a state judge found that

Texans for a Republican Majority (TRMPAC), a fundraising committee organized by DeLay, had violated election laws by failing to disclose over $600,000 in contributions. DeLay himself was indicted for conspiracy to violate campaign finance laws in September 2005. In April 2006, DeLay announced that he would not run for reelection; he then resigned from the House effective June 9, 2006.

The scope of the Abramoff scandal expanded in January 2006, when the lobbyist and two former DeLay staffers charged that Representative Robert Ney, an Ohio Republican, had been given "things of value" in return for political favors. Four months later, the House Ethics Committee announced that it was investigating Ney. In September he declared that he would plead guilty to conspiracy to defraud the United States and to falsifying financial disclosure forms, making him the first member of Congress to admit guilt in connection with the Abramoff scandal. On November 3, four days before the midterm elections, Ney resigned from Congress.

Far-reaching though the Abramoff scandal was, it was not the only case of legislative corruption exposed ahead of the midterm elections. In November 2005, Representative Randy (Duke) Cunningham of California, a Republican member of the House Appropriations Committee's defense subcommittee, pleaded guilty to accepting over $2 million in bribes from defense contractor Mitchell Wade in exchange for government contracts for Wade's firm. In a separate case, the Federal Bureau of Investigation (FBI) in October 2006 raided six offices and homes in connection with a probe into the activities of Representative Curt Weldon, a Pennsylvania Republican, fueling speculation that he had used his position to win contracts for clients of a lobbying firm formed by his daughter and a longtime friend. Meanwhile, House Republican leaders were accused of attempting to cover up allegations that Representative Mark Foley of Florida had pursued inappropriate relations with young House pages.

While the Republican Party, as the party in power, was the subject of most of the political scandals that unfolded ahead of the 2006 elections, the Democrats were by no means untarnished by allegations of corruption. The most notable were those asserting that Representative William Jefferson of Louisiana had frequently demanded bribes in exchange for promoting business ventures in Africa. In May 2006, as part of a corruption probe, Jefferson was filmed accepting a $100,000 bribe from a Virginia businessman whom the FBI had wired. Later, upon searching Jefferson's home, federal agents discovered $90,000 in cash hidden in his freezer.[2] Despite that case and a number of less egregious and less well-documented allegations of wrongdoing by members of the Democratic Party, the issue of corruption was generally a boon for Democrats and burden for Republicans during the 2006 campaign season.

In the elections, the Democratic Party managed to seize control of both houses of Congress and win a majority of the country's governorships. While this feat was no doubt the result of a confluence of several different factors, much of the early analysis suggested that a widespread perception of corruption contributed significantly to the electoral result. The *National Review*, for instance, pointed out that one-third of the 29 House seats lost by Republicans were in districts where the incumbent was tied in some way to a corruption scandal.[3] The seats formerly held by Tom DeLay, Robert Ney, Mark Foley, and Curt Weldon all fell to Democratic candidates in 2006. Moreover, according to the exit polls, corruption was rated "extremely important" by more voters than any other issue.

Opinion polls and news editorials suggest that the recent scandals have fueled both a popular perception that corruption is rampant in American politics and a growing cynicism toward the ethical disposition of political officials in the United States.[4] While these select incidents of political corruption certainly warrant the attention, ire, and calls for reform that they have elicited, they do not provide a reasonable basis for a perception of widespread corruption. To the contrary, in each of the recent cases, various political institutions have worked to identify incidents of corruption and hold the culprits responsible for their actions.

By world and historic standards, today's America is exceptionally free of corruption. The business of the U.S. government is conducted with a high degree of transparency. Any individual is able to access nonclassified government information, and the nation's press corps reports unabashedly on questionable political practices. The rule of law is firmly established and enforced by a capable bar and an independent judiciary that, given evidence of corruption, do not shrink from prosecuting either government officials or the most powerful private individuals. In fact, some argue that the problem is not a lack of tools to investigate and adjudicate corruption, but an excess of overzealous prosecutors armed with seemingly endless funds and an array of instruments with which to pursue whomever they please.[5] Nonetheless, when the range of behaviors that can be construed as corrupt is expanded to include ostensibly legal actions that would be widely viewed as misuse of government office, corruption is a significant problem in American politics.

In particular, the appointment and hiring of political cronies, the extraordinary influence of embedded special interests, and the use of no-bid government contracts to unfairly benefit a select few raise serious concerns. Additionally, although Congress has taken a few steps to limit the misuse of public office and prohibit practices that may give rise to the appearance of corruption, the federal government has more often failed to respond—or acted too slowly or inadequately—to public cries for reform. In some cases, the government has acted in a way that erodes political institutions meant to ensure responsive politics, limit favoritism, and protect government whistleblowers.

Cronyism

Administrative appointments based on loyalty or patronage rather than merit are likely to produce inept officials, unresponsive governance, and public resentment. It is for precisely this reason that the framers of the U.S. Constitution gave the Senate an "advice and consent" role in the appointment process. As Alexander Hamilton explained in *Federalist #76*, advice and consent is "an excellent check upon a spirit of favoritism in the President, and would tend greatly to prevent the appointment of unfit characters from *State prejudice, from family connection, from personal attachment, or from a view to popularity* [emphasis added]." Despite this and other checks, cronyism has infected federal, state, and local government throughout the country's history.

Ironically, one of the first accusations of cronyism was directed at President George Washington for appointing Hamilton, his trusted political adviser and former lieutenant colonel, as secretary of the treasury. While Hamilton quickly proved to be a shrewd and adept treasury secretary, there is no shortage in American history of executive appointees who showed themselves to be far less competent. Appointees of President Andrew Jackson were particularly notorious. Upon winning the 1828 presidential election, Jackson filled the executive branch with his friends and supporters, many of whom were untrained for the positions they were given and indifferent to the work they were assigned. He reasoned that rotation in the federal bureaucracy was "democratic" and argued that his electoral victory gave him a mandate to hand out jobs, a claim subsequently expressed with the phrase, "To the victor go the spoils."[6]

Under the spoils system, which was adopted by later presidents, appointments were routinely and openly given out as rewards for political support. One consequence of the system was excessive turnover, as each president replaced the hires of the previous administration with his own people. This resulted in a lack of institutional memory and experience, which exacerbated bureaucratic malaise and inefficiency. After half a century of increasingly ineffective administration, the federal government gradually replaced patronage with the merit system. In 1883, the Pendleton Act created an independent commission for bureaucratic oversight, instituted standards for hiring, and provided job security for employees brought up under the new system. Subsequent federal laws and other developments limited patronage still further, and by the turn of the century, cronyism was largely restricted to the most senior administrative positions. However, at the state and local levels, patronage remained commonplace until the 1940s, when it slowly disappeared with the collapse of most the country's political machines.

Despite institutional checks such as Senate approval of executive appointments and the gradual demise of the spoils system, presidents have continued to nominate loyal friends and advisers to important posts, regardless of merit. In fact, the use of the term "cronyism" to describe the practice was popularized by the press in reference to the administration of President Harry S. Truman.[7] The term stuck as subsequent presidents gave the press abundant occasions to use it. President John F. Kennedy made his brother the attorney general and appointed Robert McNamara, whose background was in business administration, as secretary of defense. President Jimmy Carter named his old friend Bert Lance director of the Office of Management and Budget despite his questionable business practices as chairman of Calhoun National Bank. (Lance resigned after a Senate investigation into the alleged misuse of bank funds and assertions that he had acted unethically to secure large personal loans.)

Perhaps no recent president has come under more fire for cronyism than George W. Bush. The most serious criticism has concerned appointments linked to the most significant challenges of his presidency: Hurricane Katrina and the wars in Iraq and Afghanistan.

Katrina, which ravaged the Gulf Coast and inundated New Orleans in August 2005, was the most destructive hurricane ever to strike the United States. The federal rescue and relief effort that followed was widely regarded as inept, and the Federal Emergency Management Agency (FEMA) was singled out for blame.[8] Many critics of the administration charge that 2001–03 FEMA director Joe Allbaugh, who had been Bush's 2000 presidential campaign manager, was given his job as an act of patronage and was not qualified for the position. The same accusation was directed at Allbaugh's close friend and successor, Michael Brown, who had no background in emergency management and who was discovered to have padded his resume.[9] Brown appeared uninformed during media interviews after Katrina struck, and did not help matters by sending several e-mails in the immediate aftermath of the hurricane in which he complained that he wanted to go home and seemed excessively concerned with finding a dog-sitter.[10] He resigned two weeks after the storm made landfall.

Following the Katrina debacle, a *Time* magazine probe into cronyism in the Bush administration focused on three high-level administrators who might have owed their appointments to political connections rather than merit, and whose decisions may have compromised the competence and independence of the agencies they helped run.[11] One was Scott Gottlieb, a 33-year old doctor turned stock-picker who was viewed by many as a friend of the pharmaceuticals industry. Bush had appointed him as deputy commissioner for medical and scientific affairs at the Food and Drug Administration (FDA), a position typically reserved for career scientists.[12] The magazine questioned Gottlieb's efforts to second-guess two decisions by career scientists at the FDA: their withholding of approval for a drug that was expected to yield $1 billion a year for the drugmaker Pfizer, and their move to halt clinical trials of another drug after some of the subjects experienced complications, from which one patient died. *Time* also highlighted former lobbyist David Safavian, who was put in charge of government contracts and procurements despite having virtually no relevant experience. He was indicted in connection with the Abramoff scandal in October 2005, and was sentenced to 18 months in prison a year later.

The third administrator noted by *Time* was Julie Myers, whose inexperience and background as Bush's personal assistant made Senate approval of her appointment as the top immigration official at the Department of Homeland of Security highly unlikely. In 2005, Republican Senator George Voinovich of Ohio went so far as to say, "I'd really like to have [Homeland Security Secretary Michael Chertoff] spend some time with us, telling us personally why he thinks you're qualified for the job, because based on the resume, I don't think you are."[13] Unable to get Myers's nomination through the Senate, Bush sidestepped the process by installing her during a congressional recess in January 2006.

Some accusations of cronyism have centered not on patronage hires, but on the awarding of no-bid contracts. Generally, federal agencies are required to award contracts based on open and competitive bidding. But a month into the Hurricane Katrina recovery effort, the *New York Times* reported that FEMA had awarded more than 80 percent of the $1.5 billion in new contracts without competitive bidding.[14] Many of the contractors were said to have close ties to federal, state, and local government officials, and to have overcharged the government for their services. Some of the companies had hired lobbyist Joe Allbaugh, the former FEMA director, allegedly to help them secure such deals.

Particularly contentious were contracts worth a half a billion dollars that went to Halliburton, the multinational energy services and construction conglomerate. These contracts attracted special attention because, at the time, Halliburton was under investigation for overcharging the Defense Department for services provided in Iraq as part of a two-year, no-bid contract worth up to $7 billion; the contract had initially been crafted to cope with expected oil-well fires after the U.S. invasion of that country.[15] Vice President Dick Cheney had previously served as head of Halliburton, making the administration's critics especially skeptical of such exclusive deals.

Defenders of the Iraq contract cited national security concerns and a need for secrecy. They also argued that Halliburton was the only company in the United States with the capacity to fulfill the terms of the contract. Bob Grace, president of Texas-based GSM Consulting, which the government of Kuwait had hired to put out over 300 oil-well fires after the 1991 Persian Gulf War, has challenged both of those arguments.[16] Grace cited his company's previous achievements, and on the issue of national security, he said that "secrecy about [former Iraqi President] Saddam Hussein blowing up oil wells, to me, is stupid.... I mean the guy's blown up a thousand of them. So why would that be a revelation to anybody?"[17] The secrecy argument also seemed to contradict the Bush administration's stated efforts to present Hussein with a credible threat of invasion as it tried to force him to comply with international weapons inspectors; the public award of a major contract for post-invasion recovery work would have plausibly augmented any such threat. Moreover, an open bidding process would likely have lowered the price, even if in the end the administration intended to choose Halliburton as the most qualified bidder.

In addition to hiring unqualified supporters and awarding contracts to favored companies, U.S. leaders have been accused of cronyism for abusing the power of pardon. For example, after the 2000 presidential and congressional elections, when he could no longer be held politically accountable for the decision, outgoing President Bill Clinton pardoned fugitive financier Marc Rich, who had been indicted in federal court for tax evasion and 51 counts of tax fraud. Rich's ex-wife, Denise Rich, had recently donated approximately $1 million to the Democratic National Committee, giving the pardon the appearance of impropriety. In contrast, President Gerald Ford's controversial 1974 pardon of disgraced former President Richard Nixon came just before that year's midterm elections, allowing voters to hold Ford's party responsible for his actions.

Corruption and Campaign Finance Reform

Even before the first U.S. congressional elections, political campaigns were recognized as opportunities for corruption. James Madison, for instance, complained that he lost his 1777 bid for a seat in the Virginia legislature because he refused to provide voters with alcohol on election day, as they had come to expect. Prior to the adoption of the Australian-style secret ballot in the late nineteenth century, votes were frequently purchased and voter intimidation was not uncommon. Moreover, until the direct election of senators in 1913, much of the public saw the U.S. Senate as a "millionaire's club," with seats bought by wealthy individuals or controlled by special interests.[18] The most enduring concern, though, has been the growing role of campaign contributions in electoral politics and the influence that such money may have on public policy.

During the mid-nineteenth century, as election costs increased, candidates came to rely more and more on wealthy individuals to fund their campaigns. Between 1890 and the 1920s, corporations—particularly those in the banking sector and the railroad industry—began to fill campaign coffers.

In the 1904 presidential election campaign, Democratic candidate Alton Parker accused his Republican opponent, Theodore Roosevelt, of accepting large contributions from corporations, and alleged that he was beholden to his donors' interests. After the election, several businesses did admit to contributing funds. Roosevelt, embarrassed by the revelation, supported the passage in 1907 of the Tillman Act, the country's first campaign finance reform bill. The act outlawed corporate campaign contributions, although donations from the individuals who ran the companies were still unrestricted. The Federal Corrupt Practices Act (FCPA) followed in 1910, requiring candidates and parties to report all contributions and expenditures. In 1925 the FCPA was strengthened, and in 1940 Congress for the first time limited individual contributions to political campaigns.

Soon afterward, corporations and labor unions began forming Political Action Committees (PACs) to funnel funds to candidates. Although for many years PACs were resented for their growing influence over the electoral and policy-making processes, no further significant reforms were adopted until the Federal Election Campaign Act (FECA) of 1971. FECA and its subsequent amendments limited the amount of money that PACs, parties, and individuals could donate to any particular candidate in a given election cycle. The amendments also extended the ban on direct contributions to include foreign governments and their nationals, limited the ability of advocacy groups to act on behalf of a particular candidate, provided for partial public funding of presidential campaigns, and created the Federal Election Commission (FEC) to enforce federal campaign finance laws. In *Buckley v. Valeo* (1976), however, the Supreme Court restricted the FEC's ability to regulate advocacy groups.

Over the next quarter century, the number of PACs exploded and campaign spending accelerated. Interest groups began pouring loosely regulated "soft money" into political parties. Soft money could not be used to expressly advocate for the election or defeat of a candidate, but it was otherwise unrestricted, and the parties put it to work for their candidates through creative "issue advocacy" and "party building" efforts. In 2002, after a six-year crusade by Republican Senator John McCain of Arizona and Democratic Senator Russ Feingold of Wisconsin, Congress passed and President Bush signed the Bipartisan Campaign Reform Act (BCRA), which prohibited parties from accepting unlimited contributions and limited the activity that could be described as issue advocacy. However, in *McConnell v. FEC* (2003), the Supreme Court struck down the additional restrictions on advocacy groups, citing First Amendment concerns.

Despite the enactment of the BCRA, the cost of running for public office continues to grow. The Center for Responsive Politics estimates that candidates, parties, and interest groups spent $2.8 billion on the 472 federal campaigns of 2006, a 27 percent increase over the pre-BCRA midterm elections of 2002.[19] In 2004, a presidential election year, $4.2 billion was spent on federal campaigns, an increase of more than 30 percent over the 2000 election cycle.[20]

As costs rise, candidates depend more and more on special interests to finance their election bids, and the interest groups find ways to pay. Advocacy groups exploiting a loophole in Section 527 of the tax code have been the most aggressive spenders in post-BCRA campaigns. Furthermore, the BCRA appears to have strengthened the existing advantages of incumbents by making it more difficult for challengers to raise money.[21] The law has done little to alter the public's perception that elected officials use their posts to benefit their biggest campaign donors.

Candidates themselves also appear more willing to bend campaign finance rules and engage in potentially scandalous behavior to raise funds. In 1996, for instance, President Clinton was criticized for using the White House's famed Lincoln bedroom to raise money for the Democratic Party. Guests invited to sleep there were contacted by DNC fundraisers soon afterward. Fifty-one such guests made contributions of $100,000 or more in the weeks after their stays.[22] In 1997, it was revealed that the DNC may have unlawfully accepted money from the Chinese government, and that Vice President Al Gore had appeared at a Buddhist temple where campaign contributions were raised in violation of rules that banned fundraising at religious institutions.

Unlike federal judges, who are expected to recuse themselves from cases that present an apparent conflict of interest, members of Congress are not required to abstain from votes on bills that raise such apparent conflicts. Lawmakers can also write measures that directly benefit their biggest contributors, and they occasionally do so. Although such contributors usually support candidates who would be ideologically inclined to champion their interests with or without a donation, the contributions have a significant impact on election outcomes and ultimately on legislative action. In addition to the high correlation that researchers have repeatedly found between campaign contributions and voting records,[23] which in itself creates the appearance of unethical behavior, there are several cases in which representatives appear to have voted against their own ideological principles to benefit an interest group.

Representative Roy Blunt's dealings with Jack Abramoff provide an example in which the influence of a special interest is consistent with a lawmaker's ideology as well as an instance in which the two appear to be in conflict. Blunt, a Republican from Missouri, was criticized in 2003 for endorsing three letters urging the interior secretary, Gale Norton, to block construction of an Indian casino in Louisiana. The construction project was opposed by Abramoff's clients, and the lobbyist had contributed to Blunt's PAC, but the lawmaker's actions were consistent with his moral objection to gambling. However, in 1999 Blunt lobbied his colleagues in Congress to kill the proposed Internet Gambling Prohibition Act, which would have effectively quashed the internet gambling industry in the United States. The bill was opposed by Abramoff client eLottery.

Ethics Reform and Whistleblower Protection

In 2002, the U.S. Congress responded aggressively to calls for corporate accounting reform following a spectacular wave of corruption scandals that began with the collapse of the energy-trading firm Enron, previously a favorite among investors. In February 2001, *Fortune* magazine had named the energy giant the "most innovative company in America" for the sixth year running. However, over the next several months, insider selling of company stock accelerated, internal memorandums questioning the accuracy of Enron's accounting practices started to circulate, and reports of financial problems began to leak. By the end of 2001, it had emerged that Enron executives had lied about profits and concealed debt, the company had filed for Chapter 11 bankruptcy protection, and the stock price had plummeted from a high of $90 to around 30 cents a share, costing investors billions of dollars and wiping out employees' retirement benefits. The auditing firm Arthur Andersen was soon implicated in the accounting fraud, which led to the exposure of major accounting scandals at other companies. One such firm, WorldCom, later admitted to overstating its earnings by $3.2 billion over the previous five quarters.

The corporate scandals enraged the American public, drew scorn from an administration trying to distance itself from the executives involved, and spurred Congress into action. The result was Sarbanes-Oxley, a monumental piece of legislation designed to rebuild public trust in corporate accounting and reporting by enhancing government oversight, holding executives personally responsible for company practices, and establishing stringent auditing procedures. While legislators proved eager to weed out corruption and develop new, higher standards for the country's corporations, they have been much more reticent to apply similar scrutiny to themselves or the executive branch.

In late 2005, following the Abramoff affair and other Capitol Hill scandals, Congress came under intense pressure from the press and the public to pass ethics reform legislation. Members of Congress from both parties promised to improve transparency and accountability in legislator-lobbyist relations. They introduced proposals to create an independent Office of Public Integrity, strengthen lobbyist disclosure rules, prohibit private financing of congressional travel, and establish a longer "cooling-off" period before a former representative or congressional staffer could lobby members of Congress. However, lawmakers failed to pass any such measure over the following year. All significant efforts at lobbying reform either failed in committee or passed in only one chamber.

In the 2006 congressional elections, American voters seemed to weigh in on the matter. With a few exceptions, they ousted incumbent representatives who had been involved in recent corruption scandals, and the overall result led the Republicans to lose control of both chambers. The new Democratic leadership vowed to make ethics reform a priority of the 110th Congress, but it remained unclear whether the legislation making its way through the body in the first half of 2007 would have a significant impact on entrenched political practices.

Since elected officials and bureaucrats cannot always be relied upon to police themselves, the protection of whistleblowers—employees who bring evidence of waste, fraud, and wrongdoing to the attention of the appropriate authorities—is fundamental to ensuring that governments act within the scope of the law and government officials are held accountable for their actions. Such protection also increases the likelihood that potential threats to public health, safety, and security will be neutralized before disaster strikes. Yet under current rules, many U.S. civil servants who bring complaints to their superiors, the appropriate internal auditors, Congress, or the public continue to risk retaliation, against which they often have no legal recourse.

While all corporate and most federal employees are protected from retaliation for blowing the whistle on their employers, the Whistleblower Protection Act of 1989 and its subsequent amendments do not fully cover civil servants working to guarantee food safety, prevent the abuse of medical patients, and ensure homeland security. Furthermore, the Bush administration has objected strenuously to extending such protections, arguing that they would infringe on the president's ability to manage the executive branch.[24]

Concern over the lack of protection intensified when it was revealed that top Medicare administrator Thomas Scully in 2003 had threatened to fire analyst Richard Foster if he presented evidence to Congress that the cost of a proposed Medicare overhaul bill would greatly exceed White House estimates. Foster withheld the information as lawmakers considered the bill, which passed later that year.[25]

More disturbing is the apparently common practice of retaliating against those who expose serious weaknesses in the government's security efforts. In 2000, for instance, Energy Department nuclear security specialist Richard Levernier repeatedly voiced his concern that many of the country's nuclear facilities were not properly secured. In fact, the weapons laboratory at Los Alamos, New Mexico, had repeatedly failed preparedness tests by allowing mock terrorists to steal plutonium, and officials at the facility had both falsified documents to hide those failures and destroyed inspection reports to cover up their actions.[26] When Levernier disclosed this information, the Energy Department suspended him and revoked his security clearance. After his story was featured in *Vanity Fair* magazine and on the television program *60 Minutes*, the Office of Special Counsel (OSC) investigated and ultimately vindicated Levernier, but his security clearance was never reinstated.

Revoking security clearance is a common form of retaliation by the country's security agencies, since employees have no legal recourse when their clearance is removed and they cannot continue their work without it. Republican Senator Charles Grassley of Iowa, a vocal advocate of whistleblower rights, has said of the problem, "The pulling of a security clearance effectively fires employees."[27] Having lost his job after 22 years with the Energy Department and just two years short of retiring with a full pension, Levernier told *60 Minutes*, "Given my experience, I would not do it again, even though I truly believe it was the right thing to do."

Even after the September 11, 2001, terrorist attacks on the United States, civil servants who come forward with evidence of lapses in national security are putting their careers at risk. Border security agents Mark Hall and Robert Lindeman were suspended and demoted and suffered pay cuts for emphasizing, in the months after the terrorist attacks, that the northern border of the United States was inadequately monitored and presented a significant threat to homeland security. Bogdan Dzakovic, former leader of the Federal Aviation Administration (FAA) Red Team, which is charged with testing airport security, felt similarly compelled after the attacks to bring to light weaknesses in airport security and efforts by his superiors to cover up those weaknesses.[28] For coming forward, the FAA stripped Dzakovic of all security-related duties, despite his expertise in airport security. Airport baggage screeners who followed in Dzakovic's footsteps claim that they too were punished for raising concerns about aviation security. In response to their grievances, the Merit System Protection Board ruled in 2004 that Transportation Security Administration employees had none of the whistleblower protections extended to other federal employees.[29] In all, government whistleblowers filed an average of 690 reprisal complaints annually in the four years prior to the 2001 terrorist attacks; the annual average jumped to 835 over the five years after the attacks.[30]

The OSC, which was established to enforce the Whistleblower Protection Act, is widely viewed as "inept and even hostile to whistleblowers."[31] In the late 1990s, Senator Grassley, who coauthored the law, complained that according to the OSC's 1995 report to Congress, the office sided with the government in all but three of the 603 reprisal investigations it had conducted to date.[32] Whistleblower advocates claim that the OSC under the Bush administration is no less hostile than it was under President Clinton. In 2004, the office found that only 2 percent of the 1,262 cases that year warranted an investigation, up from 1 percent in 2003. There have even been allegations of retaliation within the OSC. A group of OSC employees recently claimed that the office's head, Scott Bloch, had retaliated against OSC staff, issuing illegal gag orders to prevent them from going to Congress or the public about efforts to suppress whistleblower retaliation, cronyism, and invidious discrimination.[33]

The U.S. Court of Appeals for the Federal Circuit, which has jurisdiction over government whistleblower retaliation, has similarly failed to provide adequate protection. In deciding such matters, the court assumes that the agency involved has acted properly unless an employee offers "irrefragable proof to the contrary."[34] Both Grassley and Democratic Senator Carl Levin of Michigan, a coauthor of the Whistleblower Protection Act, have argued repeatedly that this standard is much too rigid. Nonetheless, the court continues to apply it and ruled against whistleblowers in 125 out of 127 cases between 1994 and late 2006.[35]

The U.S. Supreme Court has also recently weighed in on the issue of whistleblower protection. In *Garcetti v. Ceballos* (2006), the court ruled, 5 to 4, that government employees who are retaliated against for raising job-related concerns internally, as opposed to publicly, are not protected under the free speech doctrine of the First Amendment, and therefore have no recourse in court outside the Federal Circuit. In the majority opinion, Justice Anthony M. Kennedy suggested that federal employees might fare better by going public than by raising concerns in the course of their government duties, since they were more likely to be constitutionally protected when speaking in their capacity as citizens. Given the court's finding, and the perceived hostility of the OSC and the Federal Circuit appeals court toward whistleblowers, the recent trend of anonymous sources leaking controversial programs and questionable government actions to the press is not surprising.

Conclusion

Political corruption is much less a problem in the United States than it is in most parts of the world. Unlike in many countries in Africa and Latin America, for example, companies in the United States generally do not expect to pay bribes or accede to extortion when doing business with the government. U.S. officials are not commonly accused of pilfering state resources or embezzling public funds. Nor are they immune from prosecution when they are suspected of corrupt practices. Political corruption in the United States is also much less a concern today than it was in previous eras. And, with measures such as the Foreign Corrupt Practices Act (1977) and the International Anti-Bribery Act (1998), which work to increase transparency in international commerce and make it illegal for U.S. citizens or representatives of U.S. companies to give or accept bribes abroad, the United States is often on the front line in the struggle against international corruption.

Nonetheless, the popular perception of U.S. public servants' integrity appears to be deteriorating, and the U.S. government is frequently seen as more corrupt than those of Canada, New Zealand, Australia, and most of northwestern Europe. Transparency International gave the United States a ranking of 20 out of 163 countries surveyed in its 2006 Corruption Perceptions Index, finding that 19 countries had a lower perceived level of corruption.[36] The American public's growing sense of pervasive government corruption is apparently due to an expansion of the sphere of behavior that most Americans consider corrupt, and to the apparent willingness of politicians to engage in, or at least tolerate, technically legal practices that are widely viewed as unethical.

One example of such questionable behavior is the ever-increasing eagerness of profit-driven companies and large interest groups to invest heavily in political outcomes. Collectively, these groups now spend over $2.25 billion a year to lobby Congress, more than $2.5 billion every other year to influence legislative elections, and another $2 billion every fourth year to elect a president. Many Americans seem to have concluded that interest groups would not be spending such sums if they were not receiving a clear benefit in the form of influence over public policy.

Federal officials in recent years have elicited further contempt by failing to pass ethics reform legislation in the wake of lobbying scandals, continuing to make decisions that appear to benefit private interests without regard for the public, and failing to adequately protect whistleblowers even as they draw media attention for exposing evidence of government fraud, waste, and incompetence.

If the federal government is to quell the growing perception that political corruption is a significant problem in the United States, it must act aggressively to stamp out unseemly behavior and work to end practices that fuel the appearance of undue influence. In addition to enacting meaningful lobbying reform, Congress needs to push for more vigorous enforcement of existing campaign finance restrictions and pass additional reforms that reduce the ability of special interests to act on behalf of any one candidate. Furthermore, the current and future administrations must resist the temptation to make appointments based on favoritism and political loyalty, and submit to congressional checks on questionable executive-branch behavior.

Endnotes

1. Brian Ross, "Delay's Lavish Island Getaway," ABC News, April 6, 2005, http//abcnews.go.com?WNT/Investigation/.
2. Allan Lengel, "FBI Says Jefferson Was Filmed Taking Cash," *Washington Post*, May 22, 2006.
3. Rich Lowry, "The Culture of Corruption Loses: A corpulent Congress reaps what it sowed," National Review Online, November 10, 2006, http://article.nationalreview.com.
4. According to the five *Washington Post*/ABC News polls taken in 2006, a majority of respondents disapproved of the handling of ethics in government, a level not attained in 2005 polls by the same organizations: http://www.washingtonpost.com/wp-srv/politics/polls/postpoll_121206.htm. Furthermore, a July 2006 Harris poll asking individuals if they generally trust several types of people found that only 35 percent of respondents trusted members of Congress, down from 46 percent in 1998: http://www.pollingreport.com/values.htm.
5. Many press freedom advocates lambasted the decision to jail journalist Judith Miller in 2005 for refusing to reveal her sources in relation to the leak of the identity of CIA agent Valerie Plame, as well as threats by other prosecutors to detain journalists in similar cases. Other observers are troubled by the fact that the Plame case was pursued even after the prosecutor was unable to bring charges for the original leak, leading to the conviction of I. Lewis (Scooter) Libby, the vice president's former chief of staff, for acts of obstruction and perjury that arose from the investigation itself. Similarly, in the 1990s, Independent Counsel Kenneth Starr's six-year, $52 million probe into the real-estate dealings of Bill and Hillary Clinton failed to substantiate the core allegations, but spawned peripheral convictions. The case led many to question the wisdom of having an independent counsel, and Congress let the position expire in 1999.
6. Senator William Marcy, a New York Democrat, coined this phrase in 1831. He used it to defend the appointment practices of Andrew Jackson.

7. William Safire, *No Uncertain Terms: More Writing From the Popular "On Language" Column in the New York Times Magazine* (New York: Simon & Schuster, 2003), 60–62.
8. See Maureen Dowd, "Neigh to Cronies," *New York Times*, September 10, 2005; Spencer S. Hsu, "Leaders Lacking Disaster Experience," *Washington Post*, September 9, 2005; and Yochi J. Dreazen, "Connections Are Key to Contracts for Katrina Aid," *Wall Street Journal*, September 30, 2005.
9. Daren Fonda and Rita Healy, "How Reliable Is Brown's Resume?" *Time Magazine*, September 8, 2005, http://www.time.com/time/nation/article/0,8599,1103003,00.html.
10. CNN.com, "'Can I Quit Now?' FEMA Chief Wrote as Katrina Raged," November 4, 2005, http://www.cnn.com/2005/US/11/03/brown.fema.emails/.
11. Karen Tumulty, Mark Thompson, and Mike Allen, "How Many More Mike Browns Are Out There?" *Time Magazine*, October 3, 2005, http://www.time.com/time/magazine/article/0,9171,1109345,00.html.
12. Ibid.
13. Dan Eggen and Spencer S. Hsu, "Immigration Nominee's Credentials Questioned," *Washington Post*, September 20, 2005.
14. Eric Lipton and Ron Nixon, "Storm and Crisis: Rebuilding; Many Contracts for Storm Work Raise Questions," *New York Times*, September 26, 2005.
15. CBS News, "All in the Family," September 21, 2003, http://www.cbsnews.com/stories/2003/04/25/60minutes/main551091.shtml.
16. Ibid.
17. Ibid.
18. The term "millionaire's club" was frequently used to describe the U.S. Senate prior to direct elections. In his addresses to the Senate on the history of that body, Senator Robert Byrd of West Virginia has explained that this was how newspapers referred to the Senate at the time. The Senate has revised and published some of these essays at the following web address: http://www.senate.gov/legislative/common/briefing/Byrd_History_Lobbying.htm.

19. Center for Responsive Politics, "Center for Responsive Politics Predicts '06 Election Will Cost $2.6 Billion," news release, October 25, 2006, http://www.opensecrets.org/pressreleases/2006/PreElection.10.25.asp.

20. Center for Responsive Politics, "'04 Elections Expected to Cost Nearly $4 Billion," news release, October 21, 2004, http://www.opensecrets.org/pressreleases/2004/04spending.asp.

21. Michael Johnston, "From Thucydides to Mayor Daley: Bad Politics, and a Culture of Corruption?" *PS: Political Science and Politics* 39, no. 4 (2006): 809–812.

22. Don Van Natta Jr., "Campaign Finance: Raising the Money," *New York Times*, October 4, 1997.

23. For academic studies that find such a correlation, see Stacy B. Gordon, *Campaign Contributions and Legislative Voting: A New Approach* (New York: Routledge, 2005). Also see the work of her predecessors: A. Etzioni, *Capital Corruption: The New Attack on American Democracy* (New York: Harcourt, Brace & Co., 1984); A. Wilhite and J. Theilmann, "Labor PAC Contributions and Labor Legislation," *Public Choice* 53 (1987); P.M. Stern, *The Best Congress Money Can Buy*, (New York: Pantheon, 1988); and L.I. Langbein and M.A. Lotwis, "The Political Efficacy of Lobbying and Money," *Legislative Studies Quarterly* 15, no. 3 (1990).

24. Amy Goldstein, "Foster: White House Had Role in Withholding Medicare Data," *Washington Post*, March 19, 2004.

25. Ibid.

26. Government Accountability Project, "Richard Levernier: DOE Nuclear Security Specialist," http://www.whistleblower.org/template/page.cfm?page_id=152.

27. Robert Pear, "Congress Moves to Protect Federal Whistleblowers," *New York Times*, October 3, 2004.

28. Philip Shenon, "A Nation Challenged: Airports; FAA Is Accused of Ignoring Security Lapses," *New York Times*, February 27, 2002.

29. Pear, "Congress Moves to Protect Federal Whistleblowers."

30. Catherine Rampell, "Whistle-blowers Tell of Cost of Conscience," *USA Today*, November 24, 2006.

31. Chuck Grassley, "Government Protection: Amending the Whistleblower Protection Act to Make It More Effective," *Insight Magazine*, February 2, 1998.
32. Ibid.
33. Public Employees for Environmental Responsibility, "Statement in Support of Complaint of Prohibited Personnel Practices Against U.S. Special Counsel Scott J. Bloch," March 3, 2005, http://www.peer.org/docs/osc/2005_3_3_osc_complaint.pdf.
34. *Lachance v. White*, 174 F.3d 1378 (Fed. Cir. 1999).
35. Rampell, "Whistle-blowers Tell of Cost of Conscience."
36. See the Transparency International Corruption Perceptions Index for 2001 through 2006 at http://www.transparency.org/policy_research/surveys_indices/cpi.

Today's American: How Free?

AUTHORS

Camille Eiss is a Freedom House research analyst and the assistant editor of *Freedom in the World*. She is principal author of the chapter "Immigration: Despite Challenges, A Source of Strength."

Karin Deutsch Karlekar is a senior researcher at Freedom House and managing editor of the *Freedom of the Press* survey. She is coauthor of the chapter "The Press: Still Free and Independent."

Jason Kelly is a doctoral candidate at Columbia University, specializing in American government, congressional institutions, and the politics of redistricting. He is a coeditor of *Today's American: How Free?* as well as principal author of the chapter "Corruption: Money and Politics" and coauthor of the chapter "Political Process: Needs Repair."

Eleanor Marchant was assistant editor of the 2006 and 2007 editions of *Freedom of the Press* at Freedom House and is currently on fellowship with the Media Institute in Nairobi, Kenya. She coauthored the chapter "The Press: Still Free and Independent."

Thomas O. Melia is the deputy executive director of Freedom House and teaches at Georgetown University. He is coauthor of the chapter "Political Process: Needs Repair."

Amy Phillips is a Washington, D.C.–based writer and researcher focusing on individual liberty issues. She was formerly a research assistant at Freedom House, where she worked on international corruption and human rights research. She holds a degree in philosophy from New York University. Ms. Phillips is the principal author of two chapters: "The Civil Liberties Implications of Counterterrorism Policies" and "Rule of Law: Criminal Justice and Property Rights."

Anthony Picarello is general counsel to the U.S. Conference of Catholic Bishops in Washington, D.C. Previously, he litigated religious freedom cases on behalf of people of all faiths at the Becket Fund for Religious Liberty. He is principal author of the chapter "Religious Liberty: Still a Beacon."

Arch Puddington is director of research at Freedom House and principal author of the chapters "Equality of Opportunity in an Age of Globalization" and "Racial Inequality: America's Achilles' Heel."

Mark Y. Rosenberg is a doctoral student in political science at the University of California, Berkeley. He was previously a researcher at Freedom House and assistant editor of *Freedom in the World*. He is principal author of the chapter "Academic Freedom: Withstanding Pressures from Left and Right."

ADVISERS

Morton H. Halpern is the director of U.S. advocacy for the Open Society Institute and has a long career with the federal government, think tanks, and universities. He has authored, coauthored, and edited books and articles on national security, civil liberties, democracy and human rights, and arms control.

Michael Johnston is the Charles A. Dana Professor of Political Science at Colgate University in Hamilton, New York, specializing in political corruption, a topic on which he has written widely.

Jane Kirtley is the director of the Silha Center at the School of Journalism and Mass Communication at the University of Minnesota, where she has also been the Silha Professor of Media Ethics and Law.

Jeffrey Lax is an assistant professor of political science at Columbia University, where he focuses on American and judicial politics.

John Norton Moore is the Walter L. Brown Professor of Law at the University of Virginia School of Law, and directs the university's Center for National Security Law and Center for Oceans Law & Policy.

Jeffrey Passel is the senior research associate at the Pew Hispanic Center and formerly served as principal research associate at the Urban Institute's Labor, Human Services, and Population Center.

Noah Pickus is the Nannerl O. Keohane Director of the Kenan Institute for Ethics at Duke University, where he teaches in the Terry Sanford Institute of Public Policy. He has written widely on immigration and citizenship, and has served as an adviser for the federal government as well as public and private institutions.

Diane Ravitch is a research professor of education at New York University and a senior fellow at the Hoover Institution at Stanford University and the Brookings Institution in Washington, D.C. She has written extensively on education policy, democracy, and political correctness.

Jackson Toby is a professor of sociology emeritus at Rutgers University, focusing on criminology and adolescent delinquency. He has published numerous books and articles on criminology for both academic and general audiences.

ABOUT FREEDOM HOUSE

Freedom House is an independent private organization
supporting the expansion of freedom throughout the world.

Freedom is possible only in democratic political systems in
which governments are accountable to their own people, the
rule of law prevails, and freedoms of expression, association and
belief are guaranteed. Working directly with courageous men
and women around the world to support nonviolent civic initiatives in societies where freedom is threatened, Freedom House
functions as a catalyst for change through its unique mix of
analysis, advocacy and action.

- **Analysis.** Freedom House's rigorous research methodology has earned the organization a reputation as
  the leading source of information on the state of freedom around the globe. Since 1972, Freedom House
  has published *Freedom in the World,* an annual survey
  of political rights and civil liberties experienced in every country of the world. The survey is complemented
  by an annual review of press freedom, an analysis of
  transitions in the post-communist world, and other
  publications.

- **Advocacy.** Freedom House seeks to encourage American
  policymakers, as well as other governments and international institutions, to adopt policies that advance

288

human rights and democracy around the world. Freedom House has been instrumental in the founding of the worldwide Community of Democracies, has actively campaigned for a reformed Human Rights Council at the United Nations, and presses the Millennium Challenge Corporation to adhere to high standards of eligibility for recipient countries.

▮ **Action.** Through exchanges, grants, and technical assistance, Freedom House provides training and support to human rights defenders, civil society organizations, and members of the media in order to strengthen indigenous reform efforts in countries around the globe.

Founded in 1941 by Eleanor Roosevelt, Wendell Willkie, and other Americans concerned with mounting threats to peace and democracy, Freedom House has long been a vigorous proponent of democratic values and a steadfast opponent of dictatorships of the far left and the far right. The organization's diverse Board of Trustees is composed of a bipartisan mix of business and labor leaders, former senior government officials, scholars, and journalists who agree that the promotion of democracy and human rights abroad is vital to America's interests abroad.